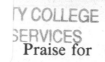
ρ_{40}

Praise for

The United States of Ambition

"[A] powerful diagnosis emerges from Alan Ehrenhalt's book, *The United States of Ambition*. This Washington-based analyst argues that what's different about American politics is not so much the voter as the politician. Voters behave basically the same as before. But for the last twenty years or so, politics has been taken over by full-time politicians, people of diverse backgrounds and beliefs whose overriding aim is to get elected and reelected."

—Leslie H. Gelb, *The New York Times*

"Every once in a while a book comes along that reaches deep and important truths about American politics. Alan Ehrenhalt's book is one of them."

—Norman J. Ornstein, American Enterprise Institute

"It's the kind of book you read and suddenly see politics in a brand-new perspective."

—Neal R. Peirce, *The Philadelphia Inquirer*

"A refreshing and invigorating book, important to anyone seriously interested in the health of democracy. . . . Ehrenhalt stands conventional political punditry on its head, which is probably why he makes so much sense."

—Dayton Duncan, *The Washington Post Book World*

"Ehrenhalt argues that [American politics today] cannot be understood by looking simply at what voters demand. We must also consider what politicians supply. . . . Ehrenhalt may well become known as the father of supply-side political science."

—James Q. Wilson, *The New Republic*

"Alan Ehrenhalt has written a brilliant book—one of the most original analyses of American politics in years. By focusing on the agenda of candidates rather than the mood of voters, he has given us a fresh and gracefully argued new way to look at how government makes policy. No one writing or thinking about the trends in modern politics can afford to ignore this vivid book."

—Ronald Brownstein, national political correspondent, *Los Angeles Times,* and author of *The Power and the Glitter*

"The most enlightening and most timely field report on America's changing political landscape since Theodore H. White's *The Making of the President* thirty years ago."

—Richard F. Fenno, Kenan Professor of Political Science, University of Rochester, and author of *Home Style: House Members in Their Districts*

"[Ehrenhalt's] stories are wonderful; they abound in the telling details that can come only from . . . a catholic love of American politics."

—Suzanne Garment, *The Public Interest*

"It is politicians and their incentives that Alan Ehrenhalt examines in *The United States of Ambition,* and it is the best treatment of this subject that I have ever read."

—Walter Dean Burnham, *Wilson Quarterly*

"A fascinating tour of the American political landscape. . . . For anyone who wants to know how City Hall has lost its clout or why Congress won't deal with the deficit, Ehrenhalt is required reading."

—*Richmond* (Va.) *News Leader*

"Alan Ehrenhalt's panoramic look at how politics are changing all across America is enlivened by some wonderful stories about real American politicians and how they do business. A vivid and absorbing account, full of insight and good ideas."

—Nelson W. Polsby, director, Institute of Governmental Studies, University of California, Berkeley

"A thought-provoking, excellently written study of the last two decades of American politics."

—*The Palm Beach Post*

"Alan Ehrenhalt, one of our nation's best observers of politics, has turned his eye on politicians and their ambitions. He asks the question, What makes them do an unnatural thing like run for office? His answers are illuminating and useful for politicians, political scientists, and voters."

—Michael Barone, senior writer, *U.S. News & World Report,* and author of *Our Country: The Shaping of America from Roosevelt to Reagan*

"Very few political writers understand both the personalities and the system of power in Washington as well as Alan Ehrenhalt. What he writes is well worth reading."

—Hedrick Smith, author of *The Power Game*

"When it comes to an encyclopedic knowledge of American politics, coupled with the rigors of political analysis, Alan Ehrenhalt has few peers . . . He has identified a revolution that has occurred almost unnoticed."

—*Congressional Quarterly*

"A persuasive cautionary analysis."

—*Kirkus*

"Ehrenhalt make[s] it eminently clear [that] there are no angels seeking office or casting ballots—and that there are no controls, either external or internal, on their behavior other than ambition, greed, and stupidity."

—*The Boston Phoenix*

"[A] thoughtful, probing look at the new-styled political professionals. . . . Ehrenhalt's portrait of American political trends is right on target."

—*Lexington* (Ky.) *Herald Leader*

THE
UNITED STATES
OF
AMBITION

THE
UNITED STATES
OF
AMBITION

Politicians, Power,
and the
Pursuit of Office

Alan Ehrenhalt

Portions of this work were originally published in
Governing magazine.

This work was originally published in slightly different
form by Times Books, a division of Random House, Inc.,
in 1991.

Library of Congress Cataloging-in-Publication Data
Ehrenhalt, Alan, 1947–
        The United States of ambition : politicians, power,
and the pursuit of office / Alan Ehrenhalt.
            p. cm.
        Includes bibliographical references and index.
        ISBN 0-8129-2027-9
        1. Politics, Practical—United States.
    2. Politicians—United States.   I. Title.
      JK1717.E36 1991
        324′.0973—dc20   90-46243

Manufactured in the United States of America

9 8 7 6 5 4 3 2

First Paperback Edition

To the memory of

Harry Barash

1872–1954

Contents

Introduction to the
Paperback Edition

It is hard to find anyone in America these days who does not believe that something has gone wrong with the country's political system. Anger and frustration seem to spill out the moment politics comes up in casual conversation and have boiled to the surface in the movement for term limitations. Against the background of a two-decades-long erosion of voter turnout, the electorate has displayed the first tentative signs that it may soon do what it has so far refused to do: simply vote incumbents out of office.

The voters are angry. But whether their rampage is entirely rational remains a legitimate question. One of the complaints heard most frequently, for example, is that politicians have stopped listening to the views of ordinary people. "They've stopped caring about us," a man from Des Moines told interviewers from the Kettering Foundation in 1991. "They don't care about people anymore." The reality of politics in the 1990s tells a different story. We see legislators dashing home every weekend for luncheons and forums and town meetings. We see members of Congress taking polls on every conceivable subject and then shrinking from any action that fails to command at least 51 percent approval. We see legislators mired in weeks of embarrassing deadlock because they fear the electoral consequences of either reducing public services or imposing the taxes those services require. We see Congress enacting a catastrophic health insurance program, only to repeal it a few months later, after a barrage of protests from the organized elderly. We see—in spite of all the rhetoric about unresponsiveness—a political system in which the elected representatives are, if anything, hyper-responsive.

Something is indeed wrong in American politics, but it is safe to say that voters have not quite focused on what that something is. There is, as evidenced by the term-limitation movement, an odd sort of feeling that the American government of the 1990s is an alien presence that has somehow been imposed on the public, rather than what it is: an assembly of citizens the electorate has freely chosen. In California recently, an irate constituent accosted Willie Brown, the speaker of the state assembly, and demanded to know when the state government was going to balance its budget and stop bothering the taxpayers for money.

Yet the fact that a lot of the complaints about American politics today are irrational does not mean they are unimportant. In the end, any democratic government requires the support of the voters. When the level of public support falls too low, it becomes difficult for that government to enforce its laws, to recruit leaders, to go about the business of maintaining a national community. Some cynicism is part of American political culture; Mark Twain made jokes about Congress, and he was not one of the first to do so. But there comes a point when the level of cynicism rises so high that it paralyzes government. We have not yet reached that point, but it may not be farfetched to imagine arriving there soon.

We all need to think seriously about the roots of our political discontent, however irrational the expressions of that discontent may sometimes sound.

Some of those roots lie outside the political system altogether. Politics reflects the society in which it is conducted, and for nearly twenty years the backdrop to politics in America has been an eroding economic prospect and a fraying social fabric. Put simply (if a little too simply): A day's labor does not earn the American worker as much as it earned him or her in 1973. Millions of families have made up for this declining real income by sending both parents to work, but at the cost of frantic schedules, diminished family time, and a more or less permanent increase in family tension.

This state of affairs persisted even through the "boom" years of the 1980s, when seemingly good economic news masked the continuing erosion of real personal income. It has burst powerfully onto the national consciousness in the depressed 1990s, especially for people in their twenties and thirties, the first generation to enter the labor force doubting an article of American faith: that they can expect to live better than their parents did.

It is not too much to say that the declining quality of economic and social life is the crucial political fact of the 1990s. Many of the people who rail against the unresponsiveness of the political system are, in part, striking out at the unexpectedly bad hand the past two decades have dealt them personally and professionally. But the economy and the society are abstractions, hard things to curse. Politicians, on the other hand, are easy to curse; we even have a national tradition of cursing them. It is quite possible to curse them and vote for them at the same time, and millions of us do just that.

All the while, of course, they are cursing each other, making our suspicions of them all the easier to maintain. This development is nothing new—negative campaigning has a long and colorful history in American politics—but twenty years ago, the prolonged attack-and-response media barrage had not made itself felt in congressional elections, let alone in those for lesser offices. The voters of 1970 had yet to witness the spectacle of a candidate accusing his opponent of corruption in TV commercials one night, followed by the opponent returning and escalating the charges the very next night, in a game of political chicken. Today, this is commonplace. In the end, someone wins the election, usually by establishing himself as the lesser of the apparent evils, but the political process sustains lasting damage.

In "Citizens and Politics," the Kettering Foundation's 1991 study of the mood of American voters, one of the most frequent complaints dealt with the name-calling that voters see as pervading all of American politics. A man in Richmond, Virginia, explained the whole system in very simple terms: "Whoever slings the most mud wins." Once people are convinced of that, it is almost impossible for them to respect the institutions that the candidates are slinging mud in order to join.

The corrosive effects of all this negativism have been made worse in the past two decades by the rise of divided government. The "normal" situation today is a Republican president and a Democratic Congress, and in 1992 more than two thirds of Americans are living in states where one party holds the governorship and the other controls at least one legislative chamber. Divided government is a recipe for partisan public squabbling that continues long after the election season ends; it brings the shrillness and negativism of the political campaign into the relations between one institution and another. With both parties free to portray the institution controlled by the other as the true culprit (as in fact they usually do), divided government makes it impossible for the voter to know for sure who should be blamed when things go wrong.

When, as in Maine in 1991, the Democratic speaker of the House labels the Republican governor an unprincipled opportunist, and the governor makes it clear he considers the speaker an arrogant autocrat, the natural tendency of many voters is to believe them both. Meanwhile, the consensus needed to solve the state's critical economic problems is impossible to obtain. All that the citizens seem to read about in the papers is the strategy each side has for checkmating the other.

But it is not merely the negativism and institutional division that is so disillusioning about present-day politics: It is the rhetoric of empty and unrealistic promises. A long time ago in American politics, elections were largely a competition between political parties, and a judgment upon the programs and platforms the parties offered. As partisan competition has yielded to collisions of individuals, programs have yielded to vague promises and declarations of optimism. It is difficult for a single candidate to offer an entire legislative program and expect it to be taken seriously; it is easy enough, however, to promise the moon, and this is what many politicians have been doing in recent years. A few modest examples:

Sen. Slade Gorton of Washington, campaigning for reelection in 1986: "There is not a single problem that, working together, we're not going to solve."

President Reagan, early in his second term: "If we keep America free, everything will be possible."

HUD secretary Jack Kemp: "There are no limits to what free men and free women, free enterprise, free markets in a free society can accomplish."

One may argue that this sort of rhetoric is in the best tradition of American resiliency and idealism, which is one reason why candidates continue to offer it and voters continue to buy it. It is nonetheless corrosive of public confidence when the candidate wins, four years pass, and everything seems to be worse.

It is dangerous when a governor takes office, as Ray Mabus did in Mississippi in 1988, announcing that his state need not be last anymore, and four years later, for a multitude of understandable reasons, his state is still last in many things. It is corrosive when candidates for governor promise that all fiscal problems can be handled through proper attention to waste, fraud, and abuse ("like squeezing water from cheese," William Weld said in Massachusetts in 1990), and it turns out the next year that the budget can be balanced only by inflicting severe pain on people all over the state who were not expecting it and do not seem to deserve it.

In present-day America, not everything is possible, most problems cannot be solved painlessly (some cannot be solved at all), and states do not rise from the bottom in four years simply by electing a new governor. The voters of Mississippi expressed their frustrations by throwing Ray Mabus out of office after one term in 1991. Others respond with a vague but deepening suspicion about politics, politicians, and American government in general.

That suspicion has been fed, in the past two decades, by a sequence of scandals that would have jolted the confidence of even the most trusting electorate. From Watergate to the Keating Five, and all the seamy disclosures in between, the 1970s and 1980s administered one shock after another to the civic consciousness. Prosecutors all over the country are now assisted in their crusades by potent legal tools that did not exist twenty years ago. They can indict politicians for "racketeering," using a 1970 federal statute that was never designed to be employed that way. They can indict them for "mail fraud" without offering evidence that the public has been cheated of anything other than the loosely defined "right to honest government."

Against that barrage, it does little good to point out that American political institutions are almost certainly cleaner than they were in the relatively scandal-free days of the past generation. When Sam Rayburn was speaker of the House in the 1950s, he used to keep a hoard of oil company cash in one of the desk drawers of his Capitol office. When a member he liked complained of financial problems, Rayburn would simply open the drawer and hand him some of the money. That does not happen anymore. The evolution from passing around untraceable cash to arguing over the tactics of political action committees is, in fact, a considerable step forward.

This distinction, however, is lost on the electorate. Voters who see one prominent leader after another removed from office in disgrace do not reflect on the evils that have been eradicated. Rather, they conclude what might be expected under the circumstances: Politicians are all a bunch of crooks.

Economic decline, negative campaigning, divided government, recurring scandal: You can mix and match them just about any way you choose. Any combination of these forces is more than powerful enough to explain why people are so disgusted by the present nature of American politics.

But the current public mood is a product of more than simple disillusionment. Lurking beneath the anger is a more positive vision, vague but intense, of what a successful American political system ought to be like. It would be a citizen politics, in which ordinary people with middle-class values take time out from their lives to offer their decency and common sense to the solution of common problems. It would be a politics in which elected officials do not need to poll constituent opinion because they feel it in their bones. Officeholders would express the voice of the people, and from that expression good public policy could not help but flow.

The current enthusiasm for term limits is essentially a product of this vision—and of the present reality that makes the vision even more powerful. The 1990s find American government increasingly dominated by a modern class of professional politicians, people who work full-time at getting and holding office. In many cases, they have done little else in their entire adult lives. *The United States of Ambition* is to a great extent the story of these people, of how they got where they are, and of how they go about doing their jobs.

Before we can even focus on attacking the fundamental weaknesses of our current political process, we must first understand the men and women who comprise it. Who are they? Is there something inherently wrong with the notion of a professional political class? Are lifetime politicians doomed to be insensitive to the problems and concerns of average voters? Is the idea of a citizen politics feasible— or even desirable—at the end of the twentieth century?

The one truth about citizen politics that is fairly easy to establish is that few of us would want to restore the version of it that prevailed in the 1950s. Any such restoration, even if it were possible, would collide sharply with other deeply held values of American society today.

Local government in the 1950s was undeniably a citizen institution. Legislative bodies met infrequently (as little as twice a month even in some large places) and usually at night so that the citizen officeholders could hold down private jobs during the day. While the amateurs in most communities were off earning a living, a small and close-knit local elite—dominated by a party chairman in some parts of the country, a state senator or a city manager in others—made most of the important community decisions in private, frequently over coffee or lunch in a local coffee shop or restaurant. This was citizen politics, and it tended to be rather efficient. What it was not was "responsive," at least not in the contemporary sense. Those who were excluded from the coffee-shop decision process by reason of race, gender, ethnicity, social class, or plain personal unpopularity, had no significant appeal from its actions. There were few public hearings and little meaningful debate in the city council or the county commission. The local elite simply did its work and moved on. The government that most of the voters got was the government that this largely unaccountable group of people wanted them to have.

State legislatures, similarly, were "citizen" institutions nearly everywhere in America up through the 1960s, with most of them in session no more than three months a year. The legislators were farmers, lawyers, Main Street merchants, and others willing to take time off from private pursuits to devote themselves to the responsibilities of writing laws and making policies. For this they were paid a modest stipend as a supplement to their regular income. While the vast majority of these citizen-legislators were decent and well-meaning, they were also poorly informed and unfamiliar with the legislative process. A docile group, they were ill-equipped to resist the blandishments of those who had access to the information they lacked—governors, party bosses, and lobbyists.

Congress, a generation ago, was not an amateur body in quite the way that legislatures and city councils were; service in Congress has been a full-time job for most of this century. Still, it was a citizen institution in the sense that most of the people who served in it had made some reputation in private life before coming to Washington, and thus were not careerists in the modern sense. They had the "real-world experience" that their present-day successors are so often derided for lacking. But it is hard to argue that the average congressman of those days used that experience in a creative, thoughtful, or even responsive way: He deliberated in closed session, cast votes that went unrecorded, and accepted the authority of committee chairmen who were under no obligation to respond to the wishes of any constituency other than the tiny one that returned them to office term after term.

The old-fashioned version of citizen politics did have some redeeming qualities, of course; in many places, decisions were made and problems were solved rather well. But by the standards of American life in the 1990s, the system was elitist, unaccountable, and authoritarian. We would never stand for it today.

The truth is, we abolished the citizen politics that used to prevail throughout the country. We did that by raising the pay and upgrading the resources of legislative bodies to the point where people would want to serve in them full-time, and we did it by expanding the scope of government itself, to the point where the old amateur institutions could no longer handle the volume of business.

Nevertheless, "citizen politics" seems like an attractive ideal to many of us these days as we contemplate the political system we have erected to replace it: one in which officeholders comprise a careerist elite whose lifetime political preoccupation has separated them from most people. The sensitivity of these men and women to ordinary voter concerns comes from town meetings and public opinion surveys, not from experiencing those concerns in their everyday lives. Indeed, the degree to which we have professionalized politics in the past two decades makes most Americans uneasy. There is something about the image of the entrenched congressional incumbent, immersed in politics as his life's work and impregnable in an elected office that pays $125,000 a year, that challenges some fundamental American notions of democracy and fairness. It is understandable that a movement would spring up to force these people to rotate out of office after a few terms and to spread the powers and pleasures of incumbency a little more widely among the citizenry at large.

There are scores of people in the current Congress—and an increasing number in state legislatures and local governments as well—whose work experience runs something like this: intern and campaign aide in high school and college; full-time aide to a public official upon college or law school graduation; candidate for and then member of a legislative body by age twenty-eight or thirty. For most of these people, politics is all they have ever done in life, and all they have ever really wanted to do. Something about a political career has been irresistible to them from the beginning: the hand-shaking and the back-slapping, the camaraderie of a campaign headquarters, the self-validation of winning, the intrigues of a committee room. These are the people who occupy center stage in this book and in our political consciousness. Their careerism has made us intensely suspicious of them as a group, but their personal charm and genuine political talent have induced us to reelect them term after term. In the past generation, they have remade American politics, both for better and for worse.

Professionals bring to any occupation or task a commitment and a discipline that amateurs find difficult to match. This is as true for politics as it is for sports, journalism, or entertainment. A state legislator or member of Congress who has devoted his entire adult life to a political career understands things about politics and government that his part-time predecessor of a generation ago did not. He knows more—not just more about campaigns and media and polling, but about the complex policy questions that are the work of the modern legislative body. This mastering of substance may not come about entirely by design (most full-time officeholders are attracted initially to politics, not public policy), but for nearly all of them, it happens eventually. It is a consequence of professionalism. Even the most politically obsessed full-time careerist soon comes to know more than an adequate amount about critical policy issues—health care, budget deficits, weapons systems—and to have some sense of what the policy options are. In terms of being well prepared for the job of legislating in complex times, the full-timers of today would run rings around the amateurs of a generation ago. To seek a return to the old system is to value ignorance over knowledge.

Still, a smarter class of politicians does not guarantee good government. While acknowledging the failures of the old days, we cannot escape the fact that the current system is failing us in its own way. It has given us government with a dangerously short time horizon, government that runs to the rhythms of the election cycle. We have bred a generation of legislators who have become conversant and even intrigued by public policy, but whose business is politics above all else.

The officeholders whose lives have been focused on politics

since adolescence do not find it easy to look beyond the consequences that a legislative act might have in the next campaign. They have trouble taking a stand that could cost them the only sort of job they have ever really wanted. They are in the business of responding to momentary fluctuations in the popular mood, rather than the long-term public interest.

This charge may be unfair to many of the individuals serving in public office in America today, for there is nothing inherently impossible about being both a political careerist and a public-spirited officeholder. Indeed, we will meet quite a few such people in the pages of this book. But they themselves usually admit, when asked, that we are moving in the wrong direction: We are producing too many officeholders who live from one campaign to the next and who find it difficult to vote for any legislation whose payoff lies further in the future than November of the next election year.

This helps to explain why we face an annual federal deficit of more than $300 billion; why we still worry about the supply of oil from the Persian Gulf; why so many of our roads and bridges are falling apart. When our political system loses the ability to make short-term sacrifices for long-term gain, we are heading toward disrepair.

The question is what to do about it. This truth is that our plight is not so much governmental as social; it is all around us in American life. To a great extent, we all suffer from the short-term disease. In the 1980s, corporations became enslaved by their quarterly profit-and-loss statements, and people ruined their lives with drugs that made them feel better for fifteen minutes at a time. We are hooked on the instant communication of fax machines, the instant heat from microwave ovens, and the mindlessly short attention span of music videos. We don't like to wait for results, and our politicians, knowing us better than we realize, hesitate to recommend anything that will try our impatience.

So is not fair to blame the short-sightedness of American government entirely on the political process. It is more complicated and insidious than that. And it will not be cured by any procedural tinkering we might apply to that system, no matter how ingenious.

Term limitation—the most popular current remedy for our political ills—fails to address the underlying realities of American government in the 1990s. A politician whose public office requires the commitment of six months campaigning and a half a million dollars expended, and whose legislative work takes up three quarters of every year, is a professional politician, whether he serves ten terms in office or is forced to retire after three or four. Simply to shuffle the cards more frequently and exchange one crew of professionals for another would do nothing to attack the problem of shortened time horizons. It might well make it worse. Would a term somehow be less precious to someone because he is only allowed four of them? Of course not. It would be more precious. Why risk any of those few terms voting for some unpopular bill whose benefits won't even show up until long after you have retired to private life? Why not vote for today?

It might be argued that term limits would at least create a larger pool of legislators who would be in their final term of office and therefore free to vote for the long-range good with political impunity. Perhaps this is true, assuming these people focus their final days in office on the public interest and not on the search for future employment. But even if true, it hardly stands as a powerful argument for term limits. Surely there must be a better reason for redesigning the political system than the manufacture of lame-duck statesmen willing to perform a few good deeds on their way out the door.

If we are going to enact procedural reforms, it makes more sense to advocate longer terms, rather than fewer terms, so that politicians who live from one election to the next would at least be living in longer blocks of time. Public financing of elections would also serve to weaken the current preoccupation with the next campaign and how to pay for it.

But what we must do most of all is to set our sights beyond the political sphere itself. We must begin thinking about our governmental problems in the context of our society's values, seeing politicians not as the source of our failings but as a reflection of them. Our aim must be to incorporate politics into a national renewal of individual responsibility and community loyalty, values that have eroded so noticeably in the past generation. Only when such a process of renewal takes hold will our politicians begin to look better in our eyes. Not that we will love them as a group; we never have. But we will be much better prepared to live with them.

March 1992

THE
UNITED STATES
OF
AMBITION

Who sent these people?

It is hard not to ask that question every now and then during a normal political year, as we find ourselves confronted with office-holders and candidates who fail to meet any commonsense definition of what political leadership ought to be: aspirants for the U.S. Senate who traffic in the basest kind of playground name-calling; governors who win election on antitax platforms they know they will have to repudiate; members of Congress who talk endlessly about cutting the federal deficit and never even begin to do it; state legislators who fall for the most heavy-handed bribery schemes cooked up by federal prosecutors to entrap them. Is it possible that this is the best we can do—that this is the best political leadership the world's oldest democracy can muster?

Who sent us the leaders we have? This question forms itself repeatedly in the recesses of our minds, even as we elect and reelect people who fall pitifully short of our ideals of statesmanship. But oddly enough, we do not pursue the issue very seriously. We love to complain about our politicians even as we return them to office. We debate proposals to limit the number of terms they can serve, in effect seeking a procedural cure for our addiction to reelecting them. What we are reluctant to do is to trace the roots of our discontent.

How did the people who govern us get there in the first place? Why are we being led by this particular set of public officials, and not some other? What sorts of people manage to win election to office these days? And if, as a group, they continue to disappoint us, term after term, campaign after campaign, is it their fault—or is it ours?

This book proposes to answer some of these questions. In order to do that, it asks the reader to begin thinking about American politics in a different way.

1

Thinking About Politicians

Above San Francisco, in the pretty little towns that spread eastward from the Pacific Coast Highway into the Napa Valley, there are an extraordinary number of elegant places to eat. Any village large enough to claim a post office, it sometimes seems, can be counted on to have a restaurant that serves stuffed quail or roulade of salmon or sautéed Burgundy snails. What are all these French restaurants doing there? Why so much gourmet cooking in such a small and crowded corner of the world? Is it because the demand for expensive food in northern California is limitless?

Not really. Restaurants need customers, of course, or they go out of business. But one could spend a lifetime studying customer taste and never understand how such a collection of haute cuisine came to be concentrated in a relatively few square miles. The truth is that northern California is full of restaurants because restaurateurs want to live there. The summers are cool; the winters are mild; the scenery is lovely; the customers are secondary. As long as there is enough business to stave off bankruptcy, Napa and Sonoma counties will always offer more pâté and goat cheese than the available diners can possibly consume.

American politics is not a restaurant, but it does have customers—voters—and people whose job it is to serve them—politicians. A great deal is written every year about political events in this country, and nearly all of it attempts to understand them by asking what is on the voters' minds. Every election year reporters and polltakers spend thousands of hours sounding out the American people on the questions of the day. The moment the polls close on election night, the television networks report their findings on why the electorate made the choices it did. In the weeks and months that follow, journalists and scholars take their turns combing the statistics for clues about just what message the American people were trying to send.

It is not the purpose of this book to disparage all this poking around in the electoral psyche. In a democratic society there is no arguing with the principle that the people doing the governing ought to know as much as possible about what the country thinks. But in the end there is only so much the electorate can tell us. Most of the time it is not trying to send any message. A great deal of what has happened in American politics in the past generation is accessible only through a different set of questions, aimed not at the customers of American politics but at the proprietors—the people who involve themselves in politics, run for office, win elections, and govern the country.

Studying the voters is, for all its statistical technology, a relatively simple matter. There are millions of them, and on any issue one chooses to take up, any random sample of a few hundred will do. It is easy to find out what the voters think.

It is comparatively hard to find out what politicians think, or even who they are and where they come from. They are not interchangeable. In any one election year, fewer than a thousand people are active candidates for Congress. One cannot draw a sample of 10 percent of them and claim to have learned anything meaningful at all. There is scarcely any choice but to approach them on an old-fashioned, unscientific, one-by-one basis.

So it is understandable that scholars and journalists tend to focus their attention on the voters, who are accessible, rather than on the candidates, who are frequently elusive. But the attractiveness of voter opinion as a field of study does not automatically make it the critical factor in understanding the results of an election. Sometimes we need to know other things.

. . .

For example:

Concord, California, is a conservative town. In the 1980s it voted twice for Ronald Reagan by decisive margins and twice for George Deukmejian, the state's orthodox Republican governor. Yet in the entire Reagan era it did not elect a single Republican to local office. It was governed entirely by liberal Democrats.

One might argue that the voters of Concord possess a finely developed sensitivity to the separation of powers and decided over the years that they wanted one sort of ideology representing them in Washington and Sacramento, and another in their own city hall. But a few conversations with people who have held office in this community turn up a different answer. Serving in city government in Concord used to be easy work. Businessmen did it in their spare time. As the city grew, governing it became a demanding, time-consuming job. The Republican merchants and insurance brokers who used to do it no longer wanted to take the time. In their place came political professionals, and all the professionals, over an entire decade, were Democrats.

The Colorado House of Representatives does the same sort of work that all legislative bodies in the United States do. There is nothing very unusual about its product. But there has been something unusual about its composition. For much of the 1980s it was nearly 40 percent female, and its instrument of leadership, the Republican Caucus, was at one point 45 percent female. No other chamber in any American legislature has come close to matching those numbers.

Some of this no doubt has to do with the fact that Colorado voters, like those in other western states, have always been more or less hospitable to women candidates. There were three women in the legislature as early as 1895. Colorado was one of the first states to ratify the federal Equal Rights Amendment. But there is a more immediate reason why the Colorado House is the way it is. The position of state representative pays $17,500 a year. It is an interesting job, and an important job, but it is no job for a breadwinner. An increasing number of House members are highly educated people who are married to well-paid professionals and do not need their legislative pay to support their families. There is no reason why these cannot be men, and some are. But the vast majority are women.

. . .

Then there is the interesting case of the Fifth Congressional District of Indiana. Its Republican loyalties are rock solid. No Democratic candidate for governor or president has carried it in more than fifteen years. In 1984 it gave its Republican congressman nearly 70 percent of the vote. But two years later the incumbent retired, and it chose a Democrat to replace him.

It helps a little, in explaining that unusual event, to know about some of the economic crises that central Indiana suffered through in the 1980s. Hard times in the automobile industry closed factories all over the Fifth District and lifted unemployment to frightening levels. It is natural enough to assume that the voters were angry about their plight and turned their anger against the Republicans—the party that was governing the country.

No doubt some of them did that. But the event becomes much clearer when one learns something about the Democrat who won the election: that at the age of twenty-two he had won a seat in the legislature by defeating the majority leader of the Indiana House; that in the ensuing twelve years he had worked full-time at politics, seven days a week; that he had raised nearly half a million dollars for his congressional campaign at a time when other underdog candidates were starved for funds. The mood of the voters had something to do with the result in Indiana's Fifth District that year, but the candidate had everything to do with it.

It is central to the folklore of our democratic system that elections reflect in some way the considered judgment of the American people. But one need not be a specialist in public opinion to realize just how far the reality differs from the myth. To begin with, most people do not vote. In a general election for president, the national turnout usually edges slightly above 50 percent of those eligible to participate, but in all other elections those who vote are a minority. Only 36 percent of adult citizens voted in the elections for Congress in 1990; in primaries for Congress the percentage is always lower; in elections at the local level it is usually lower still.

Most people who do vote cast their ballots most of the time without knowing very much about the people running or what they stand for. This was made clear by the massive voter studies begun in the 1950s by the Survey Research Center of the University of Michigan, and it has never been convincingly disputed.

The late political scientist V. O. Key, Jr., challenged the pessimism of the Ann Arbor studies in one important way in the 1960s: He argued that "voters are not fools"; choices for president do reflect the considered values and opinions of those who participate. Key felt that voting is retrospective—that citizens might not have a clear idea of which policies they want a president to pursue, but they know whether things in America are going well or badly, and they make up their minds, rationally enough, either to reward the incumbent party or to punish it for its failings. In the years since then, it has been more or less accepted that voters in presidential elections are not just choosing a friendly face or a party label but expressing themselves as best they can about what they think the country should be like.

And so they are. But a presidential election, however critical it may be, is one event held every four years. In the intervening period, in every community in the United States, dozens of elections are held to choose mayors, city councilors, state legislators, members of Congress, and countless other officials who provide the government that is crucial to people's lives, every day, every year.

I know of nobody who has tried seriously to say of these elections that, in general, they reflect the considered judgment of the voters about the choices that confront them or the people on the ballot. As Thomas E. Mann said of congressional elections a decade ago, "The burden of proof is clearly on those who would argue that a significant part of the public is aware of the candidates." The truth is, most votes that we cast in this country—even those cast by the brightest of us—are stabs in the dark. Readers can test this proposition for themselves by recalling the last time they confronted choices for their state legislature. If they made up their minds on the basis of any coherent policy choice, they are rare voters indeed.

Over the past twenty years, an average of 56 percent of the eligible voters have been unable to identify any congressional candidate in their district at the height of the fall campaign. Only 22 percent have been able to name both candidates. The figures for Senate campaigns have not been much higher. That is not to say that Key was wrong and that voters are, in fact, fools. It is simply to say, as Walter Lippmann observed convincingly more than sixty years ago, that life is too short, work is too hard, and leisure too precious for the average citizen to spend more than a small fraction of his time gathering information about the people whose names confront him on the ballot each election year. People who vote do so because they see it as their civic responsibility; they do not believe that this responsibility extends to taking up many hours of their free time informing themselves about which candidate for the legislature comes closest to matching their own views on the issues of the day.

Lippmann did not believe the American voter is a fool. "My sympathies are with him," he wrote in 1925,

> for I believe that he has been saddled with an impossible task and that he is asked to practice an unattainable ideal. I find it so myself for, although public business is my main interest and I give most of my time to watching it, I cannot find time to do what is expected of me in the theory of democracy; that is to know what is going on and to have an opinion worth expressing on every question which confronts a self-governing community. And I have not happened to meet anybody, from a President of the United States to a professor of political science, who came anywhere near to embodying the accepted ideal of the sovereign and omnicompetent citizen.

If he does exist anywhere, the omnicompetent citizen is confronted at the polls with an inevitably narrow set of choices. He is limited, for all practical purposes, to those people who have decided to be candidates. In our society that nearly always means two choices in a general election and a few more, not many more, in most primaries. There is no point in pretending that the American voter is selecting among a diverse array of clearly defined alternatives. American politics does not work that way.

It is possible to argue, as many on the left do, that narrowness of choice at the polls reflects a deliberate effort by those who possess power to maintain themselves in power. Holding a monopoly on the skills and resources needed to conduct a modern campaign, an establishment elite uses that monopoly to win all the important nominations and deny any meaningful voice to the downtrodden and anybody who wishes to speak for them.

But one does not have to believe this notion—I do not believe it myself—to realize that the limited set of choices in American elections all but determines the outcome of the voting and the government we get in the end. Our choices at the polls are not restricted by any power-hungry cabal but by thousands of potential candidates who decide on their own either that running for office is worth the trouble or that they are better off staying home and tending to family and career. If the people who want to hold office in the 1990s are a different group from those who wanted to hold office in the 1960s, the voters are going to end up with a different sort of government—whatever they happen to think about the issues of the day.

These points about voters—that they are inattentive, poorly informed, and limited to a narrow range of choices—are no secret to anybody who spends much time thinking about American politics. They can be found in any textbook of voting behavior. "American elections are hardly a classic model of democracy with rational, well-informed voters making dispassionate decisions," one popular text proclaims. "American elections provide an acceptable opportunity for parties and candidates to attempt to win or hold public office." Another political scientist, writing in 1986, was more blunt. "The picture of uninformed voters in the election booth," he said, "staring vainly at their shoes in search of cues to help in their vote decision, is in all likelihood not a hyperbole. . . . In each election year, literally millions of crib sheets are taken into voting booths to help keep the names of the candidates straight."

If voters are not making informed choices, what in the world are they doing? We know a few relevant things about elections below the presidential level in this country, but they do not explain a great deal.

We know that people are far more likely to vote for incumbents than for challengers, whether they are voting to fill seats in Congress, in a state legislature, or on a city council. It is not hard to see why. In an electoral world where information is scarce, incumbents are far more likely to be familiar, and familiarity is rewarded. But this observation, of course, begs the question of how they got to be incumbents in the first place. It is nice to have a theory of how people win second terms, but it would be more interesting to know how they won their first terms.

We know that when voters are uninformed about the candidates on the ballot, they often make their decisions on the basis of the party they prefer. Republicans do not win election to the Illinois legislature from inner-city Chicago; Democrats rarely get elected to that body from the suburbs of Du Page County. But this observation too begs the real question. If the general election in a particular place is only a formality, then the primary is the crucial event. And there is no evidence that the electorate in a primary is any better informed than the electorate in November. If anything, it knows less. How does one person emerge out of a crowded primary field and lift himself into the security of an easy general election and a safe seat in public office? There has not been a great deal written on this subject.

Officeholders do not necessarily behave as if voters were apathetic or uninformed. Congress is full of veteran members who have not faced a hint of serious opposition in years yet cast each vote in apparent fear that someone back in the district is waiting to turn it against them. This is the hypersensitivity of political professionalism. The more a person's career, livelihood, and self-image depend on remaining in office—rather than on some other work he was trained to do in private life—the more likely he is to magnify the smallest threat to that office.

In any legislative body, though, the norm of political squeamishness masks a diverse array of decisions that even the most hypersensitive legislator can make without having to worry much about public opinion back home. Consider, for example, Rep. Glenn English, a Democrat who represents a hard-pressed wheat-growing district in Oklahoma's western plains. English has built himself a secure seat in Congress by noisily trumpeting the cause of higher wheat prices at every opportunity. At the same time he has devoted much of his legislative career to protecting the Freedom of Information Act, a subject of little or no political sensitivity to his constituents. If we want to understand English's position on wheat, we need to know something about his voters. But if we want to understand his position on personal privacy, we need to know something about him—where he came from and why he believes the things he does. The voters have very little to do with it.

There are all sorts of interesting questions in American politics that we cannot answer by asking the voters, no matter how much time we spend on the task. The voters are the customers. We need to find out more about the people for whom politics is a business. We need to know what sorts of people want to be politicians. And to understand that we need to know how the work of politics itself has changed.

·   ·   ·

One thing we can say with confidence is that seeking and holding office take up more of a politician's time than they did a generation ago. It is much harder now to combine politics and a career in private life. And this is true, to a greater or lesser extent, at all levels of government.

As recently as the 1950s the U.S. Congress could reasonably be described as a part-time institution. Its members arrived in Washington on the train in January and left in the summer, when heat and humidity made the city uncomfortable. When they returned home upon adjournment in July or August, these politicians had enough time left in the year to practice law or sell insurance or do whatever they had done before they were elected.

Since the early 1960s Congress has essentially been in session year-round. It recesses for a month in August during the odd-numbered years and adjourns for campaigning a month or so before each national election, but the rest of the time it is conducting business. A member can return home virtually every weekend if he chooses, and there are half a dozen week-long recesses scattered throughout the average congressional year, but there is no sustained opportunity to pursue any career at all in private life. When someone is elected to Congress, he gives up his "regular job," assuming he did not give it up months earlier to campaign. He returns to it—assuming it still awaits him—only when he leaves office.

Not all state legislators have to cut themselves off from private life in quite the same way. In some of the least populated states, the legislatures still meet every other year for only sixty days. It is possible to combine service in the Wyoming House or Senate with almost any sort of work—law, ranching, business—and describe oneself accurately as a "citizen-legislator." But there are very few Wyomings left. In 1987 thirty-seven legislatures held regular sessions that lasted one hundred days or more, and most of those stayed in business roughly half the year. Nine legislatures met more or less year-round. When it comes to opportunities for a life outside politics, there is little practical difference between being a member of the Michigan House in Lansing and being a member of the U.S. House in Washington. It is time-consuming work.

Millions of words have been written about the advent of year-round legislating, most of them warning that it leads to too many unnecessary laws and to legislators isolated from the people they represent. We can leave that argument aside. My point is a simpler one: Full-time jobs in Congress and in legislatures attract people who want to devote most of their waking hours to politics. There is no reason to suppose that this is the same set of people who would want to do politics in their spare time.

People in local government—city council members, county commissioners, and their equivalents—nearly all have some discretion in how much time they devote to their work. Their meetings tend to take place at night and, except in the largest cities, no more than once a week. Local politicians can hold down private jobs, and most of them do. But a variation on Gresham's law has come to operate in local politics: Full-timers drive part-timers out of circulation. The city councilman who spends his days building political coalitions, meeting with constituents, and cultivating financial support sets a standard of political sophistication that colleagues pretty much have to meet if they are going to stay effective or even stay in office. Once a city council attracts its first full-time member, it is on the way to becoming a de facto full-time institution, even if it does not think of itself as one.

If it is more demanding to hold office in America than it was a generation ago, it is also far more demanding to seek office. Campaigning at any level these days is almost certain to be a time-consuming, technologically complicated, physically strenuous form of work.

To win a seat in Congress now is frequently to do what Bill Schuette did in Michigan in 1984: devote the better part of a year to meeting people and raising money seven days a week. Schuette was, as of 1984, the state of the art in congressional campaigning. "Amateur night is over in this district," he proclaimed one afternoon, more than six months before the election, as he drove from one campaign stop to another in the middle of a day crowded with political appearances. Schuette was on his way to spending nearly $900,000 on a successful campaign that included a meticulous month-by-month game plan, a summer rehearsal, and a headquarters full of computers. Running for Congress for the first time at the age of thirty, Schuette was essentially the proprietor of a small business.

It is perfectly possible to spend $900,000 on a congressional campaign and lose it badly; people do that every year. But as the enterprise becomes more complex and more sophisticated, those who want to stay in business have little choice but to move with it. There is no reason in principle why congressional campaigns have to last a year and cost a fortune. But candidates who do the things Bill Schuette did rarely lose to opponents who campaign casually and run on a shoestring.

It is not just a matter of sophistication; it is a matter of physical effort. When Jim Moody decided to run for an open congressional seat in Milwaukee in 1982, he did it by campaigning door to door virtually every day for more than a year. That was no surprise. Moody had got himself elected to the state legislature twice by doing exactly the same thing. What was surprising was the effect he had on his large field of competitors. Within a few months virtually all of them were out knocking on doors like a crew of Fuller Brush salesmen, hoping to catch the candidate who had a head start. Anyone who refused to campaign that way risked gaining a reputation as lacking the commitment or stamina to win.

In the end nobody caught up with Moody; he was elected to Congress. But the important point is that he had established a political entry barrier, and it is one that exists in many parts of the country in contests for Congress, state legislatures, and local office. Candidates win these offices by selling themselves to the voters, in person, one at a time, day after day. People who do not like to do this, people who do not like to knock on strangers' doors or who find it tedious to repeat the same thirty-second personal introduction thousands of times, are at a severe disadvantage. Many of them decide sensibly that, however interesting it might be to serve in office, the job of seeking office is not for them.

Politics in the 1990s is for people who are willing to give it vast amounts of their time. It is also for people who are not particularly concerned about making money. Time and money are related. If state legislatures met for one week every year, it would not be difficult to find a wide assortment of people willing to serve for very little pay, or even for free. But a job that is apt to require six months or more of full-time work every year is measured against a different standard.

Any time members of Congress receive a pay increase, they are assaulted by complaints from constituents who do not understand why a public servant cannot live on an annual wage several times higher than the median in every community in the United States. An annual wage of more than $90,000 (the congressional salary at this writing) seems lavish to them. But if you or I were pondering a campaign for Congress, the crucial question, of course, would not be whether we could make more than our plumber does. It would be whether a member of Congress makes more than we could make staying home and doing something else. And the answer, for most people with the capacity to win election to Congress, is that they can make considerably more money in private life.

It is an often repeated fact that more members of Congress identify themselves as lawyers than as practitioners of any other profession. But the large number of lawyer-legislators obscures the truth about who these people are. They are not, by and large, successful lawyers who left thriving partnerships to run for public office. Rather, they are political activists with law degrees. This does not mean that they are failures; it simply means that they are lawyers by training rather than by profession. Quite a few of them fit the career pattern of Massachusetts Democrat James M. Shannon, who received his law degree in 1975, won election to Congress in 1978, ran for the U.S. Senate in 1984, and later became attorney general of his state.

Shannon never practiced law before becoming a candidate. Therefore he never had to face a reduction in his standard of living by assuming public office. But nearly any successful lawyer, even in a medium-sized American town, quickly attains a standard of material life well beyond the reach of an average member of Congress, let alone a state legislator. He is very unlikely to give up that life for public office.

What is true of law is true, to a greater or lesser extent, of most other professions. They pay much better than politics. People give them up for political careers only at the beginning of the road, or at the end: before they are really launched, or after they have begun to wind down.

Jim Olin of Virginia, a former vice-president of General Electric, is one of the few Fortune 500 corporate executives in Congress. When he was in his thirties, he tried to combine his business career with service as a town supervisor in Rotterdam, New York. Told by GE to choose either business or politics, he chose business, retired in 1982 after thirty-five years with the company, ran for Congress, and won. That is about the only way anybody can combine careers in Congress and corporate business—do one, then the other. But not many people have the energy or the opportunity to accomplish it.

There is nothing particularly new about this. Nobody ever became rich on his salary as a public official. Candidates for public office have always had to accept that fact as a condition of political life. Until recent years, however, politics offered many ambitious young people another incentive—a route to prestige and social acceptance that was unavailable to them in the private world. As recently as a generation ago, no Italian-American college graduate, however talented, could reasonably expect to become president of Yale or chief executive officer of Ford or Chrysler. There was no Bart Giamatti or Lee Iacocca to influence ethnic career decisions. There was, however, Fiorello La Guardia. Politics was an outlet for the ambitions of bright young people who were rightly suspicious of how far merit alone might carry them in a prejudiced private realm.

Prejudice has not disappeared from the world, but even the skeptic must concede that careers in all fields are, to an unprecedented extent, open to talent across ethnic and racial lines. Nobody today needs to become a politician because he fears his roots will make him unacceptable as a political scientist, or a doctor or lawyer.

A political career in America in the 1990s, to summarize, is not easy, lucrative, or a particularly good route to status in life. This places increased importance on one other motive for entering politics: sheer enjoyment. You pretty much have to like the work.

You also have to be good at it. Almost as important as the question of what sorts of people want a political career is the question of what sorts of people possess the skills to do it well. Here too there is no reason to assume that the answers are the ones that would have applied earlier in this century, or even earlier in the postwar years.

The skills that work in American politics at this point in history are those of entrepreneurship. At all levels of the political system, from local boards and councils up to and including the presidency, it is unusual for parties to nominate people. People nominate themselves. That is, they offer themselves as candidates, raise money, organize campaigns, create their own publicity, and make decisions in their own behalf. If they are not willing to do that work for themselves, they are not (except in a very few parts of the country) going to find any political party structure to do it for them.

At one time in American politics, parties represented the only real professionalism that existed. A century ago, when defenders of "good government" complained that public life was being usurped by professional politicians, they did not mean candidates. They meant bosses—the people who chose the candidates. Legislators came and went, in Congress as they did at lesser levels. The institutions of professionalism were the party machines: New York's Tammany Hall, the Republican organization of Pennsylvania, the Cook County Democratic Central Committee. The leaders of these machines were the lifelong political practitioners who reaped the rewards of power and graft that the system offered.

Today's professional politicians are less imposing figures, even to those who do not like them. Their influence as individuals is modest, and their opportunities for graft are few. In most cases they do not control anyone's election but their own. Their ties to any political party are limited. They are solo practitioners. It is a different brand of professionalism altogether.

There is no need to dwell on the evidence of party decline; it is all around us. At the national level, it is true, there were some interesting signs of party renewal in the 1980s, centered in the congressional campaign committees. Both the Democratic and the Republican parties in Washington play a far greater role in recruiting and helping candidates than they did two decades ago. But that does not contradict the fundamental point that in the states and cities across America, where elections are fought and won, parties make little difference. Candidates for all sorts of offices are perfectly capable of going on about their business without them. And it is not just parties that have lost their role of anointing political candidates. Other community institutions that used to perform that task have also lost their authority in recent years.

Elections in Sioux Falls, South Dakota, for example, were never conducted on a highly partisan basis. But the successful candidates a generation ago were those who bore the stamp of approval of the town's informal leadership organization. "When we were kids growing up," a Sioux Falls businessman in his forties recalls, "everybody knew who would win the elections. The person who had been in Rotary and had been endorsed by the Chamber of Commerce always won."

What has happened in Sioux Falls in the past two decades has happened in countless other places as well. Candidates do not win because they have party support. They do not win because they have business or labor support. They win because they are motivated to set out on their own and find the votes that will make a majority. Group support helps. But it is almost never enough. The candidate who possesses every attribute needed for victory except the willingness to thrust himself forward is a losing candidate nine times out of ten.

Who sent us the political leaders we have? There is a simple answer to that question. They sent themselves. And they got where they are through a combination of ambition, talent, and the willingness to devote whatever time was necessary to seek and hold office.

In the age of the entrepreneurial candidate, character traits that used to be helpful turn out to be counterproductive. When Alfred E. Smith entered politics in Manhattan in the early years of this century, the one crucial trait he had to exhibit to win nomination was loyalty—uncomplaining devotion to the organization and leaders who placed him in the state assembly. If his loyalty to Tammany Hall had been less than total, he would not have been rewarded with a seat in the legislature, and if his loyalty had declined when he assumed office, he would have been dumped. But the people who have represented Smith's old territory in Congress or in the New York legislature in recent years have not been there because of loyalty. There has been no organization, even in the old machine strongholds, worth a pledge of allegiance. The quality that nourishes political careers today, in Manhattan as elsewhere, is independence.

Most candidates who succeeded on the basis of loyalty did not have to be especially articulate. Political organizations required spokesmen, but they did not require that all their officeholders be capable of playing a visible public role. A genial young man blessed with the support of the party organization did not need to express himself vigorously on the issues of the moment.

That is no longer true. A candidate for virtually any office has to know how to talk. Voters may not make their choices very often on the basis of public policy, but they do not like to vote for candidates who seem uncomfortable expressing themselves. More than in the old days, campaigns for all offices are exercises in communication: in town meetings, in door-to-door canvassing, on television, in direct-mail literature that the candidate has to write himself. Even if it does not matter a great deal what the candidate says, it makes an enormous difference how he looks and sounds saying it. The politics of the 1990s, unlike the politics of earlier generations, is an enterprise in which the inarticulate have no place to hide. When candidates are left to themselves to orchestrate campaigns and do their own communicating with the voters, it is only natural that the glib will survive and the tongue-tied will be drawn toward other lines of work.

In such an atmosphere, the advantage is not only to individuals who know how to talk but to professions that train people in how to talk. There are many reasons why teachers have been the fastest-growing bloc in American legislatures in the 1980s, but one of the most important has to do with verbal ability. Teachers can translate the skills of their private careers into a job in public life. And unlike lawyers, who possess most of the same skills, they can do so without making any financial sacrifice.

Politics is, then, more than in the past, a job for people who prefer it to any other line of work. About these people one more important point should be made: They tend not only to enjoy politics but to believe in government as an institution. The more somebody is required to sacrifice time and money and private life to run for the city council, for the state legislature, or for Congress, the more important it is for that person to believe that government is a respectable enterprise with crucial work to do.

That principle comes through in interviews with people at all levels of the political system. Ron Mullin expressed it one day in 1987, as he trudged down the streets of Concord, California, campaigning door to door all afternoon in 95-degree heat, an incumbent mayor seeking reelection to the city council. "If I believed government wasn't an institution beneficial to society," he said, "I wouldn't give a tinker's dam about politics. I wouldn't waste my time on it." Robert Torricelli expressed similar sentiments a few years earlier, in the midst of his successful Democratic campaign in New Jersey against an incumbent Republican congressman. "People who believe government should be doing less," Torricelli declared, "should not vote for me." Those are the sorts of words one hears from people who succeeded in politics in the 1980s, people whose zest for the game is reinforced by a conviction that they need not apologize for what they are doing.

Occasionally one hears the opposite. Randy Kamrath was elected to the Minnesota Senate as a Republican in 1981 at age twenty-five and almost immediately began pondering his retirement from a profession whose value he questioned. "If a politician likes his job," Kamrath mused one summer morning, as he drove his tractor across his southwest Minnesota farm, "then I don't think I like the job he's doing." Kamrath was in his second legislative term then, seeking a third, yet he worried that the Minnesota legislature was no place for an honest conservative. The next year the voters solved Kamrath's problem for him; they unseated him and put in a liberal Democrat, freeing him to do the farming he regards as honest work.

There are people like Randy Kamrath at all levels of the American political system—people who are highly suspicious of government yet persuade themselves to run for office, or who hate government but find themselves addicted somehow to politics as a game. But it is hard to find enough of them, in most places, to make a majority on a city council, or in a legislature, or in a congressional delegation.

In another sort of political environment, one in which parties made the important decisions, or in which it did not take much time or trouble to serve in office, belief in government might not be a crucial point. People who disliked government might become candidates and win elections in large numbers whether they found the work exciting or not. But in the current environment belief matters a great deal. Indeed, it is critical.

It may seem to some readers that, in paying all this attention to the personal qualities of the candidates, I am missing something crucial: the importance of media in the modern political process, or the dominating influence of money. Or both.

Money and television are important. It has been true for the past twenty years that TV commercials can sway election results, local as well as national. And even in the smaller media markets, commercials are expensive to produce and to put on the air. Television has pushed up the cost of campaigns for an entire range of offices to disturbing levels. It is very difficult now to win an open seat in Congress without raising and spending half a million dollars. Usually it takes more. A contested state Senate campaign, even in a medium-sized state, often costs $100,000. And it is clear to anybody who follows politics where most of this money comes from. It comes from people and interests with a stake in the policy decisions of the institution whose seats are up for grabs.

But who gets it? How did Jim Jontz, running for Congress in 1986 as a Democrat in Indiana's Fifth District, a thirty-three-year-old full-time legislator with no significant resources of his own, manage to raise and spend nearly $500,000 to get himself elected in an impossibly Republican constituency? One can argue, of course, that Jontz was simply an instrument—a tool of the labor unions and liberal pressure groups who found his politics appealing and provided most of the money. But to say that is to misconstrue the role of these groups—and their business-oriented counterparts on the Republican side—in the American political system.

Special interests reward politicians. They buy access to politicians. They seek to influence votes, and frequently they do. But they do not generate careers. They do not pluck people off college campuses or out of entry-level private jobs and lure them into politics. The candidates who raise the large amounts that campaigns now require are people who launched political careers on the basis of their own values, ambitions, and interests. They throw themselves into politics full-time, and they learn where the money is, just as they learn to campaign door to door, address a town meeting, or put together a piece of direct mail. These are the skills that make them successful.

In a similar sense it is not quite true that television wins elections. The ability to look and sound good on television wins elections. It is true that, in a number of well-publicized campaigns every year, people without any such natural ability are made presentable through the efforts of consultants whom they had the personal resources to hire, but those campaigns are exceptions. The vast majority of candidates who win elections through television are people whose commitment to politics over the course of their adult lives put them in a position to afford it and to understand how to use it.

No matter how much importance we want to place on the roles of money and media in the campaign process, we are driven back to questions about which sorts of people are succeeding in that process. Political office today flows to those who want it enough to spend their time and energy mastering its pursuit. It flows in the direction of ambition—and talent.

To recognize this fact is to begin to solve perhaps the oddest riddle of American politics in recent years: the ability of the Democratic party to thrive at so many levels of the political system in the face of a national conservative tide that has elected Republican presidents five times in the last six elections, overwhelmingly in the last three. How could it be, in the era of Ronald Reagan and George Bush, that Democrats prolonged their control of the U.S. House into its fourth uninterrupted decade; reestablished a comfortable majority in the U.S. Senate after a short Republican interlude; controlled as many as thirty state legislatures, compared with fewer than ten for the Republicans; and consistently elected more than 60 percent of the 7,412 people who serve in ninety-nine state legislative chambers nationwide?

Most of the efforts to answer this riddle have fallen back on psychological examination of the electorate. We vote for Democrats below the presidential level, it is said, to place a check on the Republicans to whom we entrust control of the White House. Or, somewhat more plausibly, we split our vote because we have different expectations about different offices. Republicans win the presidency by offering an ideology that the majority of the country feels comfortable with. Democrats win further down by delivering the personal services and generating the governmental programs that voters, on a day-to-day basis, refuse to give up.

There may be some truth to these answers, but in the end they are answers to the wrong fundamental question. Once we drop beneath the level of presidential politics, there is no reason to believe that voters are trying to tell us much of anything. They are responding in an essentially passive way to the choices placed in front of them. The best candidates and the best campaigns win. It is not really a matter of demand. It is a matter of supply. Over the past two decades, in most constituencies in America, Democrats have generated the best supply of talent, energy, and sheer political ambition. Under those circumstances it has not been crucial for them to match the opinions of the electorate on most of the important national issues of the day.

It should be clear, of course, that we are talking about large numbers of elections. We are talking about a distinction which, over time, enables Democrats to win an extra 10 percent of the seats in a state legislature, or an extra two or three seats in a congressional delegation. It adds up. It does not predict the outcome of an individual campaign. Republicans win their share of elections on the basis of talent all over the country, every election year. They just do not win an equal share.

None of this guarantees the Democratic party majority control of any legislative body anywhere in the system. But it does mean that any party, faction, or interest that wants to compete on equal terms must meet the demands of present-day political life. And doing that requires generating large numbers of people to whom politics is more important, or more rewarding, than money, leisure, or privacy. It is not absolutely necessary that these people believe in government as the ultimate social problem solver. It is helpful if they believe rather strongly in something—something sufficiently compelling to generate the sacrifice involved.

In the chapters to come, in a diverse collection of American communities and states and in national politics, we will meet dozens of people who found themselves drawn into political life in the past generation. The governmental process itself was the magnet for many of them, but not for all: There are characters in this book who were lured into politics by their religion, or by resentment against a local governing elite, or by their convictions about economic development. They are not ideologically alike. But once they entered the political system, they made two common discoveries: One was that politics was work they enjoyed. The other was that the system was wide open to their ideas and ambitions.

2

Thinking About
Power

In modern America the pursuit of office is also the pursuit of influence. This is not a truism. One can readily think of many times and places in which getting elected to a prestigious or visible office has not brought any real chance to control relevant public events. An alderman on a city council dominated by an old-fashioned party machine; a state senator in an early-twentieth-century legislature bought and manipulated by railroad interests; a junior member of a House of Representatives governed by strict seniority—none of these people derived any significant power from holding political office. Getting elected was, for them, a route to a secure paycheck, or to recognition in the community, or perhaps to another, more impressive office. Power resided somewhere else.

If these examples seem rather remote from the realities of American political life in the 1990s, it is only because we have short memories. To find the days when power and office were largely separate entities, we need look back no further than a generation or so, at all levels of the political system.

We sometimes talk of the decline of political parties as if it has been going on for a century, but as recently as the 1950s most large American cities were run by patronage organizations in which the local council—the sovereign legislature—was essentially a rubber stamp. These included not only places such as Chicago, where the boss was the mayor, an elected official himself, but countless cities of less renown where the elected officials took orders from someone who had not been elected to anything. In Utica, New York, the important decisions were arrived at over lunch at a downtown restaurant by a self-made businessman who had run for no public or party office in his entire life. "Officeholders are baby kissers," Rufus Elefante used to say.

In the Connecticut legislature, in those days, it was not much of an exaggeration to say that there were only two votes that really counted: those of the Democratic and Republican state party chairmen, neither of whom was a legislator. To one or the other of them all junior members owed the privileges of nomination and election and whatever precious patronage they might hope to acquire. What they were asked to do in return was vote precisely as their party leaders instructed them. And that, virtually to a man, was what they did.

Meanwhile, in California, the most important figure in legislative politics during the years immediately following World War II was a lobbyist, Artie Samish, who once boasted, "I am the governor of the legislature; to hell with the governor of California." And until remarks such as that brought about his downfall, so he was. To be a state legislator in California, as in Connecticut, was to do as instructed, or to risk losing the support that was necessary for electoral survival.

In Congress orders did not generally come from patronage bosses or arrogant lobbyists. They came from within the institution. But not from very many people in the institution. When Speaker Sam Rayburn needed votes for a piece of crucial legislation in the 1950s, he did not have to gather them one by one, or even in handfuls. The right combination of a dozen senior committee members and state delegation leaders could guarantee Rayburn's success—or, at least as frequently, his defeat. For the other several hundred members of the House, membership was a source of several valuable commodities: an impressive title, a chance to be quoted in the hometown newspaper, a good seat at parades. It offered a chance to be present when historic decisions were made. But it did not offer a chance to make them.

The system I am describing was, in the most important sense, a closed system. It was one in which the few proposed, and the many ratified. Of all the councilmen, legislators, and congressmen who entered the system in any given year, some possessed the ability and persistence to make their way within it and eventually become players. They were the exceptions. For the vast majority life as an elected official, a sovereign legislator, was life in the grandstand.

It is hard to think of anything in American politics that has changed so dramatically over the past generation. What used to be closed is now open. The politicians who used to be spectators are now players. They do not all play, of course; there are backbenchers in any institution. But they take on that role essentially by choice, restricted mainly by the natural limits of their ability to persuade. To win an election, at almost any level of the political system, is to win an opportunity to govern.

Stereotypes die slowly. Newspaper profiles of first-term congressmen can be counted on to include a routine passage to the effect that those just starting out are expected to spend a quiet term or two learning the ropes. This idea that there is an obligatory period of silent apprenticeship serves its purpose, especially when members have to argue with challengers who want to know why they have no conspicuous achievements to point to after two years. But it has little relation to reality. In the U.S. Congress, and to an even greater extent in less competitive institutions at lower levels, the truth is that clever newcomers have the run of the place.

There is no better illustration of this principle than the career of Phil Gramm, the Texas A & M economics professor elected to Congress as a conservative Democrat in 1978. Few of his colleagues appreciated it when he announced almost immediately upon arrival that he knew more about economics than anyone who had entered Congress in the previous thirty years. Moreover, as a free-market conservative, he was ideologically isolated on his own side of the aisle.

Yet Gramm managed within months to place himself at the center of most of the important ongoing debates. In his first term he worked on his own version of the federal budget; in his second term, collaborating with a sympathetic and popular new Reagan White House, he implemented much of it. In 1984 he moved on to the Senate, having switched to the Republican party, and in his first year there sponsored a drastic new law mandating massive spending reductions to achieve a balanced budget. Those efforts, and the arrogance that accompanied them, did not make Gramm any better liked in the Senate than he had been in the House. "You're in the Senate one year, fella," Democrat Daniel Patrick Moynihan of New York reminded Gramm after the Texan had called him weak on defense. "You don't do that to another senator."

But Gramm's personal relationships were no obstacle to gaining influence, any more than his junior status was. So permeable had the institution become that a socially isolated newcomer could accomplish in a few years as much as—or more than—the most collegial and familiar veteran. As Gramm himself said, "You don't have to worry about stepping on people's toes. They get out of the way."

Gramm is worth dwelling on not because he is a singular case but because he differs from others only by degree. In 1979, the same year that Gramm was invading the House from the right, liberal Democrat Henry Waxman of California was wresting a crucial subcommittee chairmanship from a colleague twenty years and several terms his senior; another California Democrat, Tony Coelho, was demonstrating a genius for fund-raising in his very first term that would lead to his selection at the end of that term as the chairman of the party's Congressional Campaign Committee; and Newt Gingrich, a freshman Republican from Georgia, was plotting party strategy for the rest of the century on a blackboard in his House office and persuading some of the most influential journalists in the country to drop by and listen to him.

Most of the people who entered Congress at that time, of course, were doing none of those things. They were going about the routine business of securing reelection, finding issues to focus on, and building legislative careers for themselves. No Congress will ever be composed of 535 Phil Gramms or Henry Waxmans. What matters is the permeability, the openness of it all, and the difference between this situation and the one which existed a generation before.

Does this mean that Congress in the old days was absolutely impermeable to immediate influence? Of course not. Lyndon Johnson was a sort of Tony Coelho of the late 1930s, demonstrating so much skill and energy at raising money that he was all but running the House Democratic Campaign Committee as a freshman forty years before Coelho arrived. Sen. Robert Kerr of Oklahoma was a sort of Phil Gramm of the 1950s, without the ideological zeal, but fully capable of showing up, announcing his determination to dominate events, and then doing so regardless of what his colleagues might think about him.

In the end, though, one has to distinguish between aberrations and norms. Even the least permeable institution usually finds a way to make room for extraordinary talent, but the modern Congress is open to workaday talent as well. One does not have to be a Lyndon Johnson—or a Tony Coelho—to begin having an important impact very quickly. For example, we might examine the House career of Illinois Republican Edward Madigan, elected in 1972. Lacking the boldness of Phil Gramm, the obsessive energy of Tony Coelho, and the glibness of Newt Gingrich, isolated in a House Republican party buried deeply in the minority, he simply inserted himself in the legislative process, and at the end of a decade he could claim to have made far-reaching public policy on health, transportation, and agriculture. In 1991, President Bush nominated him to be Secretary of Agriculture. It is the Ed Madigans, just as much as the Phil Gramms, to whom the openness of the modern congressional system caters.

What is true of Congress is even more true of state legislatures, and truer still of government at the local level. City councils do not have 435 members, as the U.S. House does, and few of them have traditions of seniority that newcomers are required to overcome. Until the 1980s, at least, the majority of these bodies were prone to rapid turnover. Once power at the local level began to open itself up to ambition and talent, it was ripe for taking by any bright young person with the skills to be elected.

The 1950s and early 1960s were a time of intense debate among social scientists about just who did run American communities, and two distinct ideological camps emerged: the stratificationists, who believed in an interlocking power elite of businessmen and elected officials, and the pluralists, who argued that major decisions in a community reflect a balance of competing forces and interest groups, and that those elected to office essentially govern by negotiating among them.

Floyd Hunter of the University of North Carolina spoke loudest for the stratification side with his book on Atlanta, *Community Power Structure.* He described the Atlanta of the 1950s as a place run by a network of forty people who saw each other all the time, both socially and professionally, and made virtually all the community's important decisions, including those nominally in the hands of elected officials. In the years following publication of Hunter's book in 1953, numerous other sociologists and political scientists published books, articles, and papers revealing the existence of similar elites in communities all over the country.

Those notions were challenged most effectively in 1961 by Yale political scientist Robert Dahl. In his book *Who Governs?* Dahl studied New Haven, Connecticut, in minute detail and concluded, in answer to his question, that no elite network was running the city—privately, publicly, or any other way. The old Yankee families had long since ceased to be dominant in politics, the business community was more interested in making money than in making policy, Yale University possessed only a limited sphere of influence, and the city's Italian and Irish ward politicians, preoccupied with jobs and patronage, lost interest rather quickly when the subject turned to broader questions of public policy.

By the mid-1960s the two sides in this argument had fought to an acrimonious and largely unproductive stalemate. Since then relatively little of significance has been written on the subject. While it has been conceded that Hunter's primary method—taking surveys of community leaders to find the "Top 40" influentials—is no way to determine who really holds power in a municipality, there is no consensus about what might constitute a better way. Yet the issue of community power remains important, not only to understand the communities themselves but to comprehend how the American political system as a whole operates. And it is crucial if we wish to understand how the system can change over twenty or thirty years.

After spending significant amounts of time in nearly a dozen medium-sized American communities over the past three years, I believe that Hunter and Dahl were both right, and both wrong. Dahl understood the future, the system of open access to office and power that since the 1960s has come to characterize American politics not only at the local level but at the state level and nationally as well. Hunter and his cohorts caught some of the nuances of a system that was about to expire. In that sense they were on the wrong side of the argument. But there were a great many places in America where politics still operated pretty much as they said it did.

It is necessary to tread carefully in talking about just how closed a society the average American town was a generation ago. When it comes to power and authority, as with most other subjects, nostalgia has a way of playing tricks on us. The world of our childhood, or our early youth, always seems to us a simpler place, a place where the lines of authority were clear and those who exercised it did so without fear of contradiction. The present always takes on a complexity that the past never seems to have possessed. This observation applies not only to government as such but to all the important institutions of society—school, family, and church among them.

It should serve as a warning of some sort that in the 1950s—the simpler time of closely held power that so much of this book describes—students of political power were already discussing the way it had dispersed in the decades since they themselves were young, in the 1920s. And if one chooses to go back a generation beyond that, it is not too difficult to find writers making the same point about the years of their own youth, around the turn of the century.

So if Floyd Hunter's method of the 1950s—generating consensus lists of influential people and proclaiming them to be a power elite—looks a little naive to us a generation later, then my approach—which consists in large part of just listening to aging political figures and businessmen talk about what things "used to be like"—may strike a lot of people as equally inadequate to the task. But after one hundred or so of these conversations, in a diverse collection of places, a few conclusions are simply too obvious to ignore.

In the 1950s, as in the 1980s, a young person with the determination to make his way in the political world had a reasonable opportunity to do it. A great deal of the result depended on simple willingness to work hard. But in that earlier generation, unlike the present one, a great deal of the work consisted of deference.

This deference took many different forms. In Concord, California, one joined the Chamber of Commerce and listened attentively to the opinions of the retail merchants who were its senior statesmen. In Sioux Falls, South Dakota, one was well advised to stop for breakfast each day at Kirk's Restaurant and gradually work one's way into the conversational circle dominated by the realtors, bankers, and other men of business who had emerged as the town's first citizens in the years after World War II. In Greenville, South Carolina, one patron was sufficient—the Greenville County state senator. With his help it was possible to rise very far very quickly. Without it a political career was often a fruitless enterprise. In Utica, New York, it was similarly necessary to cultivate one man, but that man was an unelected, unappointed patronage boss.

In all these places, of course, it is possible to find accounts of people who dedicated themselves during those years to running against the downtown crowd, or whatever it was called locally, and who at some point in their careers seized on a moment of popular resentment to win election and a certain amount of power. These things happened. But it is important to recognize such events for the aberrations they were. In these communities, and most others, and elsewhere on the political spectrum, the life of the maverick was commonly marked by continual frustration. The periodic glimmers of hope and once-in-a-lifetime instances of successful rebellion did not make it an attractive life to many of the ambitious young people of that time.

We need not imagine the fledging city councilman in Utica or the rookie sheriff in Greenville County taking orders in person every day from the local boss. Government by command was unnecessary. In the first place, everyone understood the relationship between pleasing one's sponsor—or sponsors—and being returned to office. There was a certain amount of leverage involved in holding office, but freedom existed within limits that were not difficult to grasp. Beyond them, it simply was not wise to venture. Equally important, the aspiring politician who had taken the time and trouble to advance his career through deference to local leaders was unlikely to desire public policies very different from the ones they desired. He was much more likely to have absorbed their values and their approach to politics and the job at hand. Deference was not primarily a matter of command. It was a way of life.

It was equally so in state legislatures all across America. The rules, norms, and cultures of those legislatures varied enormously from one state and region to another, but the vast majority had at least this feature in common: One person, or one small group, made the important decisions. The rank-and-file membership provided the votes that carried them out, and did so with very little complaint.

Where there was a competitive two-party system, as in Connecticut from the 1930s on, this scenario often took the form of domination by the Democratic and Republican chairmen, whether or not they were members of the institution. Where there was a one-party system, as in all the states of the Deep South, it took the form of domination by a cadre of long-serving legislators who controlled the courthouse politics of their rural districts and remained in their legislative seats term after term as the bulk of the membership shifted around them. Where there was essentially a no-party system, as in California, the legislative chambers frequently came under the spell of lobbying coalitions like the one that enabled Arthur Samish to proclaim himself "governor of the legislature." It was the lobbyists who provided virtually all the campaign money in the no-party states, and it was the lobbyists, therefore, who could cut political careers short by threatening to withdraw their money in the event of inadequate legislative compliance with their wishes.

All legislatures, of course, produced their share of frustrations, resentments, and occasional rebellions. No legislative body was under anybody's thumb 100 percent of the time. But the norm was deference. Whatever part of the country we are talking about— whatever level of the political system—saying no was a demonstration of individualism that one did not undertake lightly.

In the past generation, in most places, that has ceased to be true. We ought to spend a little time asking ourselves why.

In the 1950s, as in the 1980s, there were people at all levels of the system for whom politics was a lifelong fascination, even an obsession. There have always been such people. Some of them would run for office and become public officials, allowing them to spend a greater share of their waking hours on the subject that interested them.

But relatively few of these people in the 1950s, if asked the question directly, would have said that politics was their profession. They did not, for the most part, possess the luxury of treating politics as a full-time career from the beginning of their adult lives. There weren't that many opportunities. To follow the career path of so many of the current generation, from campaign work to a legislative staff position and then to a full-time campaign and public office, was almost never an option. City councilmen and state legislators did not normally have staff positions to award to ambitious young people. Besides, these officeholders could not afford to be full-time politicians themselves. It wasn't year-round work. They had to make a living some other way. Only at the higher reaches of the system—governors, big-city mayors, some members of Congress—was politics truly a full-time occupation.

So the young man angling in those days for a state legislative nomination or a city council seat was nearly always a politician second. No matter how deep his fascination with elections or with governing as a sport, politics was not likely to be his answer to the question "What do you do?" It was not likely to be his definition of himself. Thus, the lawyer, the farmer, the middle-aged businessman finding himself a candidate or an officeholder for the first time saw no particular problem in playing the game the way someone in a position of authority told him to. Politics was an interesting enterprise to be part of. It wasn't his profession. It wasn't his life.

Professionals, by contrast, don't like to be told what to do. This isn't an insight about politics; it applies equally well, and perhaps more familiarly, to any of the more traditional professions: law, medicine, architecture, academa. Professionals don't sacrifice all those years of education and training, all that sweat, to enlist in a hierarchy and defer quietly to those above. At times they may have to do it. But they don't do it very gracefully, or very well.

It is true that the modern professional politician does not have to sweat his way through long and expensive academic preparation. But if by age thirty he has managed to maneuver his way onto a city council, or into a state legislature, he has done so at the expense of years of unglamorous work that are, for him, the equivalent of professional training. "Legislator" is not, in his case, a mere title. It is the nearest thing he has to a professional identity. The odds are that he has given up his job in private life to campaign, or is about to give it up to be able to legislate full-time. It is not logical to expect someone in that position to show up for the first day of elective office and ask where he can receive his orders. He wants to legislate, to make policy.

This is as true in Congress as it is at the state and local levels. Much has been written about the decline of the seniority rule in the U.S. House of Representatives, and the consequences of its abolition in the mid-1970s. Those consequences are important. But it is worth remembering that there never really was any seniority "rule" or any insurmountable procedural obstacle locking the practice in place. Members of the House always had the right to vote for anybody they liked to be a committee chairman. Seniority was a way of legislative life that obliged newcomers to award power on an automatic basis to those who had served the longest. It was a custom that junior members had accepted quietly for most of this century. In the 1970s it ceased to be acceptable. Chairmanships turned into privileges that junior members bestowed upon colleagues who were willing to treat them as full-fledged players. This change was one small symbol of the much larger decline of deference in American politics.

If we had to explain that decline in a single word, *professionalism* would thus be the word. But to leave it at that would be to ignore some of the most important forces that have set the tone of modern political life, the forces that have been operating in the past generation on American society at large. Free political institutions cannot help but reflect the changing values of the broader society. The basis of an individualist Congress, in which authority is weak and diffuse and members arrive determined to express themselves immediately, is the culture in which those values have taken root.

The professional politicians of the most recent generation, born in the years after World War II, were educated amid the political turmoil and intellectual ferment of the late 1960s and early 1970s. They learned as undergraduates, if they had not learned from their parents, about the importance of personal freedom, self-actualization, and "doing their own thing." The dramatic events in government during their formative years were Vietnam and Watergate, both of which instructed them not only in the foolishness but in the outright deceit of those in positions of authority.

They grew up, moreover, at a time when hierarchies were collapsing all around them: hierarchies of family, school, and church as well as those of community leadership and political party. To attend college in the climate of Vietnam and Watergate was, for most people, to question the credentials of those in authority and then to watch the authorities question their own right to hold power. It was to absorb the idea of openness—open meetings, open schools, open relationships, open lives—as a positive force in itself.

Of all the people who might serve as a symbol for the presence of those new values in American politics, none is more incongruous than Jimmy Carter. Fifty-two years old in 1976, a product of the rural Deep South and of a military education, an avowed believer in discipline rather than free expression, he had very little in common with the emerging political generation. He could not legitimately be called a professional politician: He had been nearly forty years old when he first ran for a seat in the Georgia legislature. In fact, much of his initial campaign for president consisted of ridiculing professional politicians. But it was Carter who understood better than anyone else just how open the entire presidential selection process had become. The era of self-nomination had arrived. Asking for the approval of any elders, leaders, or established party factions was unnecessary, if not in fact counterproductive.

It might seem natural to think of George McGovern, rather than Jimmy Carter, as the true messenger of political change. McGovern, winning the Democratic presidential nomination four years before Carter, did challenge the party's leadership and top elected officials. But McGovern spoke for an identifiable faction within the Democratic party. He was an antiwar candidate. In that sense he was traditional. His faction might not have been very popular in old-guard Democratic ranks, but there was no denying that McGovern spoke for an organized political interest. If he had been speaking only for himself, no one would have listened. Carter, by contrast, represented no faction, no interest, no cause. He challenged no hierarchy; there was scarcely any hierarchy available for him to challenge. The door was open, and he walked in.

The story of Carter's self-nomination to the presidency has been told so many times that we need not dwell on it here. Nor is it necessary to devote great detail to the problems of governance that flowed from it. Having been nominated and elected to office without any organized allies in the Democratic party, Carter discovered that it was very difficult to find any when he needed them to run the country. The Congress that scarcely knew Jimmy Carter in 1976 was the same one that turned down most of his initiatives in 1977 and 1978 and began treating him essentially as a legislative irrelevance in 1979 and 1980, the last two years of his only term.

This, too, has been said many times. What matters most for our purposes is the notion, widely discussed and accepted in the years since Carter's presidency, that he was an aberration in recent political history, a product of Watergate and the disillusionment with traditional politics that accompanied it; or, at the very most, a reflection of the way the presidential selection system has untethered itself from normal political processes.

The truth is that Jimmy Carter represented in many ways the future of the political system, not just at the presidential level but at every level down to the city hall and the county courthouse. What Carter did—run for office as the reflection of his own ambitions and values, representing no established interest in the society—is what people have come to do in running for all sorts of offices all over the country. And the problems he encountered in the White House are familiar problems of governing as an executive at any level of the political system at the end of the twentieth century. The same forces that have brought influence to the most junior members of city councils, state legislatures, and Congress have weakened virtually everyone who has tried to direct those institutions from executive office. The more people who have influence within a legislative body, the harder it is for anyone to have influence over it.

While Carter was trying to govern America, Rick Knobe was trying to govern Sioux Falls, South Dakota. The year Carter began organizing his presidential campaign, Knobe had become mayor of that city, a twenty-seven-year-old disc jockey winning a wildly improbable victory over the commercial and political establishment. Like Carter, he had called for open government and an end to elite control. He discovered that while elites are easy targets to run against, they are difficult to govern without. Knobe was far more successful than Carter at sustaining himself politically; he lasted ten years as mayor of Sioux Falls. But he never quite solved the problem of governing the community in the absence of established power. Years later, retired to private life at age forty, he conceded the point. "I felt I was carrying the whole city on my back," Knobe said. "I was an island unto myself."

The year of Carter's political emergence, 1975, was also the year that Louis LaPolla launched his first campaign for mayor of Utica, New York. He was a loner, a city councilman with few friends or allies in the community's public life. But he was consumed by ambition for the job and the prestige it could bring him. He lost that year, and in 1979 as well, but he never lost the desire. In 1983 he finally overthrew the city's Democratic machine and took over City Hall. Like Rick Knobe in Sioux Falls, he soon discovered that the establishment he had unseated wasn't particularly interested in helping him govern; he was on his own. Unlike Knobe, he didn't particularly care. Power was not what interested him; in fact, it frightened him. "When you talk about power," LaPolla said as mayor, "you are talking about being answerable to somebody else. I answer to no one. Only the electorate."

The moral of these mayoral stories, and to a great extent of Jimmy Carter's presidency as well, is that power can evaporate. When it breaks loose from those who have held it in concentrated form, as has happened in American politics over the last generation, it does not necessarily change hands. It may be dispersed so broadly that it might as well have disappeared into thin air. And leadership, which ultimately depends upon the existence of power, may disappear along with it.

The irony of pursuing office in the 1990s is that one may reach a position of influence, find no established elite or power structure blocking its exercise, yet discover that it is more difficult than ever to lead.

That is as good a way as any of summarizing the critical flaw in the political system we have been developing over these past decades. It has allowed power and leadership, at many levels, simply to evaporate.

To make this point is to invite criticism from many people and groups who can argue justifiably that if the system they recall from a generation ago was leadership, they would just as soon not have any. It would be hard, for example, to persuade blacks in Alabama of the virtues of the political system that has disappeared in their state and its legislature over the past two decades. There was real leadership in the Alabama legislature in the 1950s and 1960s: the leadership of a small group of white men representing a few tiny districts in the middle of the state. They determined how much the residents of Alabama would be taxed, and what the tax money would be used for. They defined the limits under which any governor—even George Wallace in his heyday—was forced to operate.

Blacks were no part of this system. They formed the majority in most of the districts that sent the real leaders to the legislature, but they did not help select them. They did not hold office, and, for the most part, they were not allowed to vote. Alabama politics was a closed system in which blacks were shut out. To ask any black person whether he prefers that to the current system, in which blacks constitute nearly 20 percent of the legislature and can determine the outcome of statewide Democratic primaries, is to ask a very silly question.

It would be almost as silly to ask any of Alabama's more than 60,000 classroom teachers whether they would prefer the traditional legislature to the current one, in which power is dispersed among many blocs but teachers are the most numerous. As Alabama politics opened up in the past generation, as the conservative white lawyers who used to dominate the legislature began opting for other sorts of work, teachers stepped in to fill the vacuum, until, in one recent legislative session, 55 of the 140 legislators were teachers, retired teachers, or spouses of teachers. For them an open system, whatever its flaws, has been a ticket to real political influence. To expect them to be nostalgic about the virtues of the old ways is to expect the absurd.

A generation ago in Greenville, South Carolina, it was easy to see where political power resided. It resided with the state senator, who controlled the county budget and directed the appointment of most local officials, and with the textile companies, to whom he normally was connected. That was real leadership—sometimes one-man leadership. However, it disappeared with the reapportionment at the end of the 1960s. Today Greenville has a democratic government at both the city and the county level. To watch it operate is to watch the interplay of forces that were pretty much irrelevant thirty years ago.

Then, as now, Greenville had a large community of evangelical Christians centered at Bob Jones University, but they were not political actors. It did not occur to them to run for office, and if it had they would have found doing so fruitless. There was an establishment, and they were not part of it. Nor were most of the "country people," those living on farms or in crossroads hamlets in the outlying portions of Greenville County. The country people were an unlettered and unsophisticated group that the leaders, based in the city, did not need to pay much attention to. Today, in an open political system, evangelical Christians and country people maneuver for power in local politics and, on some issues, even tell the Greenville business community what it may and may not do. They have been the beneficiaries of the opening up of politics and the decline of deference.

Blacks and teachers in Alabama, Christians and rednecks in Greenville, all brought something to this new open politics. Blacks brought votes, once they were allowed to cast them. Teachers brought professional skills. Christians brought their emerging sense of politics as a calling. Rednecks brought a motivation generated by years of resentment against watching from the sidelines as a Main Street elite governed their community. For all of them, and many groups like them around the country, open politics has been a blessing, and anybody who insists on questioning them about the decline of deference and the evaporation of power is wasting his time as well as theirs.

It remains important, however, to weigh the benefits of openness against the virtues that the open system has taken away. All governments, liberal and conservative alike, need the capacity to say yes, to establish a consensus and act on it in the name of the governed. The community needs to do something about its declining downtown, or the state needs an income tax to finance its programs, or the nation needs to make a coherent response to the impending disasters of inflated oil prices or swollen budget deficits.

The closely held governments of the 1950s had that capacity. They did not always use their authority wisely, or for the benefit of the unrepresented majority, but we need not defend all the arrangements of that era to recognize that something important has been lost. We have replaced governments that could say yes—and make it stick—with governments that offer a multitude of interests the right to say no. We have elected and empowered a generation of political professionals whose independence and refusal to defer makes concerted action, even when necessary, quite difficult. Through their failure to act together to solve commonly recognized problems, these politicians repeatedly disappoint us. But is it their fault, or ours? That is not an easy question to answer.

The following chapters range across the full spectrum of modern American politics, from the intrigues of City Hall and county courthouse to those of the presidential primaries. They move back and forth in time as well, looking at the history of this century and speculating about how our political life might be different in the years ahead. But in essence they are about a few rather straightforward ideas. They are about a political system that is going professional and full-time, and about institutions that used to be closed and tightly controlled and are now open to virtually anyone with the skill and ambition to manipulate them. And they are about the consequences of those changes.

The main characters in this story are the politicians. Voters, who play the lead in most present-day political analysis, both journalistic and academic, are relegated in this book to minor parts. Some readers may find this a little difficult to get used to. I ask their indulgence. I do not present American politics this way out of disrespect for the electorate, or indifference to its concerns. I think that there is a great deal to be gained from looking at the whole system, top to bottom, with our focus on the people who devote their lives to the pursuit of office.

3

The Coming of the Professionals

San Francisco Bay is surrounded by vast agglomerations of suburban territory that are hard to imagine existing anywhere else. The affluent liberals of Marin County, the computer entrepreneurs of Silicon Valley, the middle-aged flower children of Berkeley—none of them would be the least bit plausible transplanted to Chicago or Charlotte. They are creatures of northern California.

Concord, however, is different. It is less than an hour by subway from downtown San Francisco, but if it were suddenly airlifted to another part of the country, it would not be entirely out of place. It is postwar subdivision suburbia, ranch houses and split-levels and an unremarkable shopping mall with 160 stores, anchored by Macy's and J. C. Penney, not Bloomingdale's or Neiman-Marcus.

There are no slums in Concord. There are no traditional ethnic groups of any visibility and only a small minority population. There are no clusters of quaint Victorian houses being restored by young professional couples. Most of the neighborhoods look more or less alike. It takes a developer to appreciate the differences between the houses built on flat land in the 1950s and the slightly more expensive ones built on hillier territory after 1960. On scales that measure family income and educational background, Concord clings to the middle. That is not because it has equal numbers of people at both ends of the spectrum, but because it has virtually nobody anywhere near either end.

Concord is, by and large, a conservative place. Ronald Reagan had no trouble carrying it in 1980 and 1984, and it voted twice for Republican George Deukmejian in his victorious gubernatorial campaigns against Los Angeles Mayor Tom Bradley. Yet throughout the 1980s it was governed without the participation of any conservatives at all. From the day the city's voters threw out the last Republican council member in 1980 until they finally rebelled nearly a decade later, Concord was governed exclusively by Democrats more than comfortable with the liberalism of the national Democratic party.

During the eighties the Concord city council was among the first in the nation to institute a comparable-worth program to boost the salaries of female city employees, subsidize a "rape crisis" center, and impose a "child care fee" on developers who wanted to build downtown. The local government fed the homeless at lunchtime in the city parks. The voters did not ask for any of these innovations, but for years they did not really complain about them either. The five Democrats who composed the city council at the end of 1982 were still there in 1989. All five were reelected at least once, without serious competition.

It was, in fact, their very record of consistent electoral success that led Concord's leaders astray. Over the course of the decade, in the absence of any sustained interest in local government on the part of the community, they proceeded to implement their own values rather than those of the people who elected them. Doing so did not seem to be a great risk, and for a long time it was not. But in the campaign of 1989 the government of Concord finally learned that it could overreach itself. The 5–0 Democratic government that had seemed so permanent suddenly was converted into a 3–2 Republican majority.

As a laboratory for studying present-day local politics in America, Concord is almost too good to be true. It offers all the important lessons: the professionalization of political life, the open path to power for those committed to using it, the opportunities all this creates for liberal Democratic government, the limits of what that government can achieve, and the ingredients of any successful opposition to it in the 1990s. Concord is thus an ideal place to begin asking questions about the players in modern American politics. But to understand the players and what brought them onstage, we need to know a little history.

For a community that is so visibly a creature of the postwar era, Concord has a long and interesting past. It has existed as a town since 1846, when Don Salvio Pacheco, a well-connected Mexican soldier and politician, settled on the 17,000 acres the government in Mexico City had made available to him. Pacheco built his own house on the current site of downtown, and the village that grew up around his cattle ranch was called Pacheco Town. Later the name was changed to Todos Santos. In 1869 it was changed again, to Concord.

There are people in town who treasure that history, descendants of the Spanish grantees who constituted the community's first elite. They devote their time to the Concord Historical Society. They produce impressive volumes filled with pictures of the place they remember. That place, however, no longer exists. Even more than in most communities in America, the historic Concord has been obliterated by the past forty years. There are only a handful of buildings that recall it and, it sometimes appears, only a handful of people who know anything about it. The families whose presence in town goes back to the nineteenth century have little to do with the politics of the city. It makes no sense to talk about how Concord has changed since 1940; there isn't enough continuity to measure the changes. A village ceased to exist, and a city, essentially unaware of its roots, grew up to take its place.

Pacheco Town had more than 1,000 residents by 1867. Three-quarters of a century later, as World War II began, Concord had only 1,373. It was a market town for the dairy farmers and grape and walnut growers who prospered through the 1920s along the slopes of nearby Mount Diablo. But the war delivered an industrial boom to all the East Bay towns in Contra Costa County, brought within easy reach of San Francisco by the completion of the Bay Bridge in 1936. Oil, chemicals, and other war materials were shipped overseas from Port Chicago, along the water just north of the city, and at its peak Port Chicago employed more than 4,000 people.

After the war Concord had no choice but to grow. There was just too much population pressure in the Bay Area for it to remain a small town. But it had some choice about what it would become. The wartime boomtowns along the Bay—Richmond, Pittsburg, and Antioch—held on to their newly attracted heavy industry and soon turned into the factory towns they remain to this day. Concord didn't want the industry—it just wanted the people. And that made sense. Concord had thousands of acres of flat land suitable for the tract homes that would be difficult to build in hillier locations nearby.

By the 1950s Concord was a fast-growing bedroom community for the blue-collar families whose breadwinners worked at U.S. Steel in Pittsburg and Shell Oil in Martinez. A fair number of these blue-collar suburbanites were actually southerners—rural people who had left Oklahoma and Arkansas in the Dust Bowl years of the 1930s, struggled to find agricultural work when they got to California, and then took advantage of the defense plant jobs that opened up in the Bay Area when World War II began. They were crucial not only in populating Concord in the 1950s but in giving it an image as a redneck town that has never entirely worn off. The city's most powerful politician of recent times, councilman, mayor, and later State Sen. Daniel Boatright, was an Arkansas-born conservative Democrat who would have been just as credible a candidate in his home state as he was in Concord.

When the 1950 census was taken, there were nearly 7,000 people in Concord. In 1955 there were more than 24,000. Early in the 1960s the population reached 50,000. By 1980, when most of the available land was used up and planners were beginning to talk about Concord as a "mature" suburban community, there were 101,844 residents—a hundredfold increase in less than forty years.

The kind of government Concord had before World War II, and for quite a while afterward, was the kind a small agricultural village needed—not very much government at all. There was almost literally no industry: The one factory, a cement plant, finally closed down in the 1940s because farmers complained that dust from it was choking them. The only people with any professional interest in public decisions were the merchants whose stores surrounded Todos Santos Plaza, in Concord's modest downtown.

The merchants were the government, such as it was. There wasn't even a city hall—the city council met in the old Fireman's Hall, where it had been gathering since 1905. The mayor in 1950 was the man who had held the office since 1938—Louis Pedrizetti. For most of his twelve years as mayor, Pedrizetti could do his job without undue strain. The city council met one night every other week; when it was not in session none of its members gave it a great deal of thought, and there is no evidence that the voters of Concord asked them to.

There is nothing at all surprising in the fact that Concord got by with a part-time merchant government in the years when it was a tiny market town. What is interesting is that it practiced something not very different all the way into the 1970s, by which time it was a city of nearly 100,000 people. The reason Concord could preserve the forms of small-town politics for so long was the presence of one unusual man: Farrel A. "Bud" Stewart. Born in 1922 in the San Joaquin Valley, Stewart came to Concord with an engineering degree in the early 1950s, took a job as public works director, and built the new City Hall, completed in 1956, which was one of the town's first real concessions to its bewildering new semiurban status.

By 1960 Bud Stewart was Concord's city manager. He would remain in that job for twenty-six years, creating a one-man permanent government that made it possible for the elected officials to treat their offices as extracurricular activity. Stewart had the soft voice and bedside manner of a kindly midwestern country doctor, but just about all the mayors and city councilmen who dealt with him over thirty years swore that he was one of the shrewdest local politicians they had ever run across. In 1986, when the youthful activist majority on the council finally induced him to leave his job—determining that they, not he, should be running the city—they decided to name the whole complex of buildings by then surrounding his 1956 City Hall the F. A. Stewart Civic Center.

Some Concord politicians are a little wistful now about the glory days of Concord's gentle power broker; others are glad the Stewart era finally ended. But there is no argument over who was in charge during the crucial years when Concord evolved from a village to a suburb. "Bud Stewart was the mayor," says Mike Pastrick, a longtime city planning commissioner. "Bud Stewart was the city government. A lot of what the council did was ceremonial." Steven Weir, a city councilman who helped ease Stewart out of office, talks about the departed city manager in somewhat harsher terms: "Stewart ran the city like a dictator. He appointed all the department heads and then he ran all the departments."

Stewart, speaking as softly as ever in retirement, isn't very comfortable talking about himself as an autocrat. But he does not disguise his nostalgia for the days when the politicians were amateurs. "They were rarely around City Hall," he remembers, "except on the days when the city council met. If a councilman walked into City Hall on any other day, bells and lights went off." When the time did come for a meeting, the members looked at the figures Stewart's staff had put together, asked a few questions, and voted yes. If the city manager needed them between meetings, he knew where to find them.

"When I first came on," says Larry Azevedo, a Republican first elected in 1968, "it was like a good old boys' club. The city manager would call me up and I'd go down to a coffee shop and two or three other councilmen would be there and we'd shoot the breeze and do some business."

There was an intimate connection between the "boys' club" that was Concord politics twenty-five years ago and the Chamber of Commerce that presided over the community's growth and development. The chamber was the political training ground. Most of the time an aspiring officeholder tried out his leadership skills there before moving on to elective office. George Krueger, a two-term mayor in the 1950s and early sixties, and perhaps the most important local politician of those days, was also a dominant presence in the chamber through his downtown insurance office. Warren Boggess, who served as mayor after Krueger, went to the council straight from the Chamber of Commerce presidency.

There was nothing very mysterious or conspiratorial about all this. Large as Concord had become by the mid-1960s, there wasn't really anything to it besides retail business and residential neighborhoods. It never occurred to the businessmen of that era that anybody else should be leading the city; nobody else seemed to want to. When a candidate had the anointment of the chamber and the active campaign help of the Jaycees, he could count on a relatively comfortable election.

Larry Azevedo is only in his mid-fifties, but he is as good a symbol as any of the way Concord politics used to be. At age twenty-five, not long out of college, he opened a sporting goods store adjacent to a new shopping center on the outskirts of downtown. He joined the Chamber of Commerce and the Elks. By the time he was thirty his friends in the chamber backed him for city council and he won. Two years later he was mayor. Altogether, Azevedo stayed on the city council twelve years. When he left, in 1980, he took with him the last remaining Republican presence in city government.

Azevedo was an amateur in politics. He ran for office as a businessman, and he left it, twelve years later, with the feeling that he was returning to his "real job" (although by then he was out of sporting goods and was running a travel agency). "I wasn't in there to make any dramatic changes," he said long afterward. "I had no design on the political life-style. . . . I found before long that it was distasteful for me to work with politicians." It is not unusual, of course, to find people at all levels of government who work at politics full-time and protest vehemently that they are not politicians. In general, they are not very convincing. A skeptic can point out in Azevedo's case that, for someone who found political life distasteful, he nevertheless managed to run for reelection twice and serve in office more than a decade.

But Azevedo is believable. He and his contemporaries in city office were skeptical not only of politics but of government. They believed in keeping the streets clean and picking up the garbage and staying out of controversy wherever possible. They were not in office to create new ways to use government. "I never carried a cross for social services," Azevedo says now with pride. "I believed that if you took care of your brick and mortar and essential services, the social services would come about." And that is the philosophy with which Concord governed itself during three critical decades in its history.

The difference between Concord politics in the 1960s and in the 1980s is the difference between the amateur and the professional—the difference, one might say, between Larry Azevedo and Steve Weir. When he ran for office in 1968, Azevedo took five months away from his business to campaign. After he was elected he was able to go back to it pretty much on a regular basis. When Weir won election to council at the same age in 1980, he didn't have to walk away from anything—he was already in the politics business full-time. Weir earned his living as an aide to State Senator Boatright; after his election he kept his job in Boatright's office for more than five years. Azevedo found himself mayor of Concord in his early thirties through a series of political events he never really planned or expected. He reaped the benefits that flowed in those days to bright, personable young men with the skill to make the right connections downtown. Weir, equally bright and energetic, reached the same public office at the same stage in life, as the climax to a political obsession that began when he was a small boy.

Steve Weir grew up in Pleasant Hill, a smaller and somewhat more affluent suburb that adjoins Concord on the south. When he was six he was helping his parents distribute literature in a campaign for a water measure. By the time he was eleven years old, in 1960, he was a member of the Young Democrats and was passing out brochures for John F. Kennedy. As a teenager he combed the voting lists of Pleasant Hill's subdivisions, searching out the unregistered to help boost Democratic turnout. By the time he got his political science degree at Berkeley, he knew as much about organizing a precinct as anybody in Contra Costa County. He became a protégé of Boatright's, and, when he was twenty-four, he got Boatright to appoint him to the county water board. Meanwhile, he went on Boatright's payroll as a constituent service aide.

Then, in the late seventies, he moved into Concord and began planning his campaign for the city council. "Concord was wide open when I came in here," he recalls. "A guy could walk in from Pleasant Hill, work the city in five years, and get elected. I had done Boatright's constituent work. I had a really good in with seniors, and I had a lot of political savvy. I put together a campaign as if I was running for my life. I ran like a man possessed." Weir was running for the city council the same year that Ronald Reagan was running for president against Jimmy Carter. And the man Weir had to beat, a nine-year Republican incumbent named Dick Holmes, sounded like a local echo of Reagan. "The next four years," Holmes said, "is not the time for free-spending liberals to gain on-the-job training. The city council must continue to strive for greater cost efficiency in all departments."

Concord liked what Reagan was saying at the national level and awarded him 59 percent of its vote. But Weir, outspending Holmes by a margin of more than 2 to 1, finished ahead of him and all the other council candidates, demonstrating convincingly that money and sheer talent were coming to mean more than ideology in the city's elections. For nine years after Holmes's defeat and Azevedo's retirement, no Republican would come close.

None of Concord's other leaders of the 1980s had quite the life history of political preoccupation that Steve Weir did. But they all shared one trait with him—they never treated politics as a sideline. When they ran for office, they gave it their undivided attention, whatever the costs might be. They knew what a campaign was all about long before they started running. "The typical person who gets elected now," said Bud Stewart in 1987, "is someone who grows up in the political process. Politics is a vocation for them." Some of Weir's colleagues in Concord politics had worked at a variety of jobs. But it is fair to say of all of them that nowhere else did they achieve the success or the public attention they were able to win as politicians.

Ron Mullin, who succeeded Weir as mayor in 1985, was a former police officer who had just finished law school when he enlisted in Weir's 1980 campaign. He spent most of the next two years building on those contacts and won a seat himself in 1982. Diane Longshore, Weir's predecessor as mayor, tried real estate and ran a home repair franchise before giving those up for politics. Colleen Coll, who served as mayor after Mullin, is the daughter of a longtime Concord politician. She dropped out of law school, then sold computers and ran promotional campaigns for a string of gas stations before finding something she could do well—organize campaigns and run for office herself. In 1987, when she won her second term on the council, her father proclaimed grandly that it was what she was born to do. "She was my pride and joy," Tom Coll said, "because at the age of ten she loved politics. She's had a lifetime of this."

Nearly everybody who holds office in Concord has another job somewhere. At an annual salary of less than $10,000, a seat on the city council doesn't provide a living wage. But for most of them a job in private life is simply a way to make a political career possible. It is a means, not an end. Some of the old-timers make fun of that attitude. "Three of five people on council now," Larry Azevedo complained a few years ago, "effectively don't have a profession. They spend all their time at City Hall because they don't have something else to do."

The people who held office in Concord twenty years ago would not have wanted the job if it had required them to spend most of their working hours at City Hall. Equally important, they would not have wanted to do what it now takes to get elected. Much of the criticism of current campaigns at all levels is focused on their financial cost. That is a legitimate issue in Concord. A full-scale campaign for the city council can cost $50,000 or more, and a campaign that expensive is beyond the reach of the average citizen starting from scratch. Still, a candidate with a background in local politics and a decent set of contacts can raise that much. The truly formidable barriers are those of time and physical effort.

In October of 1987, as the incumbent mayor seeking reelection to the council, Ron Mullin walked precincts and knocked on doors every day for a month, evenings until dark and weekends from morning until night. The only reason he limited himself to those hours was because most people were away or in bed asleep the rest of the time. And this was for a campaign in which he had no threatening opposition. Why did he go to so much effort? Because that is the way it is now done in Concord, as in many communities like it throughout America. Not to pound the pavement is to risk being labeled as somebody who isn't serious about getting elected. "It's been proven with consistency," says Mullin, "that the only way to win is to walk. You have to like going out and pressing the flesh and placing yourself at risk." As an ex-policeman, Mullin had to conquer his well-developed instinct to hang back from a doorway out of fear of what might be greeting him inside. But he did it. He wanted badly to win.

It takes a great deal of work to get elected in Concord. It does not necessarily take many votes. Except when there is an issue of unusual controversy involved, turnout rarely reaches much above 20 percent of registered voters. In many of Concord's neighborhoods the residents work outside the city, shop in Walnut Creek or Pleasant Hill, read newspapers and watch newscasts in which Concord affairs are overshadowed by those of the Bay Area in general. To the extent that they identify with any local government, it is as likely to be a homeowners' association as it is the Concord city council.

So, in a community of more than 100,000 people, 7,000 votes can be enough to win a city council seat. But finding those 7,000 votes is more a task for specialists than ever before. In an era of computerized precinct targeting, the sophisticated candidate can easily schedule his personal campaigning to place the highest priority on the precincts where the voting will be substantial and where there are pockets of undecided households that might be influenced by a personal visit. The knowledge this requires is no secret—targeting has been around far longer than computers. But the more sophisticated this work becomes, the greater the disadvantage for any candidate who is not familiar with it and has to learn in the few weeks before the election.

City council members are given four-year terms in Concord, but in the 1980s thinking about the next campaign became more or less a year-round activity, whether it was an election year or not. "The work," said Bud Stewart, "isn't sitting at your desk from eight to five. The work is cultivating your base as a political leader." Or in the words of Dale Adams, one of Concord's most prominent lawyers and a onetime council candidate himself, "We don't have people going into government as a profession. What they are going into is politics."

The members of Concord's governing majority worked reasonably well with one another on most matters of public policy. But they were not very close on a personal basis. And that too represented an important departure from the politics of the previous generation.

On the eastern outskirts of Concord is an affluent residential street that is home to four men who served as mayor of the city between 1960 and 1975. Its formal name is St. Francis Drive. Residents prefer to call it "Bullshit Hill." The term is more than just a way for the city to play a joke on its politicians. It is a symbol of the close-knit political system under which people not only made decisions together but socialized and chose to build houses next door to each other. Those days are over. "There's no old boy network," Steve Weir says of Concord now, and all his colleagues agree.

"The members don't see each other as frequently as we did," reflects Daniel Helix, who won a council seat in the late 1960s and served as mayor right after Azevedo, now his next-door neighbor. "They are living their own lives and being involved in their own pursuits. They get together thirty minutes before each council meeting starts." For Helix, one of the few elected officials of his era who were not businessmen (he had taught civics in high school), running for office was an attempt to climb the ladder socially as well as politically. "It was a chance to break out of the pack, to get out of being a faceless nobody and become somebody in the community. These seemed to be the 'in' people, and I wanted to be part of them."

There are a variety of reasons why people run for office, as there always have been, in California suburbs and everywhere else. But in Concord, in the modern era, one thing is certain. They are not doing it to improve their social lives. Political ambition and social ambition have become two different things.

However little they saw of one another outside politics, though, the leaders of the 1980s tended to have a common outlook on government and on society. They were, to all intents and purposes, a political generation. With the exception of June Bulman, who was considerably older than the others and began dabbling in politics through the League of Women Voters three decades before, all the members who made up the Concord city council during the past decade were born in the late 1940s and went to college in the late 1960s. They all brought with them into office the view of government as social problem-solver that animated national politics in the years they were going to school.

Not all of them declared themselves quite as openly as Colleen Coll, who defined her politics by proclaiming, "I am a humanitarian." But all of them endorsed Ron Mullin's contention that "if I believed government wasn't an institution beneficial to society, I wouldn't give a tinker's damn about politics." These sentiments were a far cry from those of the Republican president in whose era these liberals flourished; they were equally far from the views of Larry Azevedo and Concord's previous governing generation.

Coming from people whose first concerns were so evidently their own political futures, such declarations of governmental idealism might well sound hollow. In fact, though, there is no reason to doubt that they were genuine. Ideology and ambition are not mutually exclusive in American politics; an officeholder is rarely required to choose between saving his seat and promoting a set of values. Skillful politicians have ample opportunity to do both.

The one value that came through most clearly in any examination of the priorities of the Concord Democrats was feminism. This may be explained in part by the fact that for most of the 1980s three of the five members of the city council were women. But gender alone does not account for the array of programs enacted in Concord in that decade that reflected a feminist agenda in local government: comparable worth; rape crisis counseling; the child care fee required of downtown developers. On these subjects there was no disagreement by gender.

The comparable-worth program—"pay equity" in its formal description—is an especially interesting case. While the federal government was talking about studying ways to boost salaries in female-dominated jobs, the Concord city council was devoting 2 percent of its annual salary budget to that very goal; Concord was one of the first cities in the country to implement such a program for its employees.

There wasn't a single voice of dissent when the council approved comparable worth in 1985, but nobody who supported the measure claims that it represented the collective will of the community. It was something the five people in charge of the city wanted to do. "They were prepared to move in that direction whatever the cost might be," said Bud Stewart, who was city manager at the time. "These things weren't imposed on them by any pressure group. This was their own view of right and wrong."

There were occasional rumblings of dissatisfaction in the years after the program got started. The police department, which was not included, complained that its salaries were falling behind. Some male engineers, convinced that they were being shortchanged, chose to leave city employment. One Republican challenger referred to the pay-equity program as Concord's "million-dollar mistake." All in all, though, the dissent was minimal. Concord's liberal city government took an idea that was bitterly controversial at the national level, imposed it on a rather conservative community, and felt no ill effects politically.

It is important to stress that the council was acting in the absence of any organized opposition. When it came to social policy, Concord's Democrats saw no political reason not to proceed with their own agenda. On other questions, though, where there was evidence that the electorate was paying more attention, they were much more cautious. In election years they could overreact to seemingly minor political problems, sometimes forcing unpleasant policy consequences in the long run.

The best example was the debate over the city's utility users' tax. In 1983 the city council had eliminated a budget shortfall by imposing a 2 percent tax on gas, electric, and telephone bills. There seemed at the time to be few alternatives; the statewide approval of Proposition 13 in 1978 had strictly limited the income Concord could expect from property taxes, and the sales tax, already providing more than 40 percent of the city's revenues, could not realistically be expected to contribute much more.

The vote in favor of the utility tax was unanimous, and even after it was in place there were few complaints about it. More than 60 percent of the tax burden was on businesses, and they seemed to accept it. But early in 1985 the issue suddenly reappeared, resurrected not by taxpayers but by Mayor Steve Weir, who turned against the tax and chose to make it the central issue of his reelection campaign. Weir, claiming that the city had developed an $8 million budget surplus, asked the council to place a referendum on that year's ballot that would repeal the tax. Most voters had paid little attention to the issue, but given a chance to wipe a tax off the books, they did so by a margin of 3 to 1. And Weir was reelected that year with 11,539 votes—more than any candidate in Concord had ever received. The result was that two years later Concord once again had a million-dollar deficit, and seventeen city employees had to be laid off. Equally important in the long run, the referendum had made any future utilities tax virtually impossible, and any sort of new broad-based tax very difficult. So Concord found itself with a budget problem that seemed destined to remain for years to come.

All in all, it was not one of the finest hours in the history of Concord city government. The utility-tax debate, if it can be called a debate, was a series of events unimaginable under the political system that had been in place fifteen years earlier. The old merchant government, taking a far less expansive view of its responsibilities, probably would not have spent enough money to generate a significant deficit. If it did face such a deficit, it would have been unlikely to meet it with a tax aimed largely at businesses. If it found itself with such a tax on the books, it almost certainly would have kept it in place rather than give up the revenue. In short, it would have left well enough alone.

The political professionals who replaced this government in the 1980s were, on balance, competent, hardworking, and serious. But their intensity could be a drawback. These were people who liked to solve problems. When, amid the pressures of an election year, they faced a shortage of problems to solve, they confronted a real temptation to create new problems so they could have the opportunity to solve them.

It was becoming apparent in Concord politics, as in national politics, that campaigning and governing now required two different sets of skills. The city's leaders won election through their mastery of campaign technique, not through their demonstrated capacity for leadership. Most of the time this distinction didn't hurt the community very much. The brains and energy that made Steve Weir a master campaigner helped him become a shrewd, effective legislator as well. But there were times when politics and government did not mix very well, and at those moments government tended to be the loser.

The Democrats of Concord ran a coalition government. The coalition sounds incongruous at first, but it met the needs of all its participants for the better part of a decade. It included most of the city's business community and, especially, its real estate developers.

The city council was both committed to running an activist government and short of money with which to operate it. As the utility-tax episode proved, the council was also extremely sensitive to the political risks of paying for more government with higher taxes. But a way was found to pay for social programs at no direct cost to the taxpayer. It was downtown development. Concord's subsidized child care program, for example, was financed largely through a flat fee of 0.5 percent of the assessed value of all new commercial projects within the downtown redevelopment area. By 1988 it had brought $671,000 earmarked for child care into the city treasury. But it was a one-time fee. The only way to keep the money coming in was to keep attracting new development.

Nearly everybody in Concord politics appreciated the connection between development and liberal government. "If we're going to be doing all these things," said June Bulman, the council's senior member, "we have to have a base to support them." Colleen Coll, in the midst of her campaign for reelection in 1987, boasted of the way the system worked. "Right now," she said, "I have six developers lined up to renovate the child abuse prevention center—pro bono." But for straight talk about the way the system worked, nobody could match John Gilkison, Jr., a young political consultant who worked with most of the council Democrats. "You get business to support you," he explained, "and then you zonk them on the social programs."

For nearly three decades after World War II, Concord had little appeal to commercial developers. Nearby Walnut Creek became one of the leading centers of office development in the Bay Area, but Concord, burdened by its less-than-fashionable image as a blue-collar bedroom suburb, did not share in the boom. That began to change, though, in the 1970s. The cost of space in San Francisco forced companies to think about locating corporate offices somewhere else. When the Bay Area Rapid Transit System (BART) was completed in 1976, with Concord the terminus of one of its major lines, Chevron moved its credit-card-processing operations to a new building on the outskirts of downtown; that data center eventually came to house 2,700 employees.

But the breakthrough year was 1980. The Bank of America decided to move its enormous credit card operation from San Francisco to Concord, attracted by the presence of exactly the kind of work force it wanted. Concord offered a large pool of young married women, high school educated, eager for work that could provide a second income, and willing to perform repetitive clerical chores for a modest salary. That sort of labor force was becoming difficult to find in San Francisco. Concord's city council offered a $5 million subsidy—a $13 million piece of property near the downtown BART station for $8 million. One Monday morning in late 1983, commuters driving to work noticed that six blocks of buildings in downtown Concord no longer existed. Over the next few months five new pink-and-gray buildings were erected to replace them. By 1985 there were 4,000 people working in those buildings. The Bank of America had become by far Concord's largest employer.

The bank added 1.1 million feet of new office space to the city. But far more elaborate plans were being drawn up. In mid-1985 the council voted in favor of a master plan for downtown development that called for an eventual 5 million more square feet of downtown office space, with 2,500 new apartments and condominiums and a predicted increase of 75 percent in downtown vehicle traffic by the year 2000. "A stable of developers is in line," the Contra Costa Times reported, "to cover the city landscape with housing, offices, a convention center and a parking garage."

Much of what was on the drawing boards then has not yet been built, and much of it never will be. But there was no question by 1985 that Concord had changed irrevocably. And development had changed the city in political as well as commercial terms. For the first time in its history, Concord was an object of commercial courtship. It had something developers wanted—space. And developers had something the Concord political leaders wanted—money the government could spend.

There was an opposition to Concord's government in those years, but it was not the conservative, business-based opposition one might have expected. "I'd rather have our five liberal Democrats," said Harry York, executive vice-president of the Chamber of Commerce, "than some of the so-called conservatives in the surrounding cities." Instead, the opposition came from those who believed, for one reason or another, that there was too much development going on in Concord, and too much power in the development community.

Byron Campbell emerged in the mid-1980s as the most articulate voice of that opposition. A rich real estate investor who had moved to Concord from San Francisco, he began turning up at council meetings and digging for information about development schemes that were under way. "There is no way to raise money out there," he complained one day in 1987, "except from developers and unions—the development and building industry. You could fire a cannon in a council meeting and not hit anybody but a developer. That's the only people who go. Everything that gets debated is a done deal. The development community absolutely controls this city council."

The day he spoke those words, Campbell amounted to little more than a clever but harmless gadfly. He had fought for a height limit on the city's commercial buildings, and he had lost. He had fought to restrict major airline traffic at the small Concord airport, and he had lost. In the fall of 1987 two of the incumbent council Democrats were gliding to reelection, and one of them, Colleen Coll, was preparing to focus her liberal energies on her upcoming two-year term as mayor. The city seemed to have acquired a permanent governing majority that it did not particularly endorse but lacked any motivation to challenge.

Over the course of their years in power, Concord's leaders had been keenly sensitive to what they could and could not do politically. They never forgot they were governing a conservative community. Still, their commitment to politics as a full-time profession, and their obvious skill at practicing it, appeared to insulate them from any prospect of significant ideological backlash. As the local government began its last two-year term of the decade, its members felt as free to innovate as any group of five people in their position ever would. It was at that point that things began to fall apart.

In their search for the tax base that might underwrite a government of social activism, Concord's leaders had long been interested in acquiring for the community the one type of residential development it had never had: large homes for rich people. Over the 1980s the

arrival of Bank of America and other major employers had brought
in a core of top-rank executives who commuted to Concord from
other suburbs. Why not build them a subdivision, the city council
reasoned, so they could live where they worked—and pay taxes into
the Concord economy?

After years of discussion the council found developers who
wanted to create such a subdivision, on the huge Crystyl Ranch
property at the foot of Mount Diablo. This was not the easiest sell
to the community at large, which was nervous about possible environmental damage to the hillside, but the Concord planning commission approved a 450-home development at Crystyl Ranch by a 3–2
vote. The developers, however, found the terms of the deal unacceptable. In order to sell $500,000 houses in Concord, they said, a com-
munity that had never been associated with affluent living, something
special would be required. The Crystyl Ranch development would
have to communicate the idea of luxury to anybody who saw it. It
needed a golf course. In the developers' opinion, that would be
economically viable only if the project were increased to 700 homes.
And it would mean a few small changes in the gradient at the bottom
of Mount Diablo.

The city council reversed the planning commission and voted
4–1 in favor of 700 homes and a golf course. And as the 1989 election
approached, the council members found themselves confronting the
Save Mount Diablo Coalition, a rising protest against the traffic
congestion the new development was likely to create. A proposition
was placed on the November ballot asking the citizens of Concord
to cancel the entire idea of a fancy new subdivision at Crystyl Ranch.

While that issue was simmering, the city's voters began complaining about another kind of construction project that few of them
liked or understood. Along the median strips of Concord Avenue,
the main entrance into town off Highway 680, the city government
had begun erecting a row of metal poles, ninety-one in all, as thick
as telephone poles and ranging from 6 to 50 feet high. They were the
creation of a consultant the government had brought in, and they
were supposed to have an art deco look, part of an effort to give drab,
middle-class Concord some of the reputation of a sophisticated community in search of innovation and high technology.

The city council thought the poles would make Concord dis-
tinctive. Most of the people who saw them thought they would make
the town a laughingstock. What idiot, they asked each other,

dreamed up the idea of spending $100,000 in public money to put up ninety-one giant knitting needles on Concord Avenue? The poles did not work. And they were hard to ignore without closing your eyes in the middle of traffic.

But even the poles weren't the worst issue Concord's government had to deal with as the election approached. The worst issue was the AIDS law. Early in 1989, on the advice of its Human Relations Commission, the Concord city council had voted unanimously in favor of an ordinance forbidding discrimination against people suffering from AIDS. The language of the ordinance was not much different from what had been enacted in other Bay Area communities. Still, the council might have foreseen trouble here. A couple of years earlier, when it had voted in favor of giving city sanction to an observance of Gay Pride Week, the community had forced a reversal of the decision. A prudent politician didn't fool with gay rights in Concord.

The AIDS ordinance was in fact made to order for the man who had led the protest against Gay Pride Week, the Reverend Lloyd Mashore, proprietor of the Kings Valley Christian School. Mashore called the ordinance "a product of the homosexual agenda." He pointed out that it prohibited discrimination not only against AIDS sufferers but against those who had "associated" with them—in his eyes, a surreptitious effort to slip in a general-purpose gay rights provision without public debate. Mashore and his fundamentalist allies made sure the AIDS ordinance would be on the ballot right next to the Crystyl Ranch housing development.

In the final weeks of the campaign, the problems of the Concord city council seemed to jell into a vague feeling that the people who ran the council "just didn't listen." The fifteen candidates challenging for the three contested seats said it; the voters said it back to them whenever they campaigned door to door. The leaders had stopped listening.

On November 7, 1989, the voters of Concord did two things that surprised very few people. They repealed the AIDS ordinance, and they canceled Crystyl Ranch. But they also did something that a few months earlier would have been unthinkable. They broke up the city's "permanent" Democratic majority. June Bulman was defeated. Diane Longshore, who had chosen to step down, and Steve Weir, who had become county clerk, were both replaced by Republicans. When the council held its first meeting of the 1990s, there would be a 3–2 Republican majority. The Reverend Lloyd Mashore would be one of the members. And Byron Campbell, the antidevelopment activist, would be mayor.

The 1989 election was a vote of no confidence in the government that had been in control of city life for the past decade. "Concord was the greatest social experiment in the Bay Area," Campbell said after the returns were in. "But the liberal left became their own worst enemies. They got ahead of their constituents. Elected officials should probably be a few steps ahead. These people were a few steps ahead, around the corner, and out of sight."

It is reasonable, in the context of modern Concord politics, to call what happened in 1989 a revolution. But it is equally important to notice what it was not: a restoration. While some of what was written in the aftermath of the vote suggested a return to Azevedo-style politics—basic services at the expense of social reform—there were no Larry Azevedos in the group of Republicans who wrested control out of Democratic hands. Byron Campbell had as much in common with Concord's leaders of the 1980s as with the merchants who had run the city on a part-time basis in Azevedo's day.

Campbell had started out his adult life as an insurance investigator, checking out million-dollar policies in the elite neighborhoods of San Francisco. He noticed that his company's richest customers all seemed to own real estate. So he bought a Victorian house in an old San Francisco neighborhood, fixed it up, sold it, and bought another one. Soon he was out of insurance and into residential property full-time, and by the time he moved to Concord in the mid-1970s, he was a rich man, able to live quite comfortably on his investments and spend his time on anything he chose.

What he eventually chose to spend it on was politics. His crack that nobody but developers ever went to city council meetings in Concord wasn't quite true: He himself went to every one. He knew the details of all the development deals the council voted for. He knew how much money the council members were raising for their elections and where it was coming from. His efforts in behalf of the ballot propositions he supported evolved in five years from slapdash to highly sophisticated.

Early in 1989, when Campbell launched the campaign that would make him mayor of Concord, he was still describing himself as a concerned citizen trying to keep watch on city government. But he was more than that. He had sold the only two businesses that took up significant amounts of his time: a court-reporting business and a resort on the Russian River. He had crossed the line into a full-time political career. And he had to admit that he was no longer doing it, if he ever had been, as a sacrifice. He liked it. It was fun.

Byron Campbell was different from Steve Weir and Colleen Coll in one respect: He was running for office for the first time at age fifty-one. He had become a politician in middle age, not in childhood. But he campaigned with the same skills they had perfected in the 1980s. Campbell carefully targeted the precincts he needed to hit and knocked on 10,000 doors in a few months. He spent nearly $50,000, about $16,000 of his own money but more than that in contributions, many from developers who saw him as a winner and accepted his promises to listen to them, despite his antidevelopment record. His biggest expenditures were for consultants' fees and a series of mailings to targeted households, mailings as good as anything Weir could have done. It was a professional campaign.

"I was no amateur," Campbell admits. "I knew how to run a campaign. When I decided to run I was ready. I didn't do anything wrong. I did everything right. I didn't want to become a politician. I swore I never would. But did I steal their stuff? Yeah, I guess I did."

The self-confessed transformation of Byron Campbell suggests a lesson about the Concord revolt of 1989, or about any similar revolt against liberalism by a local electorate. There is no pendulum. There is no "swinging back" to the political life of a generation ago. The most likely reaction to a government of imprudently liberal professionals is its replacement by a different sort of professionalism.

That applies not only to campaigning but to governing as well. The life of an elected official in Concord in the 1990s will be very similar to what it was in the 1980s, even if the values of the officeholders are different. The previous group kept themselves in office together for nearly a decade by establishing an electoral base and then cultivating it week in and week out, year after year. Any successor of theirs who chooses not to do that, who argues that his time away from City Hall belongs to him and his family, is going to seem curiously inattentive. We are entering an era in which the first logical question about the part-time politician, even at the local level, will be why he doesn't care enough about the job to do it at full speed.

That does not mean we have come to admire full-time politicians as a class; it simply means we have developed a set of expectations that produces them.

Moreover, campaigns in communities the size of Concord are not going to be getting cheaper. A sophisticated campaign for the Concord city council in 1989 cost $50,000. A campaign for reelection in 1993 or 1997 is certain to cost at least that much. The candidate who wants to be returned to office in those years is unlikely to delay his fund-raising until the last few months before the election. Fund-raising for the incumbent of the 1990s, even in a city of 100,000, seems destined to harden into a year-round occupation.

We complain about the professional politicians who govern us, for we seem instinctively to find their single-mindedness unattractive. Yet the truth is that we demand such behavior from them. The leaders we get are not those politicians whose opinions match ours but those who are willing to meet the job descriptions we establish. Some of them, in the coming years, will be people like Byron Campbell. Some will be more like Steve Weir. Either way the supply of talent that a community like Concord generates will have a decisive impact regardless of what kind of government voters tell poll takers they would like to see.

Even if the professionalization of politics turns out to confer no significant advantage to any point of view, it is important to think about the long-term effects of a government such as the one Concord had in the 1980s. In the creation of government, as in the mechanics of politics, there is no pendulum. There is no swinging back.

People who believe in government as a solution to social problems employ the powers of office to implement their ideas. They establish comparable-worth formulas, subsidize rape crisis centers, impose child care fees on commercial development, and feed the homeless in city parks. Sometimes they go too far even for a quiescent electorate, as happened in Concord in the 1980s. Power changes hands. More conservative politicians are elected.

That may lead to a change in emphasis: a moratorium on innovations of the sort the previous government pursued. It may mean more concern for the provision of basic community services, and a determination to keep taxes as low as possible. What it almost never leads to is substantial repeal of the previous round of innovation. This is true in the federal government, and it is true in local government. The Eisenhower administration did not repeal Social

Security; the Reagan administration, for all its rhetoric and its substantial cutbacks in federal social spending, did not abolish the Legal Services Corporation or the Equal Employment Opportunity Commission. Nor is there much reason to believe that would have happened even if Congress had been under full Republican control. Government programs acquire an inertia and a set of constituencies that make repeal look like onerous and politically costly work, even for a newly installed conservative regime that finds them unattractive.

It seems safe to predict that at the end of the 1990s Concord, California, will still have a comparable-worth program for city workers and a child care fee for downtown development. Those programs will remain in place whether the conservative reaction of 1989 is sustained or the liberalism of the 1980s is restored. In that sense the men and women who ran Concord in the previous decade did create a permanent government, however skeptical toward it the voters might have seemed in November of 1989.

4

The End of an Establishment

Concord's experience reflects recent political change in one of its more benign forms. Part-time government yielded to a system that was, for nearly a decade, coherent and workable. The political professionals who took over from the Main Street merchants managed to make decisions and carry them out with a reasonable degree of unity and decorum. Their ideas of public policy fit together well; they created a majority coalition that survived and overcame the personal rivalries beneath the surface. Whatever fault one may choose to find with Concord's reigning liberals of the 1980s—their undiluted ambition, their obsession with campaigning, their willingness to depart from so many underlying values of their community—one has to say that they did what responsible elected officials are supposed to do: They made a government.

No doubt some communities have entered the political present more gracefully than Concord. But many have entered it more clumsily. It is possible for a governing elite to leave the scene, either voluntarily or involuntarily, and to be replaced by a sequence of officeholders that constitutes a government only in the most nominal sense. The successor to a departed establishment is not necessarily another establishment; it may be chaos. That is the best description of what happened to politics in Sioux Falls, South Dakota, in the decade and a half after 1974.

Change came to Sioux Falls in the 1970s, at the same time it was coming to Concord; but in a very different way. Concord's establishment was replaced by attrition, as part-time merchant-politicians declined to make the personal sacrifices that a political career was coming to require. The Sioux Falls establishment was dethroned in one dramatic and confusing moment.

What Sioux Falls did in the summer of 1974 was this: It unseated its eminently respectable, sixty-three-year-old mayor and replaced him with a shaggy-haired, twenty-seven-year-old disc jockey who ran because a listener dared him to on a weekday morning call-in program.

Watergate surely had an effect on the result—the vote was taken only a few weeks before debate began in Congress on President Nixon's impeachment—and so did the fact that the mayor, Mike Schirmer, all but took his reelection for granted. But Watergate was an issue everywhere in the country that summer, and plenty of complacent mayors were being reelected overwhelmingly. It is generally agreed that the Sioux Falls mutiny of 1974 reflected something important going on beneath the surface in the community. But just what it all meant is a question Sioux Falls has never really resolved to its satisfaction.

Schirmer had been in politics and the real estate business in Sioux Falls for nearly forty years—he had been president of Kiwanis and the Community Chest, chairman of the Heart Fund, and chairman of the board of the First Lutheran Church. When the incumbent mayor died in 1968, Schirmer was an obvious choice to succeed him, and a few months later he had no opposition for a full five-year term.

At the time Schirmer's full term began, Rick Knobe was working as a maintenance man in Sioux City, Iowa. Later he got a job in a music store, and it was there that he attracted the attention of Red Stangland, owner of KHCF radio in Sioux Falls. Stangland hired him to handle the morning slot at ninety dollars a week.

Knobe liked to do strange things to drum up publicity. He spent a weekend in jail to dramatize the need for a new public safety building; he deliberately got drunk on the air as part of a crusade against drunken driving. So when he responded to an on-the-air challenge to run against Schirmer, it was dismissed as one more promotional stunt. "I'm thinking of running for mayor as a joke," he told one Democratic official. He had to have himself listed on the ballot not only under his real name, which nobody knew, but also as Rick Jeffries, which he called himself on the radio. "He didn't even own a suit," recalls Stangland. "Finally his dad popped for a suit."

But Knobe turned out to have the same instinct for campaigning that he had for talking over the radio. "I have listened to enough people in three years," he said, "to know what the Sioux Falls citizen is thinking." He tapped into the frustrations of the Watergate summer, portraying Schirmer as an autocrat and promising to open up the proceedings of government to anybody who was interested. He said he would have his own office door removed. The campaign cost him a total of $1,400.

Schirmer had a hard time understanding why anybody would want to vote against him, much less run against him. And he had a point. When he took office he had found that his predecessor had been overstating city revenues, and that Sioux Falls had actually been in the red for years. He balanced the budget in a matter of months. He also presided over the completion of a new airport, launched a downtown renewal program, and attracted a multimillion-dollar federal weather observation center, built on the outskirts of town. "As time goes on," he predicted, "we will be identified as one of the important cities of the world."

Schirmer was an honest, competent, decisive mayor, and he was proud of it. His campaign reflected his self-image. It consisted in large part of TV ads in which prominent businessmen told the voters how lucky they were to have Schirmer running the city. When Knobe offered to take himself off the air to avoid "equal time" problems, Schirmer told him it would not be necessary. It simply did not occur to anyone important in Sioux Falls that a radio talk show might be the basis of a political constituency. "Knobe was much better known than the establishment thought he was," says Ted Muenster, a local businessman and political organizer. "They don't listen to morning talk shows. They're in bank board meetings." The results of the initial voting gave Schirmer relatively little reason for concern. He failed to win a majority, but that was mainly because the vote was split among five candidates. His 44 percent placed him far ahead of Knobe, whose 20 percent qualified him for the runoff by only two votes.

Only on the night of the runoff did Schirmer and the city's

leaders realize what had happened. Knobe, campaigning hard while Schirmer considered himself all but reelected, overtook the incumbent by 417 votes in a head-to-head contest that attracted a much larger turnout than the original balloting had. "The two most surprised people in that election were Knobe and Schirmer," says Evan Nolte, manager of the Sioux Falls Chamber of Commerce. Schirmer was so upset he gave his office keys to another city commissioner rather than hand them to Knobe personally. "I remember people at the country club," Red Stangland recalls, "saying this was the worst day in Sioux Falls history." More than fifteen years later it is easy to joke about those feelings, and people in Sioux Falls do. But it isn't difficult to understand why people were frightened at the time.

There is something to be said for injecting fresh air into a political system, especially one that had been closed as tight as the one in Sioux Falls. But how open do we want our politics to be? It is one thing for Steve Weir to be able to say of Concord that "a guy could walk in from Pleasant Hill, work the city in five years, and get elected." It is quite another to wake up one morning and find that one's hometown, a city of nearly 100,000 people, had suddenly turned its leadership over to a twenty-seven-year-old with no relevant training or experience, no roots in the community, and no relationship with any of its previous leaders. One needn't be an insensitive elitist, muttering over lunch at the country club, to be concerned about a decision like that. The election of Rick Knobe was a legitimately scary political event.

The way to understand the Sioux Falls mutiny, though, is not to think of it as an aberration, a moment of irresponsible mischief by an electorate insufficiently stroked by an imperious incumbent. The events of 1974 were a product of the city's past and of the developments that had changed communities all over the country in the years since World War II.

Sioux Falls grew up as a stockyards town. Apart from the presence of John Morrell, the giant meat-packing firm that arrived from Iowa in 1909, there was little to distinguish it from the other, smaller agricultural market towns sprinkled all over the rural midwestern map. Like all those places, Sioux Falls was a retail trading center whose downtown stores met the needs of local farmers and their families. But because of John Morrell, Sioux Falls had some of the atmosphere of an industrial town, dominated by a single industry.

Morrell was a Liverpool company that had come to South Dakota because the local hogs produced bacon that tasted good to people in England. By 1960 Morrell was slaughtering 6,500 hogs a day and employing 3,500 people. The stockyards, sprawling over 42 acres on the city's north side, were at one time the nation's largest. It would be remarkable if a company in Morrell's position did not play a leading role in the politics of its city, and by everybody's account Morrell did. It was a family-controlled business, and the Foster family controlled a lot of what happened in Sioux Falls.

Mayors in the Morrell years were nearly always people who proved acceptable to the Fosters. That did not, however, prevent them from dealing autocratically with others. For twenty-seven years, over three periods between 1900 and 1934, the mayor was George Burnside, who had a habit of making things happen virtually overnight with very little public discussion. When Burnside felt the city needed a new railroad spur or a coliseum downtown, the city soon had one. "The same structure existed from Day One in Sioux Falls until the midsixties," says Steve Metli, the city's planning director. "There were six old families in town plus a nucleus of Chamber of Commerce types that made most of the major decisions—where the airport should be, where the street improvements should go."

Not everyone agrees about just how many families ran Sioux Falls in the old days, or about which families they were. But there is no disputing the fact that political decisions were closely held. In the 1960s the city planning commission used to schedule its meetings at lunch hour, so few spectators could attend, and in a room so small that few could have squeezed in anyway. It was not always easy to tell where the responsibilities of the Chamber of Commerce ended and those of the city government began. The chamber's transportation committee, for example, communicated directly with the state on how to spend available federal funds.

Like any American city that prospered in the years after World War II, Sioux Falls had its share of newly won fortunes. Al Schock became a multimillionaire through his Terrace Park Dairy, which he eventually sold to the huge Land O'Lakes cooperative, and he was a force in Sioux Falls politics through the 1960s. So were two realtors, Tom Costello and Don Cook. Costello never served in any official position, but he chaired the site selection committee that located the Holiday Inn, the city's only major downtown hotel, across the street from his property. In 1963 he donated 70 acres of his land to build an airport, and the terminal was named after him.

The mayors in the postwar years were not the leaders in this business elite; they were by and large its deputies. Not all the choices worked out. Fay Wheeldon was an establishment mayor, a crony of the business leaders. He ran a brake installation business and a shoe repair shop and conferred with his friends over coffee every day at Kirk's, the local political café. "Fay Wheeldon walked into Kirk's one day," a member of this group recalls, "and they told him, 'Fay, the shoe repair business isn't very good. Why don't you run for mayor?' "

Wheeldon turned out to be an embarrassment, a mayor whose corruption was a topic of open gossip. Sioux Falls may have trusted its establishment in those days, but it was not used to a mayor whose private business was shoe repair but who somehow managed to afford a Rolls-Royce. Abandoned by his supporters, Wheeldon was recalled in 1961, to be replaced by V. L. "Clem" Crusinberry, an amiable, docile former fire chief. Crusinberry was enormously popular in the city, but he was not a strong leader. When he died in 1968 the leading citizens of Sioux Falls agreed that the city could use a mayor equally sympathetic to their concerns but better qualified to run an administration. One man met that description better than anybody: Mike Schirmer.

Schirmer took over as mayor at a time when demands for openness were starting to be heard at all levels of American government, but he didn't think much of them. He governed with the advice and consent of the business group that had dominated Sioux Falls for years. Once a month he gathered business leaders in his office for coffee, ten or twelve at a time, some invited every month and some periodically. Those were the meetings that counted. "We'd get together if there was something sticky," he says, "and when we came out we had a decision. We didn't decide things in the press or at public luncheon meetings."

One day in 1971 Schirmer got a tip from the South Dakota congressional delegation that Sioux Falls had a chance to become the site for EROS—the Earth Resources Observation System. He was told that the city had six weeks to buy up the farmland the federal government would need. Buying the land would cost close to a million dollars. Schirmer convened a lunch at the country club with three of his business allies. They called Al Schock, the dairyman. The money was raised in plenty of time. "We cracked the whip, and we cracked it hard," he recalled years later, talking about the way he governed his city. "I don't know how else we'd have done it. It was a tight fist. We got the job done."

Schirmer was operating under an unusual form of government that made Sioux Falls particularly susceptible to the will of a strong leader. It has a city commission system, in which the police department, the water department, and basic road maintenance, among other functions, are under the direct management of elected commissioners rather than appointees or civil servants, as is the case in most large cities. In Schirmer's day there were only three commissioners, including him. A strong mayor needed the vote of just one other commissioner to do virtually anything he wanted.

In fact, Schirmer had all three votes nearly all the time. His fellow commissioners were a pair of diligent subordinates who had each been in office more than a decade. Earl McCart had a degree in statistics from the University of Iowa; Dave Witte was a professional engineer. Witte was known for being especially close to Tom Costello, just as Schirmer was known for his relationship with Sioux Falls's other real estate magnate, Don Cook. "Earl and Dave and I" is the way Schirmer still likes to describe his city government. It is hard to imagine a cozier arrangement. The executive branch of Sioux Falls government was exactly the same as the legislative branch. It consisted of three people, and it took action when and if the mayor chose to act. Its constituency on the outside was the small circle of businessmen to whom the mayor owed his job in the first place.

Few political scientists would recommend this as a way to set up a local government. In the wrong hands it is a formula for small-time tyranny. But in Mike Schirmer's hands it worked well enough. He had no interest in being a dictator; he was merely doing his job. In his view he had saved the city from grafters like Fay Wheeldon and well-meaning incompetents like Clem Crusinberry. And the reward he received for his leadership was defeat at the hands of a twenty-seven-year-old disc jockey running against him on a dare.

If Schirmer was appalled by what had happened to him, Rick Knobe was not exactly comfortable with it either. "For a while I felt very guilty," he says. "Here was a guy who had been in the community forty years. He wasn't a bad guy. He did do a good job. His leadership style was extremely autocratic."

. . .

At first glance, Schirmer's tenure as mayor seems to represent the high moment of Sioux Falls's postwar business leadership. In reality it was a sort of Indian summer. The men who had made up that leadership, who had grown rich in Sioux Falls in the years since 1945, were getting old. Cook and Costello were both in their seventies by the time Schirmer became mayor. Their children maintained an interest in the family real estate investments but showed little desire to match the political involvement of their elders. It was a one-generation establishment, and it was petering out.

Equally important, Sioux Falls was ceasing to be a city whose businesses were locally owned. Al Schock had sold out his interest in Terrace Park Dairy. Several of the major banks had become subsidiaries of much larger banks in Minneapolis. And the Foster family no longer owned John Morrell. The dominant company in a one-industry town was now a division of United Fruit, with its main offices in the suburbs of Chicago. "When the Foster family left ownership of Morrell's," says a downtown banker, "there was a noticeable lack of interest in Sioux Falls. The paternalism wasn't there."

Sioux Falls was making the transition from meat-packing town to regional commercial center. It was becoming more diverse, attracting more newcomers, and acquiring a new set of business leaders who lacked the credibility to tell the city what to do, assuming they wanted to. The unity imposed by the old establishment was breaking down under the stresses of growth. Mike Schirmer, at the height of his mayoral power and in the glow of his tangible accomplishments, was an anachronism. He assumed a deference on the part of the community that, unknown to him, had ceased to exist.

Had the Sioux Falls mayoral election not occurred at the most volatile possible moment of the Watergate period, had the mayor himself not been autocratic in personal style and overconfident in his approach to the campaign, had Rick Knobe not turned out to be a prodigy of a campaigner, there would have been no mutiny in the summer of 1974. A political system that had evolved over decades would not have collapsed inexplicably overnight. But it would have fallen anyway—similar systems of closely held government were coming to an end throughout the country, amid economic and demographic changes not very different from the ones under way in Sioux Falls. The sort of power that felt so natural to Schirmer and his allies is no longer available to public officials—as Knobe and his successors have painfully found out.

To win an election the way Rick Knobe did—the same way Jimmy Carter did in 1976—on the basis of votes cast rather casually by a diffuse and largely apathetic majority, is to take office in freedom. There are remarkably few obligations to repay, few prominent supporters to reward, few promises that have to be kept. There are very few strings. But strings are exactly what a political leader needs to govern. They represent his connection to the people and institutions in the community—or the country—that must help him. Richard J. Daley, perhaps the nation's most familiar symbol of an autocratic mayor, was bound inextricably to the ward committeemen, patronage workers, union officials, and corporate executives who had, one way or another, bought into machine government in Chicago. Without them he was merely a man with a large office and a collection of bodyguards in City Hall.

Mike Schirmer's attachments—his strings—bound him to too small a group of people, at a moment when community life was changing and those people were in the twilight of their influence. Rick Knobe took advantage of that moment and won the mayor's office as the candidate of no attachments at all. Independence is a potent theme for a political campaign, as slogans such as "unbossed and unbought" and "nobody's candidate but yours" continue to demonstrate. But the mayor who doesn't owe anybody a thing doesn't have many tools to govern with either. Candidates nobody sent can be very appealing; leaders nobody sent can be dangerous.

Rick Knobe, to his credit, seemed to understand that, even as a political novice. The day after the election, he began calling Schirmer supporters to tell them there was nothing to be afraid of. And he kept repeating that message throughout his years as mayor.

Knobe did find some ways to express his individuality. He rode a motorcycle to work. He talked about shifting municipal priorities in favor of "people, not buildings." He gave speeches complaining about "big business pressure in city affairs" and accused two developers of trying to threaten him into approving a housing project. But in the day-to-day responsibilities of running Sioux Falls, it soon became clear that Knobe badly wanted the help of the establishment he had overthrown. "The things I did didn't take away any of the power of the establishment," he insisted years later. "I didn't have any desire to kill. The last thing I wanted was to alienate people who could make investments in the community. I had no desire to hammer the old guard."

Unfortunately for the new mayor, however, the city's politics had already changed irrevocably. The people who had helped run the city for years were unavailable—not so much because Knobe has personally offended them as because they took the 1974 election as a signal that it was time to withdraw. "After Schirmer left," says Evan Nolte of the Chamber of Commerce, "people that should have been in there didn't want the jobs. The confidence that existed in the old city government just disappeared." Schirmer eventually began to profess a tinge of sympathy for the man who had ousted him from power. "The business people did fall off," he said. "Knobe had to generate a whole new group. Not knowing the city very well, I imagine that was difficult for him."

In the short run the new mayor's struggles had little effect on his standing among the voters. For virtually all of Knobe's five-year first term, he struck most of them as a refreshing change from his stodgy predecessor, and his popularity remained high. Where the abrupt abdication of the establishment was to prove costly was in subsequent elections to the city commission.

When Knobe first walked into City Hall as the boy mayor of Sioux Falls, he could count on two capable colleagues in the veteran commissioners McCart and Witte. But soon they too fell victim to the combination of political changes that had overthrown Schirmer. In 1976, after fifteen years in office, McCart was beaten by Vern Winegarden, a minor city employee whom Knobe had wanted to fire for incompetence. Winegarden waved a briefcase and promised to investigate City Hall, but once installed in office he turned out to have a horrendous drinking problem. After police carried him home one night from the scene of an auto accident, people in Sioux Falls began to call him "Commissioner Winebottle." In a city government made up of three people, one-third was now dysfunctional.

The next election finished off Witte, who like McCart had established a record of three competent terms in office. Witte was defeated by Harold Wingler, an auctioneer and salesman of just about anything who promised to declare war on potholes. Wingler turned out to be as much of an embarrassment as Winegarden; he had not been in office long when police showed up at City Hall to arrest him for soliciting prostitution. Knobe publicly derided his commission colleagues as "two of the biggest political hacks I've ever seen."

Before 1974 Sioux Falls not only had an establishment but had some semblance of a political screening process. There was a power structure with the ability to persuade ambitious incompetents to remain in private life or, failing that, to influence the electorate against choosing them. After 1974 no such mechanism existed. In a community where ballots were often crowded with names and media advertising was comparatively cheap, anybody who knew how to attract attention had a chance to win.

To denounce this state of affairs is, ultimately, to collide with a fairly important set of American political values: "What right do a few businessmen have to decide who the commissioners are going to be? Why shouldn't everybody have a chance? The voters aren't fools. They know what they are doing." At some levels they do. Confronted in a general election for president by two major-party nominees with clearly defined programs, the American people very definitely understand what they are doing. They don't choose Lyndon Johnson over Barry Goldwater, or George Bush over Michael Dukakis, by accident. For all the banalities of a modern presidential campaign and all the distortions of the commercial advertising that dominates such a campaign, the fact remains that a meaningful decision is possible. Voters are exercising the responsibilities of democracy in a recognizable way. But to apply that logic to local elections in a community such as Sioux Falls is to choose civics over reality. A local political system with no informal screening process— no "elite," to use the word nobody likes to use—is a system that may find it difficult to sustain coherent government for any length of time.

Is it possible to have an open political system and a screening process? Can we find some way to sift through the parade of aspirants for city commissioner—or president—without returning to the inequities of nomination by coffee-shop clique and smoke-filled room? Solving this problem is critical to making American democracy work in the next generation.

Sioux Falls, by 1978, had a well-meaning but still inexperienced mayor trying to govern a city of nearly 100,000 people without any core of political allies and with no help from his colleagues on the city commission. "He was a leader without any following," recalls Loila Hunking, then a state legislator and later a city commissioner herself. "He was out there with some vision trying to make things happen, with a constituency based entirely on his radio audience."

Ironically, as Knobe struggled with governing his city alone, he was given a handsome victory at the polls. He was elected to a second term in 1979 with 64 percent of the vote, carrying every precinct in the city. But from that point things began to unravel. The embarrassment of Winegarden and Wingler soon broadened into a public conviction that something was seriously askew in city government. A grand jury began investigating City Hall, focusing on a whole range of problems: bidding irregularities, free hunting trips for employees, abuse of travel privileges, and illegal sale of surplus property. The Sioux Falls fire chief was found guilty of collecting pay for days he didn't work.

Meanwhile, the state Department of Criminal Investigation began looking rather conspicuously into the use of cocaine by a coterie of young people active in Sioux Falls politics, some of them friends of Knobe's. A county official was indicted. Nobody ever accused the mayor of being involved, but the whole episode tarnished his reputation, perhaps even more than the small-time graft at City Hall. Few were surprised when he announced his decision to retire in 1984, proclaiming rather convincingly that he was tired and needed a rest. Knobe had been mayor of the state's largest city for a decade. He was thirty-seven years old.

Knobe's second term produced little in the way of policy initiatives; it was mainly an exercise in damage control. And most of the city's problems were not the mayor's fault. They were the fault of a political system that no longer generated the supporting talent to run the city well. "The caliber of people in public office in the last fifteen years has not been high," a newly elected commissioner conceded in the late 1980s, "in terms of competence, intelligence, experience. A lot of them were people who couldn't get a job anywhere else."

One might suppose that a city enveloped by political chaos would begin to suffer in economic terms as well, but in the case of Sioux Falls, at least, that is hard to prove. The most enlightened political decisions are rarely enough to save a community that is on the wrong side of economic and demographic change; Sioux Falls, which found itself on the right side, seemed to prosper more or less in spite of its politics.

Never having attracted much heavy industry, Sioux Falls did

not have much to lose in the migration of factories and jobs from the urban Midwest that began during the years Knobe was mayor. The meat-packing industry developed serious problems in the 1980s, but John Morrell remained healthy for most of the Knobe period. As late as 1982 the Sioux Falls stockyards were the largest such operation in the country. Meanwhile, the city had become a major trucking hub.

The critical event, though, was the arrival of Citicorp in 1980. The nation's second largest bank moved its entire credit-card-processing operation from New York to Sioux Falls, attracted not by the city government, which was largely a bystander, but by South Dakota Gov. William Janklow, who sold Citicorp on the state's low taxes and lenient approach to interest rates.

Citicorp found in Sioux Falls—as Bank of America did in Concord—a labor force perfect for its needs, a large supply of well-educated, well-mannered, hardworking young people, willing to work for a low starting wage and not worried about whether the job was unionized. Citicorp's early years in Sioux Falls were terrible years on the farms in South Dakota, and every summer produced a new crop of high-school graduates unable to find any decent work in the farming villages where they had grown up. They were ideal clerical employees for Citicorp, and by taking jobs in Sioux Falls they at least managed to stay in the state. "Our lives were saved by Bill Janklow in 1980," says a prominent Sioux Falls banker. "The incompetence of our government didn't catch up with us. We got what we needed in spite of ourselves."

Certainly, a more effective government could have accomplished more. The city wasn't very good at roping in federal money, for example—available urban renewal funds went unclaimed for years before the commission used them to clear a blighted downtown block. For a city its size, the largest over a five-state plains-and-mountains region, Sioux Falls didn't have much of a downtown at all; despite its obvious prosperity, it wasn't attracting any of the sort of glitzy modern buildings or new convention centers that were sprouting up elsewhere in the Midwest. Still, few of its citizens were up at night worrying about those things. When Sioux Falls residents saw what was happening to other cities around them, they could not help but notice that they had plenty of jobs, decent schools, and safe streets.

Politics, however volatile it had become, was something less than a life-or-death matter in Sioux Falls in the 1980s. With the abdication of the old business leadership, it was now a game almost anyone was free to play, and a new roster of organized players came to define the rules.

Some of the players were familiar institutions simply adapting to a new political system. Labor, for example, had been a factor in Sioux Falls politics since the early days of John Morrell, whose workers affiliated with the Amalgamated Meatcutters (now the United Food and Commercial Workers). As a bargaining agent for its members, the union was not doing all that well in the 1980s. It signed a five-year contract with Morrell in 1986, but the contract called for substantial pay cuts, and worker morale was not particularly good. In the spring of 1987, when a smaller UFCW local struck Morrell in nearby Sioux City, Iowa, the Sioux Falls workers went out in sympathy. Morrell negotiated for two weeks, then began bringing in replacements. The ability of the union to negotiate for its workers was in serious doubt.

In a curious way, though, labor was more of a factor than it had been in the old days. Before 1974 unions generally composed a relatively feeble opposition to a cohesive business establishment. With that establishment gone, elections began to turn more on manpower, contributions, and technical skill. Labor had those, even if it was shrinking in membership. And it had people with the time and the willingness to pay attention to what the city government was doing, day in and day out. Ralph Morris, a retired packinghouse worker at Morrell, had attended virtually every city commission meeting held over the past twenty years. For anybody seeking a place on that commission in the 1980s, he was a man worth seeing.

Equally important was the local branch of the National Women's Political Caucus, which evolved from a single-issue protest group in the 1970s to a broad-based political organization in the 1980s. The WPC did not have numbers—its membership was far smaller even than that of labor in its shrunken condition—but it did have skills. It developed a core of activists who knew how to organize a precinct and design a media campaign. In the wide-open Sioux Falls politics of the 1980s, those were the qualities that counted.

Loila Hunking, the city's most prominent female politician, claimed that the leaders of the women's caucus had "more political expertise than any other dozen people in town." Nobody seemed surprised when the caucus allied itself with the Chamber of Commerce to lobby for a new downtown convention center, or took a prominent role in the campaign of a former police chief whose background did not include any obvious commitment to the women's movement. "You don't run a feminist agenda and achieve political power," said Hunking. "You elect people who are responsive to your agenda." If they were not feminists before the campaign, they had good political reason to become feminists once they took office.

If all the clubs, associations, and volunteer groups in Sioux Falls had been subjected to a popularity contest at any point during the decade, it is unlikely that the women's caucus would have finished near the top of the list. The city remained, after all, the conservative place it had been for much of its history. The emergence of the caucus as an important player reflects the same principle as in Concord: the triumph of talent over ideology. Political success depends more than anything else on how hard a candidate is willing to work, how hard his or her friends are willing to work, and how clever they are at going about the job.

Thanks in large measure to the women's movement, Loila Hunking became the most successful Sioux Falls politician of the 1980s. She unseated the disreputable Harold Wingler in 1983, giving Knobe, in the closing months of his last term, the first reliable colleague he had had on the city commission in five years. Elected with the support of the women's caucus, the unions, and organized Sioux Falls teachers, Hunking quickly set about entrenching herself by doing something about the potholes Wingler had denounced but never fixed. She pushed for a 1 percent sales tax dedicated to street improvements, sought—and received—help from the Chamber of Commerce, and got the measure enacted. By the time she won a second term in 1986, she was the dominant presence on the commission. Joe Cooper, the amiable, mild-mannered Democrat who had been elected to succeed Knobe as mayor in 1984, was essentially her follower.

Hunking's success symbolized the further evolution of Sioux Falls politics. Most people elected in the 1980s were not echoes of Rick Knobe, free-lance individualists proclaiming their independence from obligation and entangling alliance. Most did have some connection with organized groups and political interests of one sort or another. But there was no stable governing coalition. Events turned on which set of activists managed to talk loudest at a given moment. Sometimes it was the group that Hunking spoke for. Other times it was an entirely different set—a conservative group stitched together, ironically enough, by Red Stangland, the man who had brought Rick Knobe to town more than a decade before.

Stangland was convinced that a rapacious city government was charging exorbitant property tax rates and then wasting the money. So he organized the Taxpayers Action by Concerned Citizens Organization (TACCO), a group of activists who complained that the three-member commission system had presented a gift of unrestrained power to Loila Hunking, her liberal allies, and the Chamber of Commerce, which was making common cause with them. Stangland accused downtown business interests of mouthing free-enterprise rhetoric and then scheming to pry loose every dollar of government help they could find. He claimed that Hunking had wasted $124,000 in taxpayers' money on fees to useless consultants. In response to these alleged abuses, TACCO circulated a petition to increase the size of the city commission from three members to five. Two new commissioners could well mean two new conservative votes and an end to Hunking's control over city affairs. Within weeks Stangland and his allies had collected 4,000 signatures.

The business leadership, such as it was, considered this a terrible idea. The president of the Chamber of Commerce said it would be "a traumatic thing to cast aside something that's been so successful. . . . I hope, wish, and pray this won't result in instability." In fact, the fuss over commission reform was itself the result of a decade of instability. In any case, the voters agreed with TACCO. The commission change was put to a referendum in 1985 and was approved by 58 to 42 percent, running strongest on the blue-collar north side of the city. Stangland said the result showed "a rejection of the special interests in town."

The conservative activists moved quickly to capitalize on their sudden emergence as power brokers in Sioux Falls's chaotic politics. In the wake of its victory in the city commission vote, TACCO struck against the major policy initiative of the liberal administration—a $30 million bond issue to finance a new downtown convention center, with an eight-story hotel and a performing-arts arena. The convention center had the enthusiastic support of the Chamber of Commerce and virtually all elements of the downtown business community. In Mike Schirmer's day that would have been sufficient to guarantee its routine approval. But the fight over it was to show just how much power business leaders had lost in Sioux Falls by the mid-1980s.

TACCO collected 3,700 signatures on another petition, which sought to reverse the commission and kill the convention center. Stangland talked about "the downtown gang" inflating the value of its property and making ordinary taxpayers foot the bill. The commission and the Chamber of Commerce mounted their own public-relations offensive to save the project, with Henry Billion, a prominent automobile dealer and a living symbol of the old power structure, appearing in television commercials in which he explained how badly the project was needed. But this was not the Sioux Falls of the 1960s. Thousands of young people who had come to town to work for Citicorp did not even know who Henry Billion was. The convention center seemed to them like something cooked up over-night by some businessmen they had no particular reason to believe. Stangland's arguments, by contrast, sounded plausible. The project was defeated by a 52–48 vote.

That result made a statement about power in Sioux Falls that was impossible to ignore: There no longer existed a local business estab-lishment of any political importance. The decline of local business ownership had accelerated. Most of Sioux Falls's largest banks were now branches of outside institutions. The *Sioux Falls Argus Leader,* the city's daily newspaper, bore no resemblance to what it had been before 1974. In the old days it was owned by a local family and edited by F. C. Christopherson, a pillar of the business and political elite who saw to it that scarcely a critical word about any elected official appeared in print. By the 1980s the *Argus Leader* was a member of the Gannett chain, run by corporate loyalists who would spend a few years in Sioux Falls before moving on. None of its executives was a decision maker in local political affairs.

"I don't think we have an establishment anymore," Susan Ran-dall said shortly after her election to the city commission in 1987. In her view the benefits of its disappearance far outweighed the disadvantages. As a liberal sociology professor, a feminist active in the Women's Political Caucus, a woman of cosmopolitan interests who had once worked in the Massachusetts legislature, she was able to win an election under the new system; it is not clear her views would even have been represented in the old days. But nostalgia for the days before 1974 was not limited to those who were making the decisions at that time. "There's no permanency to the economic structure that could create an elite," said William O. Farber, a longtime political scientist at the University of South Dakota and a Sioux Falls watcher for fifty years. "There's a vacancy of power, really. It's quite unfortunate."

The vacancy of power in Sioux Falls has translated into a vacancy of leadership in local politics. It has been difficult for anyone to stay in office long enough to accomplish much. Since the mutiny of 1974, eleven incumbents have run for reelection to the Sioux Falls city commission, and eight have been defeated, for a reelection rate of 27 percent. Political commentators complain about stagnation in Congress because so few incumbents are beaten; what would they say if three-quarters of them lost every two years? A turnover of such proportions would almost certainly be seen as inimical to stable government or even sensible long-term thought. But that is what Sioux Falls has experienced.

Rick Knobe was succeeded as mayor, in turn, by two men who lacked any noticeable desire to lead, even if they had had the political resources to be leaders. The first, Joe Cooper, was a television personality with a rich, resonant voice who admitted after a short time on the job that he had had no idea what he was getting into. The second, Republican Jack White, was a genial realtor who proclaimed his intention to reestablish some stability after so many years of turmoil. "I look at myself as a conciliator," White said after his inauguration in 1987.

White did manage to preside over the relatively peaceful conduct of city commission business, but Sioux Falls electoral politics was as chaotic as ever. Two of the three new commissioners brought in for short terms by the expansion to five members were gone within two years, thrown out by the voters. One was Joe Vanderloo, a local civil defense official who spent his entire year on the commission quarreling with the police and fire departments and saw himself described by the *Sioux Falls Argus Leader* as "pushy, short-sighted and too much trouble." The other was Susan Randall, the liberal sociology professor and Women's Caucus activist, who discovered very quickly the precarious nature of the free-for-all politics she celebrated. Randall was beaten in 1988 in an election which focused on allegations that the organized feminists of Sioux Falls were simply becoming too influential. Had Randall and one other strong challenging candidate been elected in 1988, three of the city's five elected leaders would have been active allies of the women's caucus. That, as it turned out, was more than Sioux Falls was ready to accept.

The following year the voters made an even more dramatic statement: They unseated Loila Hunking, the woman who, in the absence of any other stable elected government, had essentially been running the city for the previous seven years. It was variously said that Hunking's defeat was the further rejection of feminist activism, that she had been complacent and had failed to wage a full-fledged campaign, and that she had ceased to be responsive to constituent requests.

Looking back over fifteen years of Sioux Falls politics, though, it seems clear that there was something else involved: a feeling that had taken root in the community about political leadership itself. The vacancy of power in community affairs had created a suspicion of power in elected officials. Loila Hunking was the one person in Sioux Falls politics over those fifteen years who liked power, made no apologies for it, and prided herself on her ability to use it. Mike Schirmer had once felt that way, and had governed the city effectively. But the city had stopped deferring to that sort of leadership in 1974, and the closer Hunking came to exercising it, the clearer it was that her days in office were numbered. "If you exhibit power," she said after her defeat, "you scare the hell out of people. It's kind of frightening."

Sioux Falls began the 1990s with a government that superficially resembled the government of the Schirmer years: five conservative males. But in fact it was nothing like the old government. It was not the tight little circle that Schirmer referred to as "Earl and Dave and I." It was five disparate individuals in fragile circumstances, acutely aware of the community's electoral infidelity and possessing no political motivation to think in anything other than short-range terms. Sioux Falls had acquired a form of coalition politics, but it was a form in which no coalition could be reliably expected to last beyond the lifetime of a specific issue. "Somebody that's on your side in one election," says Rick Knobe, now working profitably in the real estate and consulting business, "is on the other side in the next election." Under this system stable political leadership is very unlikely to take root. "Nobody dares take charge here," complains the managing editor of the daily newspaper.

. . .

How much does chaos cost? What harm has a decade and a half of political instability done to the life of Sioux Falls, South Dakota? One cannot deny that free-for-all politics has given a diverse array of forces the feeling that they matter in public decisions. That in itself is important. Would it really be better to have a more competent government, as the city did during the Schirmer years, in which significant elements of the community did not participate? How competent does government have to be, anyway?

It is fair to say that Sioux Falls has been in no position to obtain any public benefits that required strong political leadership in the years since the 1974 mutiny. Yet to visit the city today is to ponder the limited importance of pure electoral politics in tangible day-to-day life. Safe streets, decent schools, low unemployment—local government has done very little to bring about any of them, yet Sioux Falls has them all. Its location, the demographics of its work force, and the absence of any ethnic or racial tension have done things for the city that even the most competent government never could.

The troubling consequences of chaotic government are intangible ones, and not everyone will choose to take them seriously. In a city such as Sioux Falls, in the closing years of this century, local government has become one less thing to believe in. The bizarre election of 1974 was in part a consequence of people's declining willingness to defer to leadership, but it also helped stoke another fifteen years of that decline. It did so by the example it set.

Sioux Falls learned to say no all of a sudden in the summer of 1974, and it has hardly stopped saying it since—to its elected officials, to its business community, to plans for convention centers and hotels, even to the form of government under which it had operated for most of the century. If naysaying is simply a form of electoral expression, practiced in the voting booth once a year or so, then perhaps there is no need to be frightened of it. But what if it is addictive? Is the community that habitually says no to its political leadership more likely to begin saying no to the rest of its symbols of authority—teachers, police, judges, parents? Should we worry about that? Is there a point beyond which the fabric of social order begins to unravel? Maybe that is going a bit too far.

Or maybe not.

5

The Awakening of the Innocents

Older people who have lived their lives in Greenville, South Carolina, do not find it easy to forget what they were doing in the last few days of May 1947, though few find it pleasant to recall them. Those were days in which Greenville was briefly and unwillingly a famous place, the scene of a trial in which thirty-one white taxi drivers stood accused of the lynching of Willie Earle, a black construction worker who had killed one of their fellow drivers.

Greenville owed its notoriety that summer not to any of its own citizens, white or black, but to Rebecca West, the British novelist, who had come to town to report on the trial for *The New Yorker*. West was appalled by what she saw, not so much by the acquittal of the thirty-one men—she conceded there was no hard evidence of who had actually shot Willie Earle—but by the contempt for law expressed by the defense attorneys, one of whom told the jury that the lynching had been comparable to the shooting of a mad dog in the street.

More than forty years later, West's "Opera in Greenville" is striking not so much for its portrait of South Carolina race relations as for its insights into the community as a whole. Greenville was a southern textile town, and West found it a closed society, not just protective of its social customs but suspicious of anything that came from beyond its borders. "When they name the antagonist against whom they have to pit themselves," she wrote of Greenville's people, "they simply and passionately name the North, with the same hatred . . . that the Irish feel for the English."

Toward Greenville's white working class—the defendants, their families, and the textile workers who formed most of the jury— West felt compassionate. She saw them as victims in an elitist political order that exploited them and then distracted them by inciting racial hatred and violence. For years, she wrote, "blacks and whites snarled at each other like starved dogs fighting over a garbage can." She called the white defendants in the Earle case "the starved children of difficult history."

It is hard to imagine anybody reading "Opera in Greenville" today without feeling glad to have missed it all. The racial indignities of Greenville in the 1940s have gone the way of similar caste systems all over the South, and less painfully in Greenville than in many places. The public schools were integrated quietly in the early 1970s. The most famous Greenville native of recent times is a black man who was, during the 1947 trial, a five-year-old boy growing up on the same South Side streets that had produced Willie Earle. Rebecca West never knew Jesse Jackson, but she lived long enough to read about his first campaign for president of the United States, launched in the year she died, 1983. The irony of that transformation would have been inescapable to West had she returned to Greenville for a reprise at the end of her life, but it would have been just one irony among many.

By the early 1980s the hatred of northerners that so struck West in 1947 had evolved into a near-obsessive interest in courting them. The textile industry was in decline by then, but the antiunion, antiregulatory sentiments it had bestowed upon Greenville had made the city a magnet for dozens of corporations arriving from outside the South and outside the United States. The Chamber of Commerce advertised Greenville as the ideal refuge for entrepreneurs anywhere in the country who felt "stifled by too much government, or demoralized by trade unions." Each year the affluent East Side was sprouting new subdivisions populated by corporate executives who did not speak with southern accents and had never heard of Willie Earle.

The working-class white people whom West had found pathetic

and powerless had helped themselves to political power, not within the city, where few of them lived, but in outlying Greenville County, whose government held a veto over much that the urban business class wanted to do. Greenville's civic leaders still grumbled in the 1980s about the "redneck mentality" that surrounded them, but when it came to politics they had no choice but to treat that mentality with a modicum of respect.

Meanwhile, Greenville politics was being changed profoundly by an event that took place quietly in the same year the lynching trial attracted national attention. It was in 1947 that Bob Jones, Sr., uprooted his fundamentalist Christian college from Cleveland, Tennessee, and brought it to a 200-acre site on the eastern outskirts of Greenville. Bob Jones University was tiny then, and for nearly thirty years it was politically quiescent, except for an occasional outburst of belligerent personal conservatism by the founder or his son. But by the 1980s that had changed. Reinforced by the presence of 6,000 students and a huge residential enclave of graduates and loyalists, the Bob Jones community was the most disciplined, best-organized player in the political life of Greenville.

Once the political process opens up in a community, once the elite that used to govern its affairs departs the scene, unexpected things can happen. The field is clear for any person, any group, that wants badly enough to be there. And while very few of the country people or the fundamentalists in Greenville today would characterize themselves as professional politicians, they nonetheless have a great deal in common with people we have already met who do describe themselves that way. Politics represents to them in one case a cause and in the other a calling. They do not think of it as a sacrifice. It is what they want to be doing with their lives.

Political activity was neither a cause nor a calling to the people who dominated public affairs in Greenville for most of this century. It was a by-product of their membership in the social network that surrounded the city's premier textile families.

The city of Greenville, one soon discovers, is a small tail doing the best it can to wag a very large dog. At the end of World War II, there were 35,000 people in the city and 137,000 outside its limits but within Greenville County. In the years since then the city's population has grown to about 60,000, but the county has grown massively, to more than 300,000. That is an unusual situation for an important metropolitan area, but it is easily explained. The textile companies that came south from New England in the early years of this century located their mills outside the city limits, where they could build full-scale residential communities for their workers beyond the jurisdiction of city rules and city taxes. The workers, and some of the managers as well, lived in self-contained villages without any real law except that of the mill owner. Houses, stores, and churches were all part of the owner's property.

The city of Greenville might have moved to take more control over its surroundings by annexing the mill villages, but it never did, chiefly because the mill owners did not want that to happen, and the city fathers were responsive to what the mill owners wanted. Many of the owners lived in the city themselves; at one time Broadus Avenue boasted seven mansions owned by textile families. As directors of the city's leading banks, partners in its law firms, and investors in all the important retail businesses, the textile families dominated the politics of the city and the decisions of its elected officials. For these people, though, influencing the city was not especially important. What was crucial to controlling Greenville life was dominating the county, which cast most of the vote and elected the area's delegation to the state legislature on an at-large countywide basis.

Over the first two-thirds of this century, no state in the country was as thoroughly dominated by its legislature as South Carolina. On a variety of crucial economic issues, it reduced the governor of the moment to a role as spectator. In local politics it was supreme. Each year the legislature passed every county's "supply bill," which was in fact its budget, and fixed local tax rates. There was no county council or commission to challenge any decision the legislature made.

The real government for each county was its legislative delegation. What the delegation asked for at the annual legislative session in Columbia it invariably received. Anybody seeking a job at the state level could gain it only one way—through the good offices of the county legislative delegation. The legislature as a whole never interfered with what a local delegation wanted to do in its home county. Politics in Greenville, as in all the state's cities, was closed to anyone who was not fortunate enough to be a state legislator or well connected enough to influence one.

Sitting atop this concentration of power was a single man—the state senator. Before reapportionment in the late 1960s, each of South Carolina's forty-six counties had only one, and within his domain he was the law. He did not need to consult most of his constituents before making an important decision—his office alone imposed deference upon them. "The state senator was the all-controlling force," recalls former Gov. Richard Riley, who fought the system as a young state legislator in the 1960s. "State senators had local machines and controlled all the local people. They controlled the courts. It was too much power in one position." Nevertheless, it was a stable political system, and it endured until the emergence of one person, one vote, made it obsolete by granting the larger counties, such as Greenville, more than one seat in the state Senate.

The last man from Greenville to occupy the position of state senator in all its glory was Bradley Morrah, who served fourteen years until he unwisely decided to challenge Strom Thurmond for the U.S. Senate in 1966. "I could appoint every magistrate," he says. "That was a whole tier of government. I could veto any road in this county. I couldn't control an election for sheriff, but I could determine how much money the sheriff's office got. In my fourteen years in the Senate, I never saw a bill passed over the objections of the senator from the county." Morrah is a gentle man and, by common testimony, exercised his power lightly, but he exercised it nonetheless. When members of the legislative delegation from outlying Greenville County, rural people, worked up a bill to give the county more control over the city water system, Morrah simply vetoed it. He told them he would not allow it, and they backed down.

Morrah, when he mounted his first legislative campaign in 1940, at age twenty-four, found himself perfectly placed. His family was urban gentry—his mother had been president of the National Association of Garden Clubs—but his father had run the company store at the J. P. Stevens mill, and had done so in a benign enough way that the family name was not only known but respected.

Over nearly a quarter-century in office, Bradley Morrah was always careful not to be identified too conspicuously with the urban business elite. "I never joined the Chamber of Commerce," he recalled years later. "I didn't want to be called a stooge for the manufacturing interests." When the publisher of the *Greenville News* offered him a special insert promoting his candidacy for reelection, he turned it down. He wasn't sure that a reputation as the handpicked favorite of the publisher would do anything for him among the mill workers, whose votes he could never afford to take for granted.

Still, however sensitive he may have been to feelings in the country and in the villages, Morrah was a city man, responsive first to urban business interests, and that was true of nearly everybody who served with him in the county legislative delegation. Greenville County had eight seats in the state House, and the county delegation always included some rural men, but these were people who had made their accommodation with the city elite and its concerns. Campaigns then cost a fraction of what they do now, but running on an at-large countywide ballot, as everyone had to do, was still an expensive proposition, difficult for any candidate without access to financial help from the city.

Verne Smith, who runs a tire store in Greer, 10 miles outside Greenville, was elected to the state Senate in 1976, after the old system had broken down. He has very little good to say about the way things used to work. "In the old days," he insists, "rural people didn't have a voice in anything. We could get a man elected from here, but if he didn't support the power structure in Greenville, he didn't last but one term."

The system that had endured so long met a rather abrupt fate in the 1960s under the pressure of Supreme Court decisions requiring both the state Senate and the state House to be composed of districts equal in population. Nothing the Supreme Court said, of course, precluded a state senator from continuing to be the boss of his county, but by granting extra Senate seats to the bigger counties, it made the pyramid difficult to maintain. Instead of one state senator in each county with a peremptory claim to power, it installed clusters of colleagues who would have to fight to determine which would be first among equals. It could not work, and the legislature, realizing it could not work, bowed to the growing demands of the cities for some meaningful form of home rule. It abandoned its control over county budgets and the minutiae of local political life and allowed each county to set up a government of its own to make those decisions.

Since 1974, then, Greenville County has been governed by a council of twelve members, each elected in a separate district. This new system has been a triumph for groups that were unrepresented or inactive in the old days—blacks, rural whites, fundamentalists. It is less popular among those who had a stake in the old process and considered it orderly and responsible.

For the first few years, Republicans did rather well under the new single-member system. They controlled the county council in its first sessions and again in the early 1980s. But since 1982, as rural Democrats have come into their own as a political force, the council has been up for grabs every two years. In 1985, with the two parties split 6–6, it took thirty-five ballots to elect a chairman. In 1987, again under a 6–6 split, the chairmanship went to Mann Batson, a portly, folksy hardware dealer from the rural hamlet of Travelers' Rest. "The country is the people," Batson liked to say. "What Greenville [the city] feels it would like to have may not be the best thing for the majority of the people of the county."

It takes a certain leap of imagination to describe Mann Batson as a political activist. For one thing, he doesn't appear very active. Slow moving, slow talking, he comes across at first as the sort of man Greenville County might have sent to the state legislature under the old system. "I'm just an amateur student of history," he says. But when it comes to politics, Batson is a creature of the 1980s. In 1982, nearing age sixty, retired from his original job as a school principal and having just sold his hardware store, Batson ran for the county commission on the strength of one issue—the refusal of rural people to be pushed around by the city any longer. He challenged a Republican commissioner who had been responsive to city interests, and he defeated him.

Batson took his seat on the commission in 1983 as a member who could work at the job full-time because he had completed his other careers. He could get along on the $10,000 annual salary. And he soon discovered that the largest bloc of commission members consisted of people like him—elderly white men from rural communities who had retired from their jobs in private life. They cast the decisive votes, the ones that made Batson chairman in 1987. Like him, most of them had been drawn into politics by the rural resentment against urban domination of the county. They discovered, to their great delight, that in the political climate of the 1980s they could thumb their noses at the city and get away with it.

The urban members of the county commission routinely described Batson as an unsophisticated hick, unprepared to run a modern government in a county with nearly 300,000 people. It was hard to make the case, though, that Batson was naive about politics.

When the county tried to give him an extra telephone to use for business conversations in his home, he made a point of refusing it in the interest of fiscal prudence. "I can't talk on but one phone at a time," he said. "Why should the people of Greenville County pay to give me an extra telephone?"

Batson speaks frequently about the old days in Greenville County politics, but it is not with the nostalgia of a Bradley Morrah. He talks distastefully about the time when a rural candidate could be elected to office "only with the blessing of the power structure." Then he notes with pride that the city cannot impose its will anymore, observing how hard it has been for the city to accept that. "They just can't adjust to it," he says. And he smiles.

The city itself has undergone profound changes, not just politically but demographically. It has become a regional business headquarters.

The textile manufacturers who dominated Greenville before World War II were not particularly interested in having much corporate companionship. Comfortable with a low wage structure and secure in their nonunion environment, they were happy with Greenville as it was. In fact, when new industries expressed an interest in the area, the city fathers discouraged them. "The mills that were here controlled the water commission," a local road construction executive recalled in the 1970s. "The water commission would say, 'I'm sorry, we don't have enough water.' "

That mentality was slow to disappear, but there were signs of erosion by the late 1940s, thanks largely to Charles E. Daniel, who moved his construction company to Greenville in 1942 and immediately began preaching the area's virtues as a location for business. "As long as you can see the mountains," Daniel used to tell corporate executives, "you're in the right place." The Blue Ridge Mountains are in fact visible from nearly any office window in downtown Greenville, but Daniel was not touting the scenery. What he was touting was the Appalachian work ethic. He was promising companies a ready supply of Scotch-Irish mountain folk who were glad to have steady work, willing to labor diligently for modest wages, and too ornery and independent to be good union material.

Daniel was instrumental in the move of dozens of corporations to states all over the South, but the city he changed most was Greenville, whose tallest building is still the twenty-five-story structure on

Main Street that was named for him and completed in 1965, the year after he died. By 1975 Daniel International was the second-largest general building contractor in the United States. And Greenville was hosting or wooing Michelin, General Electric, W. R. Grace, and a flock of other corporations who would not only offer jobs to locals but import their own personnel with a bewildering variety of accents, American and foreign. "So many Yankees have come in," one local businessman noted in 1979, "that the courthouse crowd just doesn't have the power anymore."

In the 1970s one man symbolized the open political environment that corporate migration was helping to create in Greenville. But he was not a Yankee. He came from Austria. Born in 1920, Max Heller had fled the Nazis at age seventeen, found his way to South Carolina, entered the textile business, and made enough money to retire at fifty and take up politics. He was elected mayor in 1971 and reelected overwhelmingly in 1975. Had local law not barred him from a third term in 1979, he could have had it for the asking.

Heller, as a European, a Jew, and a moderate Democrat, could not have been more different from Charlie Daniel and the corporate executives who were pouring into Greenville. But he shared with them one important value: He had little use for the "closed town" mentality of the textile owners. Years earlier, when Heller had been blackballed by the Poinsett Club, it had been Buck Mickel, Charlie Daniel's nephew and successor as head of Daniel Corporation, who had gone to Heller and offered to resign in protest. Heller told him not to bother. In the 1970s, when Heller was mayor and the club finally offered him a membership, Heller informed them he was not interested.

For a construction executive like Buck Mickel, a policy of economic development meant more business, more profits, and a more sophisticated city that would in turn attract still more business. To Max Heller, it meant opportunity—especially for people like him, who were never fully accepted in the old textile town. But there was enough common ground for Heller to serve eight extremely successful years as the city's strategist and symbol of development, growth, and progress. "Greenville as a community is wide open," he was able to boast after he had left City Hall. "If you come in today as a plant manager, tomorrow you will be asked to join something."

Heller based his mayoralty on the argument that Greenville

needed a downtown befitting its status as an international business center, and he launched a massive urban renewal program aimed at transforming Main Street from the blighted corridor it had become into a showpiece that would impress widely traveled visitors. In fact, Heller staked his entire career on downtown development. When he came up for a second term, he told business leaders he would not run again unless they committed themselves to his program. It was not a very risky gamble; they gave him the backing he wanted.

Heller lobbied the Hyatt hotel chain for years to build a new Hyatt Regency in downtown Greenville. He and Buck Mickel traveled to Chicago to pitch the project to the firm's aging chief executive, A. N. Pritzker. Heller was the right mayor to make that proposal; the Pritzkers, too, were Jews of relatively recent European emigration. "If Max had been from Spain," Mickel joked later, "we wouldn't have had a hotel." As it was, the Hyatt chain not only built the hotel but invested $2 million in it, and since 1982 it has stood on Main Street as the glitzy, chrome-and-concrete token of the new Greenville, with a ballroom and conference wing identified in huge letters as the Max M. Heller Convention Center.

Heller and his allies in Greenville's burgeoning corporate community represented one important element in the complex political system that was emerging in the post-textile era. As the 1980s began they seemed to be the dominant force in both city and county politics. But they soon learned that that was not the case. The real alignment of Greenville politics was made clear to them in the controversy over the most emotional issue Greenville confronted in the 1980s: whether to build a new coliseum downtown. As in Sioux Falls, it was downtown development that generated conflict between the commercial leadership and the newest contingent of political activists, and, as in Sioux Falls, the commercial leadership was rudely awakened.

As a centerpiece of their downtown program, Heller and his supporters wanted an impressive place to stage sports events and entertainment, one that would attract people from all over the Carolinas and beyond. Other communities smaller than metropolitan Greenville were building huge new facilities; all Greenville had was its cramped, dingy Memorial Auditorium, too small to attract many first-class bookings. Aside from the Miss South Carolina Pageant, an occasional rodeo and a country music festival, it did not make much of a contribution to what the business community saw as economic progress.

At the very start of the Heller administration, the city had wanted to tear down the old auditorium and build the new coliseum on the same site, as the opening wedge of downtown redevelopment. That idea had been defeated in a referendum. But a decade later, with the Hyatt Regency about to open and Main Street spruced up with trees and flowers, the need for a new coliseum seemed even more pressing. It was a way of guaranteeing that there would be enough business to fill the hotel and maintain the shops and restaurants that had opened up in the blocks around it. Without a big-time coliseum, the city council feared, the dream of a vibrant downtown Greenville might never be realized.

The problem was that the land on which the auditorium stood was owned jointly by the city and the county. Any move the city wanted to make—especially the multimillion-dollar bond issue that would be required—had to have the county council's approval. It took nearly ten years, but in 1981 the county council voted 9–3 in favor of building the coliseum and spending $18 million in taxpayer money to issue the bonds that would pay for it. The city appeared to have won. In fact, it had provoked a rural revolt.

What the county council had done, the county voters could undo by referendum. Lem Dillard, a peach farmer from Greer, began circulating petitions for a countywide vote on the coliseum, and the local Farm Bureau gave its assistance. Dillard had no interest in going downtown to see shows. He said it was dangerous on the streets at night. More important, he said, a coliseum was not something the voters should have to pay for. If it was such a good thing, private enterprise would be building the coliseum on its own. Before long it was common talk in the rural areas that the Greenville Chamber of Commerce had suckered the county council and was now trying to sucker the people with a $100,000 advertising campaign. "The downtown people wanted it bad," said Verne Smith, the state senator from rural Greer, "but they didn't want to pay for it. They wanted us to pay for it." All these years, people here had felt downtown Greenville was exploiting the tax structure of the whole county. Now they believed they had proof.

The city forces tried to fight back with arguments that it was a matter of regional pride, that other cities were making money by building coliseums, that it was a test of whether Greenville was as important a place as Greensboro or Florence. The opponents, said the chairman of the pro-coliseum citizens' group, "seem to think Greenville is and should remain a backward, stale, second-rate town." In the end, none of those arguments mattered. The coliseum went down to an embarrassing defeat, 34,920 votes to 24,910, or 58 percent to 42. It carried twenty of twenty-eight precincts within the city of Greenville, most of them black or upper-income, but was trounced virtually everywhere else. Several of the Republicans on the county council who had voted for it were swept out of office and Mann Batson and a cohort of his "country people" voted in to replace them. Democrats took over control of the council. All in all, it was a rout.

When the results were in, something else became clear. It had not been rural votes alone that had killed the coliseum. The fundamentalists had played a crucial role as well. The eight precincts within the city that had voted against the project were all heavily populated by graduates, employees, and supporters of Bob Jones University. In the heaviest Bob Jones precincts, the coliseum went down by more than 3 to 1. The fundamentalists were worried not so much about the costs of the enterprise as about what a coliseum might do to the cultural life of the community. To them a coliseum meant rock concerts, sexual overtones, and the sorts of people who would come to Greenville just to partake of those temptations. It might, in the long run, mean drugs on street corners. Whatever it might do for the local economy, they wanted no part of it. So a potentially close election turned into a landslide.

The fundamentalist community had been gathering political strength in Greenville for most of the preceding decade. One strength it had was numbers. Just under 60,000 people voted on the coliseum issue; participants estimated that between 10,000 and 15,000 of them had some association with Bob Jones University, either on their own or through a family member. But more important, the fundamentalist community had the skill, organization, and discipline to make those numbers count. In the aftermath of the coliseum vote and other elections in the early 1980s, it came to be said increasingly often in Greenville politics that anything opposed strongly enough by the "Bob Jones crowd" simply could not be done.

It had not been that way very long. Bob Jones University had been in the community nearly forty years, but for about thirty of those years the Bob Jones people had largely avoided local politics, seeing it essentially as a distraction from their more important work of saving souls. The only political attention the school attracted came from the ill-tempered comments of its leadership.

In 1960 Bob Jones, Sr., had declared that it was "dangerous and unwise" to elect a Catholic president of the United States. In 1970 Bob Jones, Jr., had stated that the four student demonstrators shot by police at Kent State University had "got exactly what they were entitled to." Those comments and others like them were printed and broadcast all over the country and gave Bob Jones University a widespread reputation as a school run by crackpots. That image was not helped by the protracted legal dispute over its continued teaching of the merits of segregation, a dispute in which it eventually lost its status as a tax-exempt institution.

Within Greenville, however, the school was for decades anything but ferocious. Its people tended to stick to themselves. "For all those years we considered politics to be a dirty business," said Terry Haskins, a Bob Jones student in the 1970s and now a state legislator. "There was a rethinking of that point of view." The change did not take place gradually. It occurred in one turbulent year, 1976, the year the fundamentalists signaled their newfound political activism by the simple expedient of taking over the local Republican party.

It might seem reasonable to think of the fundamentalist political offensive of 1976 as a by-product of that year's presidential campaign, in which the Democrats nominated a self-described "born-again Christian" and Ronald Reagan's candidacy generated enthusiasm on the Republican right all over the country. In fact, though, presidential politics had very little to do with the political awakening of fundamentalists in Greenville. More important was the work of Al Janney, a traveling fundamentalist minister who went to the pulpits of the city's biggest Baptist churches on a series of bright spring Sunday mornings. Churches such as Southside and Hampton Park Baptist can draw as many as 2,000 parishioners at a time, and Janney was telling these crowds that in the climate of Watergate and pervasive moral decay they had no choice but to enter politics.

So they did. They packed the Republican party precinct caucuses, and when the GOP held its county convention in Greenville that summer, they showed up 600 strong, with floor leaders, walkie-talkies, and a rigid discipline far out of proportion in a meeting they could have controlled easily on the strength of numbers alone. "We came on too strong," Haskins reflected later. "We went into the convention too well organized. When the man with the walkie-talkie stood up, you stood up." When the convention adjourned, the entire county Republican leadership had been replaced. Fundamentalists held all the important party positions. The "regulars," most of whom had come into politics with the Goldwater campaign in 1964 and had held power ever since, left to form their own organization, the Piedmont Republican Club. Bob Jones III, who by then had succeeded his father and grandfather as president of the university, managed at once to be proud, restrained, and embittered. "The citizenry is awakened from its lethargy," he proclaimed. "But it was in every respect a movement of the people, not of Bob Jones University." He accused the ousted party officials of "inflamed bigotry against this institution."

In the short run the 1976 coup was a disaster for all concerned. With its factions bitterly opposed to each other, the Republican party lost virtually all its state legislative seats in Greenville County, even as Gerald Ford was carrying the county against Jimmy Carter by more than 3,000 votes. For the next four years there were essentially two Republican parties in Greenville. But by 1980 the two sides were working together, dividing the important offices and rewards in a rapprochement that Democrats in the city like to joke about as "the marriage made in heaven." And that arrangement held up throughout the decade that followed. The fundamentalists and the business executives who made up the local GOP remained wary of each other and continued to travel in different social worlds. Buck Mickel and Bob Jones III never became close friends. But the two sides needed each other, and they cooperated. "When it came down to moral questions," said Terry Haskins, "the fundamentalists and the traditional Republicans were in agreement. We agreed on everything except where to go to church."

More than a dozen years after the coup, the signs of Bob Jones University's influence in Greenville are everywhere. "They are the fundamental base of the Republican party," says Frank Holleman, who served much of the 1980s as local Democratic chairman. "Without them, we've got the advantage every time."

Not everybody agrees with that assessment. It is arguable that, with the influx of northern businesspeople in recent years, Greenville would have tilted to the GOP side in the 1980s anyway. But few Republicans would want to test that proposition. "Any Republican running citywide looks to Bob Jones University first for support," concedes Mike Burton, a longtime local GOP leader. "The Republicans could elect candidates here without the Bob Jones vote, but it would be very difficult."

The political awakening of 1976 coincided with the ripening of the single-member district system, and that system has benefited the Bob Jones community, just as it has benefited the rural Democrats farther out in the county. Bob Jones is a community in a geographical as well as a political sense. It normally controls one of the six city council districts, one of the twelve seats on the county council, one seat on the school board, one seat in the state House, and one seat in the state Senate. Before the late 1970s the Bob Jones constituencies on the east side of town frequently were represented by people diametrically opposed to their views. As late as 1978 the state representative for most of the Bob Jones precincts was Sylvia Dreyfuss, a liberal Jewish Democrat. That does not happen anymore. These days, when elections are held in the districts that surround the university, anybody who does not have a Bob Jones connection does not have a realistic chance.

Beyond their East Side political enclave, fundamentalists win more than their share. The city council, county council, and state House each have one seat outside Bob Jones territory that has been held for most of the 1980s by somebody affiliated with the university. The county treasurer for most of the 1980s was a Bob Jones product. "We have tried not to seem to run the town," Bob Jones, Jr., said in 1984, leaving some doubt about whether it was the reality or the appearance that he was disclaiming. "If there is something that needs speaking out against, we speak out against it for righteousness' sake, for the sake of Christ and the Scriptures. But we try to stay out of city politics, city elections."

In the same interview Jones made clear his conviction that the university had had an effect on community life that went beyond mere political involvement. "I believe God has blessed Greenville because of Bob Jones University," he said. "The financial prosperity, material prosperity which has come to Greenville in these last thirty-five or thirty-six years I think comes largely because of God's blessing on this institution."

"I have to give them credit," Max Heller once said, reflecting on the Bob Jones influence in local politics. "They don't back dummies."

Far from it. Perhaps the most striking aspect of the fundamentalist awakening in Greenville politics is the political talent it has generated in a relatively short time.

An education at Bob Jones is, in fact, pretty good preparation for a career in politics as it is now practiced all over the country. Preaching, like running for office, is largely a matter of presenting oneself to the public. Candidates for office do not speak to large crowds very often anymore, as they did in Greenville fifty years ago, but they do need to be persuasive and articulate, whether they are performing in a television studio, in someone's living room, or on a door-to-door canvass. They need to know how to talk.

Bob Jones students learn that. They are all required to take speech both semesters freshman year. There is a disproportionate emphasis on dramatics, especially Shakespeare. That is not because the university is attempting to inculcate Shakespeare's values, or because it wants its students to become professional actors. It is based on the assumption that people who learn how to speak effectively will be good at saving souls. Many of them do turn out to be good at preaching. Others turn out to be good at politics.

Moreover, they tend to look upon politics as a calling. However critical they may be about the programs that liberal governments have enacted in recent years, they have managed to maintain a belief in the political process itself. Unlike conservatives all over the country who see that process as a dirty and unpleasant business, the fundamentalist conservatives in Greenville manage to run for office without sounding embarrassed about it. "They have a conviction," says Heller, "that they are going to save the world. And they want to save it from the inside."

Sometimes they are not only unembarrassed but driven. Paul Wickensimer grew up in southern Ohio, steeped in fundamentalist religion and curiously obsessed by politics. When he was fourteen years old he started going to city council meetings in his hometown. When he was eighteen he decided the local fire fighters needed a raise and lobbied the council to get it. Then he attended Bob Jones University and began looking for a way to practice politics and religion at the same time. He went to work for the telephone company but set his sights on a county council campaign. He began working for other fundamentalist candidates, gradually built an organization out of Bob Jones loyalists and Southern Bell employees, and won himself a seat. "The Bible says in the Book of Romans that government is ordained by God," Wickensimer explains. "I'm in it because it's a calling. If you feel the good Lord is going to bless you as a result of what you are doing in politics, it sustains you."

Dayton Walker graduated from Bob Jones, then spent seventeen years working for the campus radio station (called WMUU, for World's Most Unusual University). He was one of the men with walkie-talkies at the county Republican convention in 1976. He went into the real estate business after that but stayed active in politics. In 1985 there was a city council vacancy, and he went after it. He had unanimous support on campus and in the Bob Jones precincts on the East Side. Nobody of any consequence bothered to run against him.

Walker describes himself not as a fundamentalist but as a biblicist—one who believes not only that the words of the Bible are literally true but that they supply the best answer to all difficult questions, political as well as religious. When he is asked a question about his political career, his first response is to see if there is a line of Scripture that fits. If he finds one, he quotes it, citing the exact chapter and verse. "The Scripture requires us to be good citizens," Walker says. "We must do what we can as the salt of the earth to hold back the tide of anarchy. The responsibility of the politician is to God. I'm sorry for politicians who don't realize this. They are going to have to answer to God someday."

It is not easy to hold back the tide of anarchy from a seat on the Greenville city council. It is not simple, even for a person using Scripture as a guide, to know what the moral decision is in local politics. But Dayton Walker and his fundamentalist colleagues try. They do not always come up with standard conservative solutions. Walker agonized for a long time over whether to sponsor an ordinance restricting smoking in public places. As a conservative he believed in the concept of individual freedom. But as a biblicist he felt smoking is poisonous to the body and therefore improper in the eyes of God. He decided to sponsor the measure and brought along his fundamentalist backers, and Greenville enacted a tough ordinance banning smoking in most public places.

It is possible, talking with Dayton Walker, to get the feeling you are listening to a religious zealot who happened to have strayed into politics. It is not possible to get that feeling talking to Terry Haskins. He is a fundamentalist; he is also as hard-nosed a politician as

Greenville has. Democratic party officials refer to him derisively as a "ward-heeler." But none of them questions his effectiveness as a politician.

As a student at Bob Jones, Haskins was involved in the 1976 takeover of the local Republican party. The next year he was elected chairman of the local Republicans. In 1979, as a law student, he managed the city council campaign of a fellow Bob Jones graduate, who won the election by seventeen votes. Then he moved into a city council district where the incumbent was retiring. "We didn't look for a house anywhere but in city council district one," he says. He won the council seat in 1983 and moved to the state House of Representatives two years later.

Haskins was searching constantly for ways to inject his religious values into politics. On the city council he wanted to prevent prostitutes from loitering outside a downtown Greenville Baptist church. So he got the council to pass an ordinance declaring that any convicted prostitute found near the church would be assumed to be soliciting. Haskins knew as well as anyone that the ordinance could not stand up to a constitutional test. But nobody has challenged it, and it remains in effect.

Haskins left the city council after two years because it didn't pose enough moral questions for him. "You very seldom get into questions of morality," he says, "or ones where church and state even come into play." The legislature seemed a better match for his interests—preventing the government from involving itself in the affairs of fundamentalist churches and their adherents. In the state House, Haskins engineered a bill making it easier for fundamentalists to educate their children at home, and another allowing parents to exempt children from sex education programs advocating contraception or family planning.

After a couple of terms in the legislature, though, Haskins had changed in a subtle way. He was no longer a Christian venturing into politics—he was a highly skilled professional politician with Christian values. He didn't just work on moral issues, he worked on everything, and with everyone. "A politician who only gets involved in abortion, home schooling, blue laws, or pornography," Haskins argues, "and does not get involved in helping decide where highway money goes or in insurance reform, that politician is going to be totally ineffective on the moral issues, because he has no influence in the areas that other legislators are interested in." In 1989, as he began his third term, Terry Haskins was elected minority leader of the South Carolina House. That victory, thirteen years after the fundamentalist invasion of the Greenville GOP, represented the triumph and the political maturity of the Bob Jones activists.

Haskins is right about one aspect of local government—it is not, for the most part, high moral drama. There is no way to pinpoint the effect that the arrival of a group of skilled fundamentalist politicians has had on a city and county government devoted mostly to providing basic services. Still, the fundamentalist presence has changed the tone and style of Greenville government. Decisions are turned inside out to see whether they might have a moral component. "There's no such thing as an evil pothole," says Mayor Bill Workman, "but there are ethical and unethical ways of dealing with potholes." Or so a substantial number of the elected officials in Greenville seem to believe.

Workman's very career has been a convincing demonstration of the fundamentalist influence on Greenville politics and government. When he won his first term as mayor in 1983, it was as the clearly labeled candidate of development and the business community. He was solidly pro-coliseum, and he complained about "archconservatives" who obstructed the government-business partnership.

His first four years in office softened some of those tensions, but not all. When Workman ran for Congress in 1986, he was challenged for the Republican nomination by three fundamentalist opponents and won the primary largely because the Bob Jones community did not unite behind any of them. Lingering skepticism about him among some of the Bob Jones loyalists held down his Greenville vote in the general election and proved a critical factor in his defeat. After that, though, Workman began spending a substantial proportion of his time as mayor cultivating fundamentalist support for his economic development ideas. He took pains to stress the contributions fundamentalists made to the city's public life. "What could be a greater strength for a political system," he asked, "than to have 10,000 people committed to the Judeo-Christian value system involved in politics?" It is an argument he made with conviction; it is also an argument he could not afford not to make.

It would be hard to find two politicians with less in common than Terry Haskins and Mann Batson, the intense Christian moralist who started campaigning in college and the folksy hardware man who ran for office to enliven his retirement. But both these men tell us something about the political life of the day, in Greenville and elsewhere. Both entered politics on the strength of an issue—religion in one case and rural rights in the other. Both were trying to send a message to the community at large. That is, they were speaking *to* the community, not *for* it. We can contrast them with Bradley Morrah, Greenville's state senator of a generation ago, who ran for the legislature as a promising young man steeping himself in the values of the social and economic network that made the important decisions. He was learning to speak for the local governing majority in the corridors of political influence.

To describe the Greenville power structure, circa 1940, as a majority, is perhaps to use the term in a curious way. An affluent downtown establishment that looked contemptuously upon the county's rural voters, that discouraged blacks from voting at all, might better be described in some other way than by the word *majority.* Still, they thought of themselves as a kind of majority, a group of people making decisions for the welfare of the community as a whole. If it was frequently an illusion, it was one that sustained their political participation over more than half a century. Morrah thought it was a very important idea, the idea of elected officials representing what they at least believed was the community as a whole.

In Greenville today, as in hundreds of places across the country, there is no group sufficiently presumptuous to keep up that notion of broad political trusteeship. As Loila Hunking says of Sioux Falls, "Politics now is the politics of coalition." Local government is the coming together—and the coming apart—of collections of minority interests. Mann Batson's "country people" are important, as are Terry Haskins's fundamentalists. Downtown business is important. But when business leaders speak in Greenville now, it is clear that they are speaking for their segment of the community, not for everyone. The Chamber of Commerce proved that one more time in the fall of 1990, backing another attempt to promote a new coliseum by county-wide referendum. Once again the plan went down to decisive defeat. The citizens of Greenville no more intended to defer to an economic elite in 1990 than they had in 1983. The idea that prevailed in Bradley Morrah's day, of a political establishment exercising its power for what it considers the common good, is a relic of the receding past.

6

Life After the
Machine

When one talks about political power in the old days in Utica, New York, one is not talking about the consensus of a few families, or of a secretive business elite. One is talking about Rufus Elefante. Utica was a machine town, and Elefante was the boss. He never ran for office—he always derided officeholders as "baby kissers"—yet, for the better part of two decades after World War II, Elefante was the decision-making process in Utica. When he wanted to say yes or no on an important question of public policy, he did not need to take a vote. He simply instructed the government on how it should proceed.

Today, in his late eighties, Elefante watches in some bewilderment as Louis LaPolla, a man from another generation and political culture, serves as mayor of Utica. Elefante pursued power and disdained public office; LaPolla dreamed of public office his entire life and has held it continuously since he was twenty-three. Elefante was the center of a tight political organization built on loyalty; LaPolla prides himself on being a loner. "I answer to no one," he says, "only the electorate." Elefante's city council was for years an eighteen-member rubber stamp; LaPolla's consists of nine people, each a political faction unto himself. Elefante, for better or worse, governed. LaPolla presides.

In Utica we come upon the critical elements of political change in their starkest form. We witness the transfer of authority, at least nominal authority, from a private citizen to a career officeholder. We watch a closed political system—closed to anyone unwilling to swear loyalty to an organization—evolve into an open one, in which free-lance campaigners move in and out of office on the basis largely of their personal ambition and energy. We see the process by which power does not so much change hands as evaporate altogether. A few years ago the *Utica Observer-Dispatch* sent one of its reporters on an extended assignment to determine the city's top ten power brokers. He managed to come up with only three names. That was not because he found a sinister triumvirate running the city; it was because he couldn't detect anybody else with a broad-ranging influence over city affairs.

One can trace Utica's political metamorphosis by following the rise and fall of its political restaurants. Utica has always had a city hall, but for two decades after World War II, Marino's Restaurant was the real seat of government, the place where Elefante's Democratic machine dispensed favors and made the decisions that kept the town going. It was an old-fashioned Italian restaurant crowded with high-backed wooden booths, and the booth a customer chose depended on the sort of help he wanted. There was one for jobs, one for welfare complaints, one for party politics, each booth maintained by an Elefante lieutenant. A businessman who wanted a building permit was sometimes advised to head for Marino's back room, join a card game with some of Rufie's boys, and lose as much money as possible. After Marino's fell victim to the wrecking ball in 1972, there was Uncle Henry's Pancake House. Few went there for the food; regulars remember it as ranging between mediocre and inedible. There were those, in fact, who doubted whether pancakes were "Uncle Henry" Cittadino's true calling. They remembered his conviction in 1959 on charges of running a house of prostitution. Nevertheless, Uncle Henry's was Elefante's main political meeting place for years. The waitresses spent as much time taking Rufie's messages as they did serving food. Wherever the lunch took place, the meetings often adjourned to a more private spot. On days when the city's Common Council met, Elefante liked to finish eating, then take off for a drive with the city clerk to instruct him on how the council meeting was to proceed.

Uncle Henry's has gone the way of Marino's, and it has had no successor. In the absence of power, there is no real need for one. "There is no organization that dictates things," says Steve DiMeo, the city planning director. "There isn't even a fixed coalition. You can't count votes." By and large Utica is glad it abandoned machine rule, and there is no evidence it would like to go back. Still, one doesn't have to search very far to find traces of nostalgia. "If you want things to happen," says Utica College political scientist Richard Emmert, "the pieces have to be put together. Rufie controlled the mayor, he controlled the council, he put them together. Nobody can do that now."

Utica, one might say, is an extreme case. Most American cities did not concentrate power nearly as much as Utica did, and most of them, perhaps as a result, have not swung so far over to free-lance politics since the old system fell apart. But these differences are a matter of degree. Because Utica provides a dramatic illustration of so many important American political trends, its story is worth telling in some detail.

Not only was Rufus P. Elefante never elected to any public office, he was never an important official of any political party, cither in Utica or in surrounding Oneida County. "I was a leader, period," he says. "I elected my own candidates."

Elefante started in the simplest possible way, gathering up as many votes as he could find in the Italian neighborhoods and trading them for favors from the party leaders citywide. There was no question that Italians were treated with contempt by the affluent families who controlled the Utica of Elefante's youth. He portrays himself as a sort of ethnic civil rights leader. "When I was a kid," he says, "all I heard was wop, guinea, and grease ball. We weren't even third-class citizens." His generation remembers the story of the Utica mayor, early in this century, who invited reporters in one evening to hear his remarks on Garibaldi and the inspiring story of Italian independence. Then, his speech finished, he put away his papers and sat down. "That ought to satisfy the dagos," he said.

Rufus Elefante was born into the Italian ghetto of East Utica in 1903. His father was a laborer. Rufie himself was a high-school dropout but a political prodigy. At age sixteen he was driving a truck for the city's GOP boss, "Pop" Bolotierri. At eighteen Elefante was Republican leader of the First Ward. He did not switch to the

Democratic party until the 1928 presidential election persuaded him that the Republicans were prejudiced against Catholics. Then he became a Democrat with a vengeance. He organized priests in East Utica to strike back at bigotry by urging their parishioners to vote for Alfred E. Smith of New York, the Catholic Democratic presidential nominee.

But another decision Elefante made in 1928 turned out to be more important to his future. He invested the influence he had in the gubernatorial campaign of Franklin Delano Roosevelt. Elefante staged a huge rally for FDR at the corner of Mohawk and Bleecker streets, in the heart of Utica's Little Italy, when most of the other upstate cities were giving the candidate a cool reception. FDR never forgot it. During Roosevelt's four years as governor, and even during the twelve years of his presidency, Rufus Elefante was taken care of. One time Roosevelt even showed up at Marino's for lunch. In the depths of the Depression, when Utica needed to buy out its private water company, Roosevelt's Reconstruction Finance Corporation backed the bonds that made the purchase possible. At one point in the mid-1930s, there were 5,000 people in Utica on WPA jobs.

In those years Elefante's Democratic machine still had to struggle to control the city's politics. Republicans won their share of city elections. And within the machine Irish Democrats continued to make many of the important decisions. But in the years after World War II, the situation changed. The Italian community was casting close to a majority of the city's vote and could no longer be treated as junior partner. Meanwhile, Elefante found the perfect vehicle to power in Boyd E. Golder. A celebrated athlete, kindly coach, and volunteer for virtually every charitable cause in Utica, Golder was a superb political candidate. A Roosevelt Democrat, he was a natural vote getter among the blue-collar ethnics who had backed the New Deal with enthusiasm. He already knew many of the working-class families from his days coaching baseball, football, and basketball for the Utica Knights of Columbus. The boys he coached were nearly all Italian Catholics; Golder himself was German Protestant. That made his credentials as a humanitarian even more impressive.

Golder won his first term in 1945, a few months after FDR died, and was mayor of Utica for ten years. His integrity was rarely challenged. The city loved him, and he loved being mayor. He lobbied for the establishment of Utica College, so that the children of Italian bricklayers and textile workers could get a decent education within the community and stay to create an ethnic professional class. Golder was a local FDR in all but one important respect: He wasn't running the government. Elefante was. "Golder was Mr. Clean," remembers Virgil Crisafulli, who came to Utica College to teach economics in the late 1940s. "Behind the scenes, Elefante was the power." In 1950, when Mohawk Airlines began discussing a move of its headquarters to Utica, its executives were surprised to find that the negotiators for the community were Elefante and the county Republican chairman, with whom he was on quietly friendly terms. Golder was conspicuously absent.

Forty years after the fact, Elefante leaves no uncertainty about who was running the show. "We made him lead," he says of Golder, "and we gave him the support. There were fifteen Democratic aldermen out of seventeen, and we controlled them all." Not that Elefante hovered over them at meetings. He hardly ever showed up at City Hall. "There was no reason for us to appear at City Hall," he insists. "It would have been stupid on our part. It would have appeared that we were dictating to the council. We were, but not there. . . . I communicated with the clerk. He ran the Common Council." It could all be managed from a booth at Marino's.

By the mid-1950s Elefante was running a classically successful urban political machine, one whose hold on Italian votes in East Utica and Polish votes in West Utica enabled it to control the Common Council, elect and unseat city officials, and provide more than enough public jobs to perpetuate itself in power.

The money that lubricated the machine was in part union money. While Elefante was building his Democratic organization, Rocco DePerno was building a power base in the Teamsters, forming an alliance with Elefante that created a virtually seamless political web. Dues from Teamster members paid for a considerable amount of the generosity the machine was able to bestow on its friends. All in all, the machine probably took in far more money than it needed to spend on election campaigns. When the Democrats controlled City Hall (virtually the entire 1950s), city employees were required to kick back to the party 4 percent of their salaries each election year. In off years they had to pay only 2 percent. But those kickbacks alone, allies of the machine agree, were sufficient to pay the campaign expenses. Union money and all other sources of machine income were more or less available for Elefante to dole out as he saw fit.

Elefante's debts to his allies, both financial and political, were "strings" of the sort that modern politicians try to avoid, or at least try to avoid acknowledging. They were limitations on his personal freedom as a political actor. To him, however, they were strengths, relationships that maintained his control and in the long run made him freer to move the city in the way he wished. They were the ingredients of a system: a machine to those who did not like it, a government to those who did. They were the old-fashioned arrangements that the Rick Knobes and Jimmy Carters of American politics campaigned against and then found it difficult to govern without.

Elefante himself was growing rich, in large part through the indirect awarding of local government contracts. He did not like to take a city paycheck, so city business was given to private companies friendly to the machine, and they subcontracted work to Elefante's enterprises. In this way the trucking firm of Elefante and Mazza supplied sand and gravel for Utica roads and hauled stone for the maintenance of the barge canal. The wrecking company Elefante Associates handled demolition work. Elefante himself owned some of the land on which the Utica-Rome branch of the State University of New York was built. Not everybody in town approved of these arrangements, but they were legal. Elefante did not hold any office with which his business deals could conflict. He was a private citizen.

Elefante understood politics as it was explained early in this century by George Washington Plunkitt, the Manhattan ward boss and sage of Tammany Hall. "The politician who steals," Plunkitt said, "is worse than a thief. With the grand opportunities all around for the man with a political pull, there's no excuse for stealin' a cent." Elefante lived later, but he lived in Plunkitt's world. In accordance with the code of ethics they shared, he did not steal.

Elefante was in many ways a public-spirited man. The immediate postwar years were a crucial time for Utica, a time in which the city lost what remained of its once thriving textile industry and had to find replacement jobs in a hurry. By and large that was done. General Electric came to Utica in the late 1940s to manufacture radios, built an aircraft equipment plant on the outskirts of town in 1951, and by 1960 was employing 6,000 people. Nearby Griffiss Air Force Base, a survivor of numerous Pentagon efforts to close it, was by then providing nearly 20 percent of the jobs in the metropolitan area.

Elefante claims at least partial credit for virtually all the economic development that occurred during the postwar "loom to boom" years. Maybe he stretches the truth a little; many of the changes that kept Utica afloat might well have happened anyway. Still, compared with the stereotypical ward boss, Elefante gave a considerable amount of thought to the broader needs of the community. If power and patronage were the most important things to Elefante, they were not the only things. "I worked for Utica," he insists today. "Please believe me. I loved my Italian people. I wanted them to progress."

Here again the world of Elefante is the world of Plunkitt and Tammany Hall fifty years earlier. Plunkitt took great pains to draw the distinction between responsible political bosses and "looters." "The looter hogs it," Plunkitt said. "I never hogged. I made my pile in politics, but at the same time, I served the organization and got more big improvements for New York City than any other livin' man." That is as good an epitaph as Rufus Elefante could ask for.

In the closing months of 1957, there was no reason to suspect that the salad days of the Elefante machine were numbered. Boyd Golder had retired as mayor two years earlier, after a final term in which he had acted more independently than Elefante appreciated, and had been replaced by a younger Elefante protégé, John McKennan. At the end of his first two years, McKennan was reelected with the biggest margin any Utica mayor had enjoyed in half a century. But the machine was about to begin its long and painful decline, and Utica's reputation and self-image were about to change irrevocably.

On October 25, 1957, the gangster and labor racketeer Albert Anastasia was murdered in the barbershop of the Park Sheraton Hotel in Manhattan. A few weeks later, amid the chaos that his death had created in organized crime, representatives of all the important Mafia families in the United States gathered in the upstate village of Apalachin to rearrange the power and proceeds of American criminal life. That series of events brought Utica a barrage of disastrous publicity. It turned out that the city had sent a three-man delegation to Apalachin, led by liquor dealer Joseph Falcone, a close acquaintance of some of Utica's leaders. On more than one occasion in the weeks before his death, Anastasia himself had turned up in Utica. Once he even checked into a hospital to avoid his pursuers. Another time he attended a funeral in the city, and Elefante had to station police all along the cemetery gates to discourage Anastasia's enemies from dispatching him then and there.

The presence of gangsters in Utica was no shock to most of its citizens. But in the climate of widespread interest in the Mafia and organized crime, the national media began paying close attention to the affairs of this unpretentious industrial town, singling out Utica as a symbol of corruption and disgrace. The *New York Journal-American* sent a team of reporters to Utica, and they returned with tales of wide-open gambling, prostitution, loan-sharking, and police and politicians in cahoots with the criminals. The paper labeled Utica "Sin City." *Newsweek* went further. "Utica," it said, "is the town the gangsters own. . . . It is the headquarters town for the big-time mobster operations in most of the eastern half of the nation."

Nobody ever established the truth of those allegations, but by the middle of 1958 there were eight investigations under way into corruption in Utica. By the time the last one ended, nearly four years later, twenty-two residents of the city had been sent to prison (Uncle Henry Cittadino, the future pancake man, was one of them), and numerous city officials loyal to the machine had been forced to resign, including police chief Leo Miller, who told investigators that he had been keeping one house of prostitution under surveillance for twenty years but had not accumulated enough evidence to make an arrest.

Nobody involved in the investigation went so far as to call Utica's political boss a mafioso. But his willingness to run a wide-open city had become a public issue that was impossible for even the gullible to ignore. "Elefante certainly wasn't Mafia," says William Lohden, whose investigative reporting led to a 1959 Pulitzer Prize for the Utica papers. "But he closed his eyes. He did his thing and they did theirs."

Rufus Elefante was never charged with a crime. Called repeatedly before a special grand jury, he refused immunity, labeled the entire affair a "persecution," and proclaimed himself "clean as a hound's tooth" when the prosecutor left town having failed to secure his indictment. "Those were Republican DA's investigating," said Elefante's lawyer, Stephen Pawlinga, years later. "If they had anything, they would have put Rufie in prison. Not one of the whores ever came forward to say she had given Rufie any money. They didn't have anything."

But there was nothing Elefante could do to prevent the political earthquake the scandals generated. In 1959 John McKennan announced his premature retirement as mayor. In his place Utica elected Frank Dulan, a Republican protest candidate who had been seeking office for years on one issue: the bossism of Rufus Elefante. In 1953 he had challenged Golder, ridiculing the distinguished mayor as the willing stooge of a corrupt machine. But Utica was doing pretty well at that time, and there weren't enough people prepared to believe it. In 1959 Dulan was an easy winner.

The Utica newspapers had a great deal to do with that change. The *Observer-Dispatch* editorialized day after day in the late 1950s against what it saw as the stench of boss rule. It struck much closer than Elefante ever expected with a series of stories showing how the city was buying tires at higher-than-market prices from companies with which the boss himself had an affiliation. For a period at the height of the controversy, reading the newspaper in Utica amounted to watching a serialized debate between the boss and the editors about what local government was supposed to be like. "We believe," Elefante said at one point, "that government must be tolerant of human weakness." The *Observer-Dispatch* went after that one with everything it had. "If human weakness is intended to cover prostitution, gambling and stealing and corruption within a city administration, it is well that we have a government that is less tolerant."

But as far as Elefante was concerned, the Utica papers were taking minor transgressions that existed in any normal American city, inflating them to enormous proportions, and advertising to the entire world—including prospective investors—that their own community was a place of unparalleled wickedness. "With my connections," Elefante boasts, "I could have remade Utica. Albany and Washington were open to me. But the newspapers kept knocking me, and knocking me, and knocking me, and made me out to look like a goddamn mafioso." There is no question that the whole affair destroyed the hegemony of the Elefante machine. Elefante retained his control over the Utica Democratic party and over individual members of the city council, which kept its Democratic majority. But the mayoralty, the one office necessary for full control of local political life, was gone, and it would prove extremely difficult for Elefante to win back.

Over the 1960s the Elefante machine gradually became a heavy burden, not just to candidates running on the Democratic label but to the economic life of the community. Before 1957 the machine held out the promise of stability to companies interested in locating in the Utica area. At the very least business executives knew they could sit down with Elefante, as Mohawk Airlines had done, and work out the terms of their role in the area. And whatever they agreed upon would stick. After 1957 the machine was known to outsiders for the stories of corruption and bossism. It was a reason not to come to town. "The effect was devastating," said Frank Scalise, a veteran local official and onetime mayoral candidate. "Salesmen wouldn't even come here anymore."

Even had there been no scandals, it's not clear Utica would have escaped the aura of decline that has enveloped it in the last quarter-century. Other northeast industrial towns of similar size have had just as much trouble attracting industry, preserving their inner cities, and preventing massive population loss. But few of them began to suffer at the time Utica did, in the 1960s, a period of steady economic growth almost everywhere in the country. During that decade some of the city's major employers, such as Savage Arms and Univac, began deserting Utica. They were not fleeing to the Sunbelt; most of them resettled elsewhere in upstate New York or in New England. They were simply expressing their distaste for a community made notorious by the scandals of the previous few years. Whatever chance Utica had to rise above its problems and build a new future, the "Sin City" image almost certainly took away.

It did something else as well: It deprived Utica of the political talent it could not afford to do without. Even before 1957 the city had a distressing amount of trouble attracting its educated people to public life. In part this was the inevitable consequence of ethnic rivalry: The ruling Democratic party was in the hands of the Italians, Irish, and Poles; the more affluent Yankees and Germans, who in those days constituted virtually all the residents with higher education, saw local politics as something alien to their values and experience. They were professional people. They didn't want to start at the bottom of a hierarchy and spend years paying homage to Elefante. There were exceptions, like Boyd Golder. But after 1957 the talent pool just about dried up. Politics was an enterprise that Utica's elite avoided at all costs. "They chose to stay out and keep their hands clean," says Joe Tierno, a veteran Utica labor organizer. "The art of politics was something generally perceived as beneath consideration." One active Democrat remembers an evening in 1975 when he asked a prominent Utica banker to consider running for mayor. He got a blunt response. "What," the banker asked, "and ruin my good name?" F. X. Matt II, president of Utica's Matt Brewing Co. and perhaps the most widely respected local businessman, has resolutely avoided running for office his entire adult life. "If I take a controversial stand," he once explained to a reporter, "I alienate half the people who drink my beer."

Those young people who were not avoiding Utica politics were generally avoiding the city altogether. As economic stagnation set in, the population began an inexorable decline: 100,000 in 1960; 91,000 in 1970; 75,000 in 1980; fewer than 70,000 by 1986. The generation that might have provided political leadership and exercised power in the postmachine years was moving elsewhere in search of careers and opportunity.

Those who did stay and fight it out in Utica politics tended to be people who carried heavy baggage—long histories of personal dispute and family quarrels that made it difficult for them to build a constituency behind any new idea. "It's a difficult place to practice politics," argues Tierno. "It's very incestuous. You go to someone you consider a natural ally, only to find that his cousin or his uncle is beholden to your opponent and he can't help you." Utica politics in the past quarter-century has produced more than its share of sound and fury. But it has generated very little leadership. The community threw its political system wide open to talent, then failed to produce the sort of talent that could run it effectively.

After Frank Dulan left the mayoralty in 1967, Utica tried its own version of Camelot, in the person of Dominic "Dick" Assaro, a reform-minded liberal Democrat who idolized Robert F. Kennedy. During his four years in office, Assaro proclaimed an idealistic new urban agenda, brought in former Kennedy campaign workers to staff City Hall, and even imported RFK himself for an occasional well-publicized visit. But very little happened. Elefante's forces still controlled the city council, and any mayor needed council approval for any action of importance he wanted to take. In the Golder era that was no problem. By Assaro's time it was a critical obstacle to action.

The machine soon concluded that anything, even a Republican, was better than a reform Democrat. "I didn't like Assaro," Elefante says, "and he didn't like the organization. So we took him out." In 1971 Elefante simply withheld his assistance from Assaro, making possible the election of Republican Michael Caruso, a wealthy and passive cheese manufacturer who seemed far less troublesome.

Caruso did indeed provide little outright opposition to the Elefante machine. He also provided little noticeable government for the city.

Two years later, at the height of the national Watergate furor, it was time for another breed of Democrat: Edward Hanna, a crude, volatile, and eccentric businessman who declared his distaste for politics as an institution and a profession. "I hate politics," Mayor Hanna raged. "I can't stand it. Politics is infested with wrongdoings. The phonies and the fakers and the blue bloods have been draining and straining this lousy town too long." Improbable as it may sound, Hanna and Elefante tried to live with each other. At the age of seventy-two, Elefante even accepted his first and only public office, as a member of the Utica water board. But the rapprochement could not last. Hanna was more interested in polishing his reputation as a stubborn independent than in cultivating whatever political power a relationship with the machine might bring him. He soon denounced Elefante and removed city deposits from banks affiliated with the machine.

In short-run political terms, this strategy worked. Denied renomination by the Democrats, Hanna formed his own Rainbow party and won a second term. "I beat 'em all," he boasted afterward. "I beat the political machines and I beat the unions. I told 'em all to go to hell, and I fought 'em." But when it came to governing, Hanna's two terms as mayor brought little besides managerial chaos and grandiose development schemes that could not succeed. Hanna pledged to remake the streets of downtown Utica into a promenade that would remind visitors of Paris. He ordered the construction of a 150-foot clock tower and a brand-new park in front of City Hall. He filled City Hall with so many tropical plants that employees began to complain that they were working in a hothouse. Some of the schemes were paid for by Hanna himself. But his most important legacy was a $600,000 deficit and a reduced city bond rating from Moody's.

Early in his administration, Hanna had brought in Mason Taylor, the retired editor of the *Observer-Dispatch,* as an unpaid adviser. After a few months Taylor quit and wrote a bitter letter of resignation. "The course you are pursuing," he wrote, "will lead to chaos and could result in the collapse of the governmental structure to the point where some higher governmental authority might have to intervene." Nothing like that happened. But the debacle of Edward Hanna's mayoralty did make possible a last hurrah for the machine, one that Elefante, in his midseventies, must have thought he would never live to see. In 1977, tired of Hanna's tirades, the Utica voters replaced him with a machine loyalist of the sort they had not elected in two decades: Stephen J. Pawlinga.

Pawlinga was a Colgate graduate and a successful lawyer, but, almost alone among his generation of Utica professionals, he had cast his lot with Elefante right from the beginning of his career. He had been Elefante's defense lawyer in the 1958 investigations, and soon after that he had been made city Democratic chairman. Now, nearly twenty years later, Hanna's failures had given him and the machine an opening.

Pawlinga dedicated his administration to getting outside help for Utica and did pretty well at it. He became one of President Carter's most conspicuous fans among America's mayors—he campaigned for Carter in New Hampshire in 1980—and that helped him pry loose some $15 million in various kinds of federal urban assistance during the four Carter years. Within the city, though, Pawlinga never managed to establish himself as a legitimate leader. He spent his entire six-year mayoralty on the edge of defeat. "I had to pull every stop I ever knew," Elefante says, "to get Pawlinga reelected." After his first term Pawlinga was beaten for renomination and had to scratch his way to reelection as an independent. Two years later he survived the primary by only 270 votes. In 1983 he lost the general election.

Some of those problems were the result of Utica's financial distress; Pawlinga had had to impose a new sales tax to cover the deficit Hanna had left behind. Some of the problem was Pawlinga's personal vanity; he told some audiences that he was "born to be mayor," others that the job was his destiny. But Pawlinga's main political problem was Rufus Elefante. Although Pawlinga insisted that he used the services of the boss only for patronage, not public policy, the common perception was that "the old man" was telling the mayor what to do. An Elefante machine stalwart sat outside Pawlinga's office passing judgment on the decisions of the day. And Elefante's personal popularity was appallingly low. Surveys consistently gave the aged leader a favorable rating of about 20 percent, and an unfavorable of about 50. And the Utica newspapers, which had been relatively gentle to Elefante during his long years out of power, began unloading on him again, editorializing about the evils of boss rule in their city.

Pawlinga, undeniably intelligent and energetic, was never able to translate his energy into real leadership. It was only a matter of time before his administration collapsed under its many liabilities. "The city simply outgrew the political machine," said newspaper editor Tony Vella. "It wanted to be free of it." The stage was set for Utica's mayor of the 1980s: Louis D. LaPolla.

Throughout the Pawlinga years, LaPolla had been the machine's main electoral irritant. It was he who had denied Pawlinga renomination in 1979 and come within 270 votes of doing it again two years later. In 1983 the city GOP chairman asked him to consider switching parties, and he agreed. By that year, LaPolla's mayoral ambitions were an old and familiar story in Utica, and after two failures few political leaders thought he was ever going to make it. He seemed to agree with them. On election night he was in his car when a local radio station reported that "Utica has a new mayor tonight." LaPolla turned to his wife and said, "Oh my goodness, I think I won."

At a time when political organization had ceased to count for much in Utica campaigns, and ideology was more or less irrelevant, LaPolla had made himself mayor largely by wanting it more than anything else in the world. Raised in a public housing project by a mother who was employed as a maid, LaPolla worked his way through Utica College, then became a sixth-grade teacher in the city schools. But he began running for office almost as soon as he could vote.

Two generations earlier, all over urban America, politics had been the salvation of the smartest young men from working-class backgrounds, men like Rufus Elefante, whose ethnicity and lack of formal education cut them off from careers in the professional world. By the 1960s those obstacles were disappearing. Anyone of superior ability could rise as far as his talent would take him. When LaPolla became an adult in the mid-1960s, Utica's brightest graduates were scrambling to take advantage of professional opportunities outside their hometown, in corporations, law firms, and academia. Local politics offered them nothing they wanted or needed. The young people who chose political careers were the ones drawn instinctively to the political life itself, and those whose modest records did not permit them grandiose professional dreams. Louis LaPolla met both criteria.

He worked hard, but nobody ever wrote him up in a yearbook as "most likely to succeed." He craved a status and a prestige neither he nor his family had ever had, and he saw political office as one of the few available ways to get it. "Yes, I wanted the job," he said from behind his desk in City Hall twenty years later. "I knew I couldn't go to law school. I knew I never could be wealthy. I thought I could gain respectability in politics. I dreamed of being on the city council. I dreamed of being mayor."

Is it possible that Louis LaPolla represented the best Utica could do for leadership in the 1980s? Was it unrealistic to hope that the city might be governed by its brightest and most public-spirited young people, rather than merely by the most dogged and personally ambitious? Given the constraints of Utica's history and the demands of a life in local politics, such a hope may indeed have been too much, for LaPolla turned out to be the best candidate Utica could muster. And a career in politics was by far the best choice he could make for himself.

He ran for the council at age twenty-three, pledging to work for the demolition of an abandoned bridge he and other residents of his ward considered a safety hazard. He won the election and never stopped agitating until the bridge was torn down, several years later. Over more than fifteen years as a city councilman, LaPolla proved to be a loner. He rarely disclosed how he planned to vote until it was absolutely necessary. "My best and only friend," he says, "is my wife." What he excelled at was campaigning. LaPolla never developed much skill as a public speaker, but he was fantastic as a one-on-one campaigner. "I'm a workhorse," he says. "I'm a door-to-door guy. I ring 8,000 to 10,000 doorbells every time I run." He has a memory for detail that has to be seen to be believed. If a Utica resident tells LaPolla his name and the street he lives on, the mayor can nearly always come up with the exact address.

During three terms in office, LaPolla has not made many changes in the routine that got him elected. He shows up everywhere. "We have five senior citizens' centers. I go to their birthday parties every month. I serve the food. I go to 90 percent of the wakes. If I know one person in the family, I go. I'll get invited to three weddings on a Saturday night. I go to all of them. I'm not selective."

In the office LaPolla spends a good deal of his time talking to constituents about the most routine problems of urban life. "They call me for potholes, they call me for garbage." He does not go home at night until he has personally answered every phone call he has received during the day. He pretty much has to return them himself, since he has reduced his office staff from Pawlinga's six mayoral aides, some of them deputized to make important decisions, to three routine clerical positions. When LaPolla wants to show a visitor a report or a document, he goes into a storage room and looks for it in the files.

In many ways LaPolla is the reincarnation of the old-fashioned urban politician: favors, personal contact, and personal service. He takes pride in what he says is his reputation as the "pothole mayor." But in the days of machine control, personal service translated into both votes and governmental power. The success at the polls that placed Elefante's loyalists in office created a network of obligation and loyalty that enabled them to function as a team once they got there. In the LaPolla era personal service translates only into votes, and into votes for just one candidate. Popular as he is, LaPolla is not much help to any of the council candidates, and rarely do they need to vote with him out of political indebtedness. "They are an independent group of people," says planning director Steve DiMeo. "They don't defer to any type of leadership."

It is sometimes hard to find even the slightest hint of teamwork on Utica's council. In the first three years that the Republicans controlled the council, in the mid-1980s, there were three majority leaders, and each of them quit or threatened to quit over the lack of cooperation from his colleagues. The third leader, Michael Cerminaro, tried to resign in the summer of 1988 but was forced to stay on because nobody else wanted the job. Meanwhile, incessant arguments erupted between LaPolla and the Republican councilmen over the routine business of the city. One of the subjects was trash collection. It was generally agreed that to meet its growing waste disposal expenses, Utica needed to impose a garbage "user fee," through which residents would pay for each trash bag they disposed of. But it took months to end the deadlock among the Republican majority over how the fee would be structured and collected. Lacking political influence over the individual members, the administration was unable to broker any sort of compromise that could command the needed votes. In the course of the argument, one Republican councilman accused LaPolla of "unconscionable ineptness" in his entire garbage removal policy. LaPolla accused the councilman of "grandstanding and posturing." Still another GOP member said the council as a whole was guilty of "backbiting and back stabbing."

The garbage dispute was a good example of Utica politics in the late 1980s. But it was only one example. All kinds of policy disputes seemed to linger forever. The Common Council borrowed $700,000 in 1986 to build a new firehouse and replace two of its existing stations. But it could not agree on where to put the new structures, and three years later the funds were still unspent, while the city faced an obligation to repay the loan whether it built the stations or not.

The elections of 1989, which replaced the council's Republican majority with a 5–4 Democratic advantage, merely added new partisan tensions to the existing confusion. During the year following that vote, the council refused to appropriate money to pay for new police cars because it said LaPolla had not consulted its members on the choice. Councilmen began introducing city ordinances to repair individual streets and cut down individual trees, arguing that LaPolla's administration was ignoring routine maintenance requests from his critics' constituencies.

Meanwhile, Utica ignored a mandate from the state to reassess city property, which it had not done since 1947. Some sections of inner-city Utica actually stood to have their taxes lowered by a reassessment, but as a result of forty years of inaction, taxes in more affluent areas would have increased enormously, and the residents of those areas managed to persuade the council to defeat two reassessment bills. They possessed the power to say no; the power to say yes—to build coalitions for the common good—was not often in evidence.

And as Utica declined in population, the bickering continued for nearly a decade over the closing of some underutilized public schools. The schools are not under the control of the mayor or the council, but the city's conspicuous inability to resolve the dispute reflected the overall vacuum in political power. "The quality of the school system is a problem," said school board member John Balzano. "But we're complicating it with all this bickering. I'm becoming a believer in the notion that there has to be a recognized leader. Someone has to answer for something."

In economic terms it was hard to escape the feeling that the city of Utica was turning into little more than the depressed core of its reasonably healthy metropolitan area. Greater Oneida County found itself attracting numerous industrial plums in the 1980s, including several insurance companies and a new facility established by New

York City's Irving Trust Company. Unemployment in the county was below the national average for much of the decade. But Utica itself missed out on many of the benefits of this resurgence. Some of its leading downtown employers, such as Blue Cross, fled the city to become part of the out-county boom. Utica's population continued to decline alarmingly, and to age steadily, leading to concerns that the city would eventually be little more than a warehouse for senior citizens and poor people. As its tax base declined, taxes themselves had to go up to cover the losses, leading more people to leave for the suburbs. There was widespread agreement with the views of Ed Peterson, an executive with General Electric: "The long-term economic solution is outside the city." What role that left Utica itself was not easy to determine.

The city's clumsy efforts to govern itself in the 1980s added up to a graphic demonstration of politics in the absence of authority. And they made Rufus Elefante look better than he once did even to some who used to fight him. "The city was never any better off than it was in the machine days," said Frank Scalise, once an antimachine candidate for mayor. "The streets were clean and the garbage was picked up. . . . We fought so hard against a single source of power that we've dispersed it all, and now we're like the government of Italy." Elefante himself, a connoisseur as well as a practitioner of political power, watched it all in sadness. "There's nobody you can talk to and get things done," he lamented in retirement at age eighty-five. "And it's no good. Believe me when I tell you, it's no good."

But that did not appear to be the majority opinion of the Utica electorate. Mayor LaPolla, despite his remarkable lack of influence over his council, enjoyed continuing popularity as he served his third term. Much of his appeal stemmed from his determination to destroy the governmental remnants of the old Elefante regime. He struck a responsive chord by firing numerous city patronage employees, most of them machine loyalists who had been there for years. He reduced the police force by 200 positions, the fire department by 40 positions. He put the machine-controlled police department under the supervision of a public safety director, brought in from outside the city.

All this seemed to please the voters. It was widely agreed in the 1980s in Utica that a government whose honesty cannot be questioned is worth a great deal, whatever the cost in political power. "LaPolla has convinced people that you can have clean government," says political scientist Richard Emmert.

It is important not to confuse the occasional outbursts of nostalgia for Rufus Elefante's days of authority and deference with any widespread desire to return to them. Nearly everyone appreciates the value of a leader who makes the trains run on time, but it is no longer fashionable or even acceptable to keep them on schedule if that means trampling on the sensibilities of open, participatory government. Whatever its problems in governing itself, Utica does not want Rufus Elefante back. Louisiana does not want Huey Long back, either. Nor does Chicago want Richard J. Daley. In 1989, when Daley's son was elected mayor, it was not simply a reflection of nostalgia for the elder Daley's simpler times but a response to the younger Daley's conspicuous pledge not to be the autocrat his beloved father had been for twenty-two years.

Richard J. Daley, like Rufus Elefante, followed the literal requirements of the political process. City council meetings were held; members spoke; votes were taken. But very few decisions were made at those sessions. The decisions were taken in private, in small gatherings of the leader and his lieutenants. The formal council meetings in Chicago were scripted. Utica's script was written during Elefante's early-afternoon automobile rides with the city clerk. At the time this state of affairs did not strike many people as offensive. Today it would. It is not good form to script the meetings of a legislative body anymore, at any level of the system. City councils, legislatures, and chambers of Congress are expected not only to meet in public but to do real business while they are in session. Private arrangements made beforehand are objects of automatic community suspicion. The citizens of Utica may be disturbed by the spectacle of a Common Council engaged in endless personal bickering, but they find it preferable to a rubber-stamp council à la Elefante.

In present-day American politics, an elected official can be called few names worse than "rubber stamp." It is an accusation that comes up in every campaign year at all levels. One does not want to be caught practicing deference too conspicuously. And it is not only the candidates and officeholders who reject the politics of deference, it is the people. They are suspicious of it. Which is to say, once again, that they are suspicious of power itself, at least in large concentrations. In the end it was not just the image of corruption, or the crudeness of their style, that made Rufus Elefante and bosses like him unacceptable leaders for the 1980s. It was the concentration of power in one person, no matter how carefully he might profess to exercise it.

"Why should the citizens of Utica," the *Observer-Dispatch* asked in an editorial in 1981, "have to go to Uncle Henry's to get a job or have a tree cut down? Who elected or appointed Rufus Elefante to a position with so much power? Machine government is an affront to something on which our entire society is supposedly based—the principle of democracy." A visitor from another time or place might pose a different question: Why is machine government a greater affront to democracy than a government of leaderless individualists prone to petty rivalry and endless bickering? In modern American politics that question is rarely asked.

7

The New Governing Class

Gloriam spreti honoris auctam.
I shall enhance my reputation by refusing office.

So said Cincinnatus, the Roman general and hero. He was a born politician, but he hated politics. In 458 B.C., with Rome under ferocious Aequian assault, Senate leaders were convinced the Republic was doomed unless Cincinnatus came out of retirement and took control. As Livy tells it, they found him on his farm, plowing, and pleaded with him to return to public life. He wiped the sweat off his face, asked his wife to bring him a toga, and accepted a six-month term as absolute dictator of Rome. It took him two weeks to vanquish the enemy, crack down on corrupt public officials, and bring in a reformist government. Having done those things, Cincinnatus resigned as dictator, five and a half months ahead of schedule, and resumed full-time farming. Politics, as he saw it, is a necessary evil. He had no intention of making it a career.

It is safe to say Cincinnatus would not understand the Wisconsin legislature. He would not understand, for example, David Clarenbach, Speaker pro tempore of the state Assembly. As he turned thirty-five in 1988, Clarenbach was completing his sixteenth consecutive year as an elected official. He had never held any other sort of job, either in public or in private life. He loves politics, and he is not embarrassed about admitting it. When anybody calls him a professional politician, he dares them to run against him on that issue. Nobody has ever come close to beating him.

Clarenbach is a key member of the Democratic majority that has run the Wisconsin Assembly for two decades without interruption. Republicans last elected a Speaker in 1969. In 1990, while the state's Republican governor was easily winning reelection, Democrats were adding three more seats to their already comfortable Assembly advantage. And it is not hard to see why. In this state the GOP has become the party of Cincinnatus—the party of those who, in the final analysis, would rather be doing something else for a living. The Democrats are the party of those who believe, with David Clarenbach, that "I can't think of anything I'd rather devote my life to."

Every two years Democrats and Republicans battle for legislative control in Wisconsin in what is advertised as a debate about which party best reflects the views of the electorate. Within the corridors of the state Capitol, however, the biennial elections are recognized for what they really are: a competition to attract candidates who have the skills and energy to win and the desire and resourcefulness to stay in office. This is the competition that Democrats keep winning. Republicans know it perfectly well. "For me to recruit a Republican to run for the state Senate is very difficult," says Michael Ellis, the chamber's Republican leader. "Democrats can go out and find a whole slew of people making less than $30,000 a year [the maximum Senate salary is $33,622] who want to go out and change the world. You come in here at eight o'clock on a Monday morning and all the Democratic parking spaces are filled. This is their career, this is what they do with their lives. It's it. Republicans will show up at nine o'clock on Tuesday when the session starts at ten. They leave at four on Thursday. They come and vote on the bills and then they leave. The Democrats come back in on Friday to work out what they are going to do the next Tuesday and Thursday." David Helbach, the Senate majority leader, has an even more succinct way of putting it: "The Republicans hate government. Why be here if you hate government? So they let us run it for them."

Reasonable people may differ on just how much enthusiasm for politics is ideal in a legislator. But in Wisconsin, at least, there is little disagreement about what has preserved the Democratic majorities of the last twenty years. In an era when the legislature meets most of the year, pay is comparatively low, campaigns are grueling, and fund-raising an onerous chore, an enormous advantage goes to the party of enthusiasts. The Cincinnatus syndrome has produced years of Republican frustration. More important, it has produced an entire army of Democratic legislative leadership, during a time when the governorship has bounced back and forth between the parties. Who are these Democratic leaders? Why are they so attracted to politics? What sort of government have they given the state? And how have they themselves changed in the process?

The most important thing to say about these Democratic leaders is that they represent a generation, not just in a chronological sense but intellectually and emotionally as well. They are the student activists of the late 1960s, now turning forty and remarkably protective of the institutions they once questioned.

David Travis, the Assembly majority leader, is one of them. During more than a decade in office, he has performed a multitude of institutional tasks: chaired the Reapportionment Committee, served on the Joint Committee on Finance, chaired the state Sentencing Commission, which exists in part because of legislation he wrote.

But Travis did not enter politics to do any of those things. He entered politics for one reason: Vietnam. When he graduated from the University of Wisconsin, Milwaukee, in 1969, he escaped the draft by four numbers in the lottery. He became a full-time antiwar campaigner, and when one of his candidates got elected to the state Senate, he went along as a staff aide. Later he ran the Senate Democratic caucus. In 1978 an Assembly seat opened up in Madison, where he was living. Travis got it, and he has held it ever since, a full-time political practitioner, as he has been virtually all his adult life. He sees himself explicitly as part of a group. "A lot of people," he says, "arrived in government here out of opposition to Vietnam. That was intertwined with civil rights, the Peace Corps, the environment. We were out to change the world. We have a whole group of people running the government who were politicized by the war."

For Spencer Black, another legislative leader of the same generation, the environment was everything. He was born in the South Bronx, grew up in New York City, went to high school in Manhattan, graduated from college on Long Island, and, by the time he got his degree in 1972, had had enough of cities and of the East altogether. "I'd rather be in a prison in Wisconsin," he says, "than in a penthouse in New York." In what almost seems a personal revenge on the indignities of urban life, he became a midwesterner, an outdoorsman, even a gun owner. But most of all he became an environmentalist.

Black got a job with the Wisconsin Historical Society, joined the Sierra Club, and soon became the club's state chairman. Then he quit to work at the state Capitol as a lobbyist for a coalition of five environmental organizations. That was in 1979. Ten years later he was still lobbying on the same issues. But he was doing it from the inside. He had become chairman of the Natural Resources Committee of the Wisconsin Assembly. "If you lobby long enough," Black says, "you reach the conclusion that you would rather have a vote. In many ways, I am doing what I did as a grass-roots activist for the Sierra Club, only I am doing it from a more powerful position."

By the time he announced for the Assembly, in 1984, when he was thirty-four years old, Black already possessed the political skills he needed to be a strong candidate. "I was used to organizing volunteers, motivating volunteers, motivating people to give money." He had gained that knowledge in the environmental movement, just as Travis had picked it up in the antiwar movement. He is still using it. Black has never forgotten how important it is to influence a legislature from the outside. Even as a key committee chairman, he spends as much time generating publicity as he does negotiating with other members. He writes an environmental column for small weekly newspapers all over Wisconsin and travels across the state holding legislative hearings at night to get press in the dailies. "I tend to see my most important role as public relations," he says, "using the press, influencing public opinion."

To become an institutional power in the Wisconsin legislature, Black did not have to modify his environmental views to any significant degree. Militant as he might be, he is not far from where most of the Democratic majority is on environmental issues. The institution has moved left to meet him. "Vietnam, the environment, these are internal values for people here," Black says. "We've grown up with these issues. It gives us something in common."

Stan Gruszynski offers another story. For him the issue has

always been power, and the absence of power. As a college student he complained that Polish-American farm families like his never seemed to have any control over their incomes and lives. He began fighting against the power arrangements that seemed to him to lock them and inner-city poor people into lives of squalor. "I was a crusader," he says. After college he went home to Marinette, along the border with Upper Michigan, to agitate for farmland preservation. Then he got a job in his home county with the federal Office of Economic Opportunity, in its Community Action Program, until the Nixon administration closed the program down. He worked four years for Robert J. Cornell, a liberal Democratic congressman. Then he left to become an organizer for the Industrial Areas Foundation, a community action group dedicated to the principles of the late radical activist Saul Alinsky. In 1984 he was elected to the Assembly.

Five years later he was part of the establishment, chairman of the Assembly's Democratic caucus. But, at thirty-nine years of age, he was still a Saul Alinsky man. "A smart organizer," he said, "looks at all the options and calculates. I can look at the legislature from the inside out, and from the outside in. Alinsky said you do what you need to do to get things done. I became comfortable with the idea that power is going to be exercised one way or another. So it might as well be me." Past caucus chairmen were generally passive, presiding over meetings and simply moderating the debate. Gruszynski chose to be different. When the fifty-six Democratic Assembly members became unruly, he raised his own voice to keep theirs down. He treated running a legislative caucus as a variant of community organizing, a search for people willing to emerge from the back benches and commit themselves to action. "Alinsky was always on the lookout for leaders," he says. "Leaders mean power. We can always use more."

David Clarenbach is younger than Travis, Black, or Gruszynski, but his career reflects all the political currents that produced them, and more. He grew up in a family that amounted to a workshop in political activism: His father was an antiwar delegate to the 1968 Democratic National Convention; his mother chaired the National Organization for Women. When he was sixteen Clarenbach was campaigning to register black voters in Mississippi, spending the summer as a houseguest of Fannie Lou Hamer, the civil rights pioneer. He returned to Madison to crusade for the rights of high school students and fought successfully to get them represented on the local school board.

His timing was perfect. The eighteen-year-old vote became effective in 1972, and Clarenbach was already developing a citywide reputation in Madison as a student-rights agitator. Suddenly there was a built-in constituency for a bold political move. The average eighteen-year-old wouldn't have realized that, but Clarenbach was no ordinary teenager. He was already a professional politician. He went after a position on the Dane County Board, a forty-one-member body that was at the time more conservative than liberal. He announced his candidacy in a district where 30 percent of the voters were students, 30 percent senior citizens. He went after both. In the middle of the campaign the incumbent died. Clarenbach outpolled four older opponents. At eighteen he was a county supervisor.

At that point he began to realize just what a marketable political commodity he was. In 1974 a vacancy came up on the Madison city council, and he won it. For a while he was an alderman and a county supervisor at the same time. But he wanted to be in the legislature, and at age twenty he knew more about how to get there than almost anyone in Madison. He filed in an open district and won the nomination without any primary opposition. Then he won a comfortable victory in the general election; he got 40 percent of the vote, a Republican got 30 percent, and a Socialist 20 percent.

Clarenbach showed up in Madison in January of 1975 with shoulder-length blond hair and a legislative agenda that featured legalization of marijuana and unconditional amnesty for draft evaders. "He came in as a liberal flake," said Joseph Tregoning, a long-time Assembly Republican, "and an immature one." Clarenbach doesn't really disagree. "In a much larger bowl than the city council," he admits, "I was an equally isolated fish." Today Clarenbach's hair is short, he wears conservative suits, and he is Speaker pro tempore. He is not a gadfly. He is a parliamentarian. He presides over the Assembly more than anybody else, and his ability to move a bill or handle a debate is unsurpassed. "If you want to roll through bills," says his colleague Stan Gruszynski, "Clarenbach can do it faster than anybody. He speaks so fast you can't keep up with him. It's a pride he has taken in knowing the process, knowing the rules, establishing decorum."

Clarenbach has not changed much ideologically. He ran in

1974 as a gay rights advocate, for example, and in 1982 he became the author of Wisconsin's gay rights statute. In promoting that law, however, Clarenbach demonstrated how much he had changed in his approach to politics. In the spring of 1981 he had gathered enough votes in the Assembly's Democratic Caucus to have gay rights language included in the annual budget bill. The caucus had bound its members on the budget; even Democrats uncomfortable with gay rights would have had to support it. Clarenbach didn't make them do it. He made sure everyone knew he had the votes, then withdrew the language, in the interest of party harmony. The next year a gay rights bill became law on its own. "That was part of my transition," he says now. "I was willing to ride roughshod over colleagues in my early years. Now I'm more sensitive."

Clarenbach's willingness to back off in the first gay rights confrontation was a key factor in his selection as Speaker pro tempore in 1983. But so was the detail work he had been performing for colleagues for years. The Assembly is loaded with full-time legislators, but most of them are home in their districts when the legislature is not in session. For Clarenbach, who represents Madison, the Capitol is the only office. He spent years roaming the corridors on off days, striking up conversations with whoever happened to be around, asking if there were any favors he could do for them.

The less somebody agreed with him on the issues, the more determined Clarenbach was to do him a favor. "It's the conservatives who need me more than anyone," he argued. "The rural people. They are woefully underrepresented in the Assembly. I provide the bridge." It was that record of careful bridge building that made David Clarenbach the gay rights crusader and celebrated student radical of 1975 into David Clarenbach the presiding officer and parliamentarian of 1990. He did not have to change his mind about any important issue. Like Spencer Black on the environment, he simply reached out for influence in the institution as it swung closer and closer to his point of view.

Clarenbach insists he doesn't plan to spend his whole life in the legislature, but when you ask him what else he would like to do, he talks about other elective offices, not jobs in the private sector. What if he lost an election and found himself, for the first time since age eighteen, holding no political office? "I'd shed a tear," he says, "then I'd have to work for a living."

. . .

David Clarenbach's career helps explain why the Wisconsin legislature governs as it does. But it provides little insight into why Democrats control it the way they do. Clarenbach's district in Madison is a liberal Democratic stronghold. If he were not there to represent it, someone else would almost certainly be voting on the same side of the issues. To understand Democratic control, it is necessary to look at a Democrat from a different sort of district—someone like John Medinger.

Medinger represents La Crosse County. A Republican county, La Crosse cast its presidential vote for Gerald Ford in 1976, Ronald Reagan in 1980 and 1984, and George Bush in 1988. But in every one of those years, and in the midterm years in between, it elected John Donald Medinger to the Wisconsin Assembly. Long-term Democratic control of the legislature has been built in districts like this one, in the sparsely populated counties of the state, north and west of Madison. Wisconsin has a solid core of Democratic votes in Madison, in Milwaukee, and in a few southeastern industrial cities, but not enough to give the party control of the Assembly or the Senate. To win control they must take a respectable number of the seats outstate, where they are rarely successful in gubernatorial campaigns and almost never in the presidential vote.

Medinger's district is that sort of place. It has been a piece of the Democratic Assembly majority since he first won it in 1976. How has he held it all those years? By carefully tailoring his voting record to the district's underlying conservatism? No. The opposite. By spending most of his waking hours on constituent service and making sure the voters are thinking about service rather than issues when they go to the polls. And by escaping any high-quality Republican opposition at all.

Nothing but elbow grease could possibly explain how Medinger won in the first place. "The year I got elected," he says, "I was twenty-eight, living in an apartment, no family, no kids, no property, long hair, hippie glasses. I was making $7,500 pumping gas and driving a school bus. My opponent was county treasurer." Medinger outcampaigned him and won. He became a highly unconventional representative for La Crosse County. Some of his conservative neighbors were surprised when he and his wife adopted two black children. He voted for gay rights, and, with the lone exception of gun control, virtually all the items on the liberal Democratic agenda in

Madison. In 1988 he was given a rating of 100 by the Wisconsin AFL-CIO.

But all the political risks of Medinger's career in Madison were overcome by the friendships it is possible to accumulate in a full-time legislative career. He drives the 137 miles to Madison and the 137 miles back three times a week even when the legislature is not in session. When he is in La Crosse, he is in perpetual motion: "If I don't have anything to do at home, I go sit in a coffee shop and shoot the breeze. I might be home two nights a week to tuck my kids in. I go to every pancake breakfast and every rummage sale. I am always looking for something to do. If there's nothing else, I go to a basketball game and mingle with the crowd. It's what you do back home that's important. Not what you do in Madison." The year he got a 100 rating from the AFL-CIO, Medinger was rated at 29 by the Wisconsin Association of Manufacturers. But the La Crosse Chamber of Commerce endorsed him for reelection.

"There are some Republicans in my district who could run against me," Medinger said in 1989, "and make my life miserable. . . . But the Republicans can't come up with candidates who will put in hundred-hour weeks. So they don't make it." The following year he was reelected to his eighth term.

What is it about being a legislator that has driven John Medinger and his Democratic cohorts to work so hard for so many years for so little money? Part of it is simple fun: Anybody who had done the sorts of jobs Medinger had done until his first campaign—pumping gas, driving a bus, working construction—would immediately recognize the position of state assemblyman as by far the most interesting and prestigious occupation he had ever held. It is no surprise that anybody in that position would work like a demon to get the job and then do the same to keep it. But even for the most enthusiastic politician, some aspects of the work cease to be fun after a few years. Floor debate and strategy sessions maintain their allure rather well over a long career, but fund-raising and door-to-door campaigning generally do not. As they become senior legislators, nearly all the Wisconsin Democrats come to see the job as a trade-off between tasks they love and tasks they simply endure.

After ten years and six campaigns, David Travis clearly felt that way. "This is a very rough business," he said in 1989. "It's not fun to knock on doors when it's 100 degrees. I did that last summer. In campaigns I get dry heaves in the morning. I get back spasms. It's a very high-stress occupation." Yet he has been putting up with the stress for a more than a decade. That is because he is a believer in government. He may doubt himself, he may doubt the Wisconsin legislature, but he never doubts that government itself is an institution worthy of his participation.

We have all grown accustomed in recent years to polls that document the decline in public approval of government. To a great extent it was distaste for government that made the Reagan presidency possible. But while there is no reason to deny the validity of those public opinion polls, there are other opinions that matter. For Democrats such as David Travis, government in the last twenty years has not been a failure at all. Thanks in part to their help, it has dealt with most of the societal problems that led them into politics in the first place. It has not solved them all, but it has, in virtually every case, taken serious aim at them.

"To me," says Travis, "the seminal issues since World War II have been racial segregation, health care, and Vietnam. Vietnam ended. Segregation has been attacked. Health care is now available to all older people in this country. It shows me that over twenty years in this country the government did something right." John Medinger feels the same way. "I came here to change the world," he admits, repeating a phrase that seems to turn up in conversation with nearly all the Wisconsin Democrats of his generation. "I think we've won more than we've lost."

There have been three bursts of legislative reform in Wisconsin politics in this century. One came before World War I, during and just after the governorship of Robert M. La Follette, Sr. The second was in the Depression years, under the administration of La Follette's son Philip. The third took place in the 1970s.

The driving force behind this third wave of activism was the Democratic governor of those years, Patrick J. Lucey. He will never achieve the national reputation of the La Follettes, but in many ways he should. A behind-the-scenes man in state politics for over twenty years and a longtime party chairman, he won the governorship in 1970 and devoted to it the same intensity he had used to make a fortune in real estate when he wasn't dabbling in politics. Lucey's election brought in a Democratic Assembly, and in the first year they overcame the Republican Senate and reorganized the state tax structure, diverting money from wealthy suburbs for use in poorer communities. They revamped the university system, bringing thirteen campuses under one president and one board of regents. In 1972 they passed consumer protection and environmental impact bills that placed Wisconsin in the forefront of state action in those fields.

Lucey was reelected overwhelmingly in 1974, and that year he swept in not only another Democratic Assembly but a Democratic Senate, the first since 1893. The next legislative session went after ethics and campaign finance, establishing one of the first public financing programs for state elections in the country. By the time Lucey left office in 1977, to become President Carter's ambassador to Mexico, he had generated what political analyst Neal Peirce later called "a plethora of new initiatives, the likes of which had been unseen since 1911."

Those were the formative experiences of Wisconsin's current legislative leaders. Most of them were in Madison during the Lucey years in one capacity or another. Tom Loftus, the Speaker for most of the 1980s, was an aide to the Assembly's Democratic majority in the first Lucey years and a member of that majority in the later ones. David Clarenbach was an intern and then a member in the second Lucey term. Stan Gruszynski and David Travis both served as staff director of the Senate Democratic Caucus. For a liberal Democrat in Wisconsin in the 1970s, government was fun. It turned dozens of young academics and staff aides into active political candidates willing to invest their efforts in moving from the sidelines to the more exhilarating experience of holding office. "You fought big fights and you won," says Loftus. "It was heady stuff. The sky was the limit. And that's a psychology that has served us well. We expect to win elections, and we expect to win in the legislature."

Mordecai Lee came to the Assembly in 1976, fresh from a legislative aide's job and holding a brand-new Ph.D. in public administration. His first day as a member in 1977 was the fulfillment of a childhood fantasy. "It was hard to believe I was really there," he remembers. "I kept wondering when somebody was going to come on the floor and ask me to get off." But Lee brought something more important than enthusiasm—he brought his training and self-identification as a "policy professional," someone with the skills to evaluate laws and write good ones. Not all his Democratic peers in the legislature had Lee's academic credentials, but nearly all of them shared his sense of professionalism. They were not the amateurs and part-timers of the old days; they saw their work as a science and spent whatever time it might take to do it right. "Everybody had an agenda in those days," Lee recalls. "Everybody had a legislative program."

After Lucey's departure in 1977, the opportunities for activism declined. The following year's election brought in a Republican governor, Lee Sherman Dreyfus, who was more interested in cutting taxes than in thinking up any new government programs. By the time the Democrats reclaimed the governorship, with Anthony Earl in 1982, a massive recession had deprived state government of the resources to finance many elaborate initiatives. Still, the Wisconsin legislature in the 1980s managed to keep up its reputation as a haven for liberal experiment. It simply found cheaper experiments. In 1982 it enacted the nation's strongest gay rights and sexual privacy laws. In 1985, responding to the feminist sentiments of its majority, it passed a marital property law, rewriting a 150-year-old statute to guarantee spouses a 50 percent share in family wealth. The next year it passed comparable-worth provisions aimed at benefiting female state employees.

Perhaps more important, the generation of Democrats who came to power in the 1980s stood guard successfully against Republican efforts to repeal legislation that had taken effect in the Lucey years. Neither Dreyfus nor Tommy G. Thompson, the more conservative Republican governor who unseated Earl in 1986, launched any serious assault upon the Lucey legislative edifice. "The Lucey years made a major policy shift," says John Bibby, political scientist at the University of Wisconsin, Milwaukee, "and because these folks are here, we haven't turned back." Nor has the legislature turned back from its increased dependence on full-time professionals as leaders. Legislative activism may have slowed down in the 1980s, but the legislative activists are more numerous than ever. The legislature will never again be the province of the part-time farmers, merchants, lawyers, and insurance salesmen who dominated it for so many years before 1970. Conservative Republicans who regret the change are reduced to little more than sniping at what they see as its ill effects.

Wisconsin's Republican party has spent much of the past decade trying to understand how it became a more or less permanent legislative minority and trying to see if there might be a way to turn the situation around. The GOP leaders who worry about that problem find themselves in an impossible position. They don't really like the idea of a legislature dominated by professional politicians, but they have finally begun to realize they are never going to unseat a party of pros with a party of amateurs.

Michael Ellis, the Senate Republican leader, reflects that ambivalence. In one breath he denounces the Democratic majority as a bunch of fuzzy-headed liberals who never worked for a living. The next moment he is wishing he had people of similar political dedication on his side. "If you come out of a textbook and right into this building," he complains, "you have a pure philosophy, but no broad-based experience. Your view is a rehash of other people's thoughts that you have read or listened to but not experienced. It's almost a sophomoric view of the world. It's pristine, and it's unrealistic." Ellis would love to have a state Senate dominated by the farmers and small businessmen who ran it when he arrived at the end of the 1960s. He thinks it would make more sensible laws. It might be a Republican Senate. But he knows it is not going to happen.

David Prosser, the Republican leader in the Assembly, isn't quite so hard on professional politicians. He is one himself, more or less; he has a law degree, but he has done little besides politics since he got out of law school. Prosser thinks it is a waste of time to wish the 1950s were back or to denounce the Democratic pros. What the Republicans need, in his opinion, is some pros of their own. "The Republican party can't have citizen-legislators," Prosser says, "and expect to take power back in this state."

The GOP was very slow to realize that fact in Wisconsin, as it has been in other states, and its slowness cost it dearly. Democrats have benefited not only from the natural political talent of their candidates but from the willingness of party leaders to recruit budding politicians and nurture their careers. And the vehicle for that nurturing process has been the legislative staff.

Twenty years ago, in the twilight of Republican control, staff was minimal in the Wisconsin Capitol. There was one aide for every two senators, one for every four assemblymen. The Speaker got two staff positions. The party caucuses, staffed for the first time with Ford Foundation money in 1963, received state funding for a few full-time jobs only in 1967. Today the caucuses in both chambers are heavily staffed. The Speaker and the party leaders are entitled to as many as half a dozen people working for them directly. Each member of the

Assembly has a personal assistant; each senator has two. Anybody who is a committee chairman (and a majority of the Democrats are) gets another one.

Much has been written about how this explosion in staffing has changed the legislative process, making legislatures both more competent and more prolific (conservatives might say hyperactive). Those effects have been felt in Wisconsin, as in most other states. But in Wisconsin something else has happened as well: The staff has become a farm system for aspiring Democratic politicians. In the Assembly, at the end of the 1980s, the Speaker, Speaker pro tempore, and Democratic caucus chairman all had been legislative aides at one time or another.

Joe Strohl, who was Senate majority leader at that time, described the system this way. "People get out of college, go to work in the Capitol, back home to run for office, and then back to the Capitol as legislators. They are good candidates because they have connections with the establishment up here and they have access to finances."

The Democrats begin developing candidates as early as four years before the election. Those being recruited find themselves on party mailing lists, are offered campaign training, receive visits from incumbent legislators, and are promised financial help when the time comes. By the time they run, these people tend to be creatures of Madison as much as they are creatures of their home districts; most would not have gone home at all except to further their political ambitions. A few staff aides become candidates not out of personal ambition but out of loyalty to a leadership that has marked them out as good potential candidates. "If we can't find somebody to run for a seat," said Tom Loftus, "we'll send an aide up there to do it. We shanghai them."

There is no reason why two parties can't play this game. Republicans do not get as many legislative aide positions as Democrats do, but they have more than enough to use as a political talent pool. It is worth a try, and in the past few elections the Republican party has begun trying it. "We're finally waking up," says Brian Rude, a former GOP aide who became assistant minority leader in the Senate at the age of thirty-three.

In almost every respect other than party affiliation, Rude fits the mold of those who have come to dominate the legislature on the

Democratic side. A lifelong political animal, he graduated from college in 1970 and left the state to take a staff job with the Iowa Senate. Then he came back to work for the Wisconsin Senate. Along the way he traded in his initial hard-right sympathies for a moderate Republican outlook, but he never lost his consuming desire to serve in office. Five years after he got his college degree, he was a member of the Assembly; two years after that he had moved up to the Senate; in 1989 he became assistant minority leader.

Rude's rapid rise generated a noticeable number of candidacies around the state from other Republican staff assistants. Rude thinks it is the only way. "We're finally waking up," he repeats. "We are building our own group who start as aides and either have limited private-sector experience or none." The irony of that strategy has not been lost on the Democratic leaders who have traditionally found themselves targets of Republican complaint about the inadequacies of the professional politician. "They used to be critical of us for having no real-world experience," says Joe Strohl. "Now they are depending on Capitol staff themselves."

But in trying to rebuild on a new base of professional talent, Republicans are up against an annoying obstacle: the reluctance of some of their traditional business supporters to accept the realities of political change. When Brian Rude left his legislative staff position to run for office, he also started a job in his hometown of La Crosse doing public relations for the Trane Corporation, a manufacturing company. When he was elected he asked to stay on part-time, acknowledging that his political duties would allow him to come in only one day a week. The company fired him.

In the old days of Republican control, numerous GOP legislators held corporate jobs and managed to keep them while in office. But in those days being a legislator did not require even half-time effort. A legislator could still devote most of his energies to private business. In the 1980s that became impossible. Corporations that wanted to keep legislators on their payroll had to get used to having them gone most of the week, most weeks of the year. The average corporation is not willing to do that. "I've never seen anybody survive in the Wisconsin legislature that worked for a large corporation," says Tom Loftus. "It's not something that gets people ahead in the corporation."

Business has been making a mistake. In every election Wisconsin corporations use their political action committees to invest huge sums in Republican legislative campaigns, and the GOP has not won a majority in either chamber in more than fifteen years. The same money, used to subsidize low-show corporate jobs for talented politicians who wanted to be full-time legislators, might have done considerably more to close the talent gap in Wisconsin politics. That is the argument of Michael Ellis, the Senate GOP leader. "Corporations ought to have built into the management sphere public service," Ellis says. "That would help them create a more level playing field and fight off some regulation." There is little evidence, however, that corporations have started taking his advice.

Nor is there any evidence that the Democratic legislative majorities are in jeopardy. Republicans, after seeing their strength decline in the 1970s to only one-third of the Assembly and less than one-third of the Senate, performed more respectably in the 1980s. Still, the goal of equal numbers has been elusive. The 1984 election brought them within striking distance in both chambers—52–47 in the Assembly, 19–14 in the Senate—but since then, despite well-financed efforts in both 1986 and 1988, they have lost ground again. It seems extremely unlikely that the Wisconsin legislature will change back to a Republican institution any time soon.

But it will change. The generation of Democrats that were leaders in the 1980s—the generation that launched its political life on the issues of Vietnam and civil rights—will be easing its way out of power in the next few years, running for higher office, accepting government appointments, even deciding in some cases that after twenty years and more in politics it is time, in early middle age, to try something else. The next generation of Democrats will be different. David Travis learned that several years ago when he and some of his senior colleagues began pushing the Assembly to pass legislation urging Congress to bring all U.S. troops home from Lebanon. He noticed that the enthusiasm for this effort seemed to fall off sharply among those under age thirty-five. "It was the older people like me who took this seriously," said Travis, the 1960s antiwar activist. "The younger ones didn't see why we needed to bother memorializing Congress." It wasn't that these people thought the troops ought to stay in Lebanon; they just thought the legislature had better things to do with its time.

The generational differences also crop up on issues much closer to home. Shirley Krug, a three-term member of the legislature, votes as a liberal Democrat just as Travis does. Back home in Milwaukee she helped found an organization to lobby for a transfer of money from defense programs to job creation. But at thirty-two, a full decade younger than Travis, she does not share his positive approach to government as social-problem solver. In between her service as a legislative aide and her election to the Assembly, Krug went to graduate school in economics—"I thought it would be a good background for the legislature"—and emerged with a belief that some social ills are best cured by a reliance on market therapy. "Government can't do everything," she proclaims. "Individuals have to have a commitment to themselves and their families. Equal outcomes are not going to occur. Sometimes being against government spending is the correct liberal position."

Krug has managed to combine feminist politics and skepticism about government spending in some very clever ways. When the legislature debated comparable worth, she argued that the best route to equality was not to raise the salaries of women who were paid too little but to reduce the salaries of men who were paid too much. A version of this actually passed the Assembly before falling victim to a gubernatorial veto. Later she voted, contrary to most of her Democratic colleagues, against a bill to expand pension benefits for state employees. She said it did not meet the test of sound market economics. That is a test that the older generation of liberal Democrats does not often impose. "For our generation," jokes Tom Loftus, "the market is where you buy cereal and meat. It doesn't solve social problems."

Of all the rising stars in the youngest Democratic generation, Walter Kunicki has been the brightest. He was an assemblyman at twenty-two, vice-chairman of the majority caucus at twenty-five. By 1989, he was cochairman of the Joint Committee on Finance. Early in 1991, at age thirty-two, he became Speaker of the Wisconsin Assembly. A nurse by training, he has spent virtually his entire adult life as a full-time politician, and he is a tough and ambitious one. "I happen to be a very competitive, very assertive person," he says. "I have to feel my career is advancing in order to be happy." While advancing in the legislature, Kunicki has used his position to secure some tangible legislative achievements, and generally they have been along traditional liberal lines. He was in large part responsible for the fact that the Wisconsin budget includes a standing annual appropriation for the homeless. But Kunicki did not enter politics to pursue any crusades, and he does not view issues as a means of self-expression. He is in politics because it is what he prefers to do, what he prides himself upon doing well.

In 1988, when the Republicans mounted a well-financed effort to take away Democratic Assembly seats, it was Kunicki who designed much of the Democrats' counterstrategy and recruited the candidates who actually increased the Democratic majority. He found good candidates, people his age and younger, people who liked politics and saw the same opportunities in it that he had seen. It has never been a mystery to Kunicki why his party controls the Wisconsin legislature. "We're good at elections," he says. "We view this as a profession. We view government as a business."

The people of Wisconsin have never chosen the Democratic party en bloc to be the legislative majority. The question is not put to the electorate that way. Like their counterparts in Concord, California, and in congressional districts across the nation, Wisconsin's voters have elected individual Democrats who outperformed their opposition at the tasks a modern political career requires. The electorate has not sent them to govern; it has merely maintained the conditions under which they could send themselves.

There has been no permanent grant of power. Given enough time in control, the Democrats in Wisconsin might make a misstep— as the ones in Concord did—and move so far beyond public opinion that even an inert electorate would notice. Or economic disasters beyond the legislature's control might create an antimajority sentiment strong enough to override the candidates' individual advantages. Or the Republicans might finally generate the talent to compete on an equal basis. Then again, none of those things may happen. Indeed, it is not too difficult to imagine the Wisconsin legislature holding its first session of the twenty-first century with Walter Kunicki, forty-two years old and in his third decade of membership, instructing a whole new generation of Democratic enthusiasts in the secrets of professionalism and power.

8

Free and Equal

Shaun McNally is the sort of person we have met many times in this book. In his background, his style, and his outlook on political affairs, he is very much like Steve Weir in Concord, or David Clarenbach in Wisconsin. Like them he has managed in a decade of adult life to be social activist and campaign tactician at the same time. He threw himself into a series of campaigns in college, accepted a job with a congressman upon graduation, then took time out to serve in the Peace Corps and work for a welfare agency in his hometown of Norwich, Connecticut. In 1986, at the age of twenty-nine, he was elected to the state legislature. McNally is a modern legislator—a modern politician. He is creative and articulate, and hard to lead. He does not defer.

In 1987, his first year as a state representative, McNally began to have some doubts about the leadership of the man who had recruited him for his first campaign, Connecticut House Speaker Irving Stolberg. He thought Stolberg was condoning inflated estimates of state revenue, worrying more about the short-term political climate than about the long-term economic result. So at the start of his second term, when some dissident House Democrats told him they were plotting a coup against Stolberg's leadership, McNally said to count him in, even though many of his most deeply held political values—in favor of legalized abortion, in favor of gay rights, against capital punishment—were closer to Stolberg's than to those of the cabal.

Early in January 1989 McNally provided one of the thirty-one renegade Democratic votes that gave Stolberg a humiliating defeat and installed a more conservative Democrat, Richard Balducci, as Speaker. A few days later McNally got his reward. Balducci dumped Stolberg's choice for chairman of the Planning and Housing Committee and made McNally chairman instead. He was thirty-one years old, the youngest chairman in the legislature.

McNally was the beneficiary of some old-fashioned conspiratorial politics, the kind that has always surrounded legislatures. But he did not repay his gift in the time-honored way. A few months after the coup, Balducci and the new leaders were having budget problems of their own. They were forced to look for nearly $800 million to meet the state's unexpected fiscal shortfall. They faced a very difficult task in selling any package of new taxes and spending cuts that large to the bloc of liberal Democrats still upset about Stolberg's defeat. In that situation, Balducci felt he had to have the absolute loyalty of his insurgent group.

McNally was a key member of that group. But he wasn't on board. He thought the tax increases in Balducci's budget plan were much too high and the spending cuts not nearly deep enough. He put together his own list of spending reductions, and then, when they weren't deployed in the way he had suggested, he organized the opposition to his new mentor's budget. He wrote Balducci a letter of resignation from his committee chairmanship. It wasn't accepted. Ultimately the leadership budget plan got through, with McNally giving it a grudging vote on final passage.

In the months after that, McNally suffered no ill effects from his lapse of loyalty. He kept his chairmanship and his role as a significant player in budget politics. "I've had people threaten from leadership positions that my bills would be killed," he said, "but most of them seem to get through. I've had people say they were going to line up a Democratic opponent for me, but they haven't had much success. What kind of patronage can it cost me? I don't even want patronage. That's not what I'm up here for."

Such are the manners of the modern legislature. People like Shaun McNally do what they have to do. Leaders don't have much alternative but to accept it. "I made a choice," McNally says. "I was going into politics for life. This is it for me. If you are going to invest your life in it, you can't be dishonest about it."

McNally's self-definition as a professional underscores the way the meaning of that term has changed in the past generation, in Connecticut and in American politics. In the 1950s, when a legislator in McNally's position described himself as a professional, he meant a member of a political party, an organization, someone who grasped the rules of that organization and worked patiently to secure the benefits membership brought.

Those benefits were several. Patronage was perhaps the most tangible. For most of this century, it drove politics in Connecticut more than it did in most places in America. To sit in the legislature in Hartford was to have an opportunity to bring home to constituents an array of state jobs, from judgeships to minor clerical positions, and landing them was the badge of effectiveness. The only way to qualify for these fruits of office was to be a team player, to practice the political self-discipline that party loyalty required. A professional was someone who understood that.

At a more personal level, a professional was someone who took pride in the very fact of holding office, seeing it correctly as testament to years successfully spent navigating the currents of political competition in a local community and political party. The emblem of that success, of course, was renomination, and the only way to achieve it was loyalty. That was especially true in Connecticut, where until 1955 there were no primaries for state or local office. Nomination took place by vote of the party's town committee, and from its decision there was no recourse. The professional was someone who, whatever outlets he might seek to express his individualism and personal values, knew how to stop short of endangering his career.

To be a professional in Shaun McNally's sense means, of course, almost exactly the opposite. It means a commitment of vast amounts of time and energy in pursuit of values and goals that seem much too important to be subordinated to teamwork or party discipline. It means developing a personal base of constituent support that makes independence politically possible. It means joining a legislative body with the clear intention of becoming an immediate participant in its decisions. One doesn't work months on end and give up all other gainful employment for the privilege of going to Hartford to sit around and take orders. That would be, in the most modern sense, unprofessional. "I think it should be possible to be part of the process," McNally says, "without being part of the team." In the legislature of the 1990s, it is very possible. It is, for a politician with talent, fairly easy.

In the generation before Shaun McNally, legislative bodies all over the country accepted the notions of leadership and deference as part of the natural order of things. But hardly any accepted them quite to the degree that the Connecticut legislature did. By nearly any available standard of measurement, Connecticut is one of America's most affluent, best educated, most sophisticated states, and it has been throughout this century. But for nearly all those years, through most of the 1960s, it was home to the most disciplined form of political bossism. Not the most venal or abusive form, by any means, but old-fashioned bossism nevertheless.

Some of that tradition was a matter of law. The absence of primaries helped keep the system intact through the first half of the century. Reinforcing it was the straight-ticket party lever in the voting booth, which discouraged voters from dividing their ballots between the parties and tied candidates all over the state to the fortunes of the party as a whole in a given year. More important than procedure, however, Connecticut politics produced party leaders capable of taking creative advantage of its habits of deference. The greatest of them was J. Henry Roraback. He is not a famous name today, even in his home state. But his career is worth recalling. He was a political leader who demanded and received deference in awesome proportions.

The reader of the 1990s may be prepared for the historical fact that Roraback, as Connecticut Republican chairman from 1912 to 1937, pretty much controlled the nominating process in his state through the exercise of patronage powers over the town committees. That is the way many of us imagine old-time political bosses to have operated. What is jarring to modern sensibilities is the extent to which he dictated the substantive business of the legislature itself.

Roraback was rarely seen at the Capitol. He operated out of a suite on the third floor of the Allyn Hotel in downtown Hartford. To that suite, at the close of each day of the legislative session, was brought a box containing the bills that had been introduced in the Connecticut House and Senate that day. The next morning the bills would be returned to the Capitol with the chairman's instructions on whether they should be allowed to progress further.

Roraback could count on his instructions being followed because he personally appointed the chairman and the membership of the legislative committees. All the members of the important committees were Republicans. No Democrats needed to apply. In some years that composition merely reflected the overwhelming GOP majorities in the legislature as a whole, bolstered by rural overapportionment: In 1926, for example, Republicans outnumbered Democrats 237–25 in the House and 34–1 in the Senate. But even in years when Democrats made up a respectable minority—and there were years like that in the Roraback era—there was nothing for them to do in Hartford but sit and watch. As the larger cities in the state became increasingly Democratic, that disenfranchisement meant an urban disenfranchisement as well. In 1925 the appropriations committees of the Connecticut legislature did not contain a single member from any of the five largest cities of the state.

But Roraback's power was more than a matter of partisan control. Republicans with the slightest tendency toward self-expression were just as unfortunate as Democrats. When the Republican leadership in Bridgeport chose to contest some of Roraback's patronage appointments, the chairman simply had a bill passed suspending the city's right to levy taxes.

Meanwhile, as the reader probably suspects by now, Roraback's private interests were well taken care of. President of the Connecticut Power and Light Company, as well as five smaller utilities, the chairman was well positioned to demand legislation that preserved his own economic monopolies, and the legislators were in no position to refuse him. Connecticut Power and Light was a heavily subsidized corporation; it owned the water in the Housatonic River, the river whose energy was vital to much of the heavy industry that guaranteed the state's livelihood in the early years of this century.

Some currents, however, were beyond even Roraback's control. By the time of his death in 1937, the Republican party was losing its grip on state politics. As in the other industrial states of the Northeast, ethnic working-class voters were making the Democratic party competitive in statewide elections. Wilbur Cross won the governorship for the Democrats three times during the Depression years, and while Cross, a genial and elderly college dean, was sympathetic enough to small-town conservative values to get along with Roraback quite well, it was clear in those years that the period of Republican hegemony had ended; an era of close partisan competition had begun.

By the close of World War II, the equation of Connecticut politics was this: The GOP could count on controlling the House of Representatives, thanks to the built-in overrepresentation of the state's overwhelmingly Republican small Yankee towns, but the Democrats, in years that were more or less favorable to them nationally, could expect a legitimate opportunity to elect a governor, and very possibly a Democratic state Senate to help him out. This system generated the same degree of deference as in the Roraback years but required a different form of leader. It was the system that prevailed in 1946 as John Bailey began his long career as Connecticut Democratic chairman.

In the hands of Bailey, a graduate of Harvard Law School but a protégé of one of Hartford's classic ward politicians, the role of the political boss evolved into something far more subtle than Roraback would have felt comfortable with. Leadership for Bailey meant keeping one's own forces under strict control and using that control to exert the maximum possible leverage in negotiation with the other side. Bailey's margin for error was never as great as Roraback's had been. When Democrats controlled the state Senate, it was never by more than a few votes. Bailey had to keep every Democratic member loyal in every situation, and he did it by employing, if somewhat more gently, the primary weapon of the Roraback regime: patronage. Sometimes the rewards were personal and direct: In 1949 there were twenty-three Democratic state senators, and twelve of them had state patronage jobs.

Democrats held the governorship as well as the state Senate that year, so Bailey had far more than those twelve appointments available to keep his legislative contingent compliant. With a Democratic governor in office in Hartford, the party chairman could dispense as many as 500 seats on numerous state boards and commissions, most of them superfluous in governmental terms but critical to keeping a legislative majority under control. A legislator who behaved himself could count on seeing a fellow townsman appointed to the Commission on Fire Prevention; the Soldiers, Sailors and Marines Fund; or any of several dozen other state bodies. A legislator who strayed not only had to forget about winning any of these patronage plums for a local ally but had to worry about the governor's awarding one to his hometown political enemy, a fate considerably worse than being ignored.

When the governorship was in the opposing party's hands, the chairman lost most of his leverage over patronage appointments. But the expectation of patronage in the future, and the unchallenged party control over the local nominating process, maintained legislative deference to virtually the same degree. In 1951, when the governor was Republican but the state Senate was Democratic by the slimmest possible margin, 19–17, Connecticut Democrats achieved a level of discipline that all but defies credibility: In the entire legislative session that year, on all the roll-call votes that took place, not one Democrat ever defected from the party leadership position. It was a triumph for John Bailey, and a triumph for traditional leadership. The members practiced their profession as they had been taught to practice it. They did as they were told.

Bailey roamed the halls of the Capitol in those years, directing his troops, plotting strategy, carrying copies of bills in the breast pocket of his coat. Sometimes, in those days before Xerox machines, the copy he had was the only one in existence. If he chose to lose it, the entire legislative process had to begin on it all over again. In the frantic closing hours of a session, that was impossible. The bill would die.

That a political party chairman, a man never even elected to public office, could simply throw away legislation strikes us not only as unfair but as bizarre. But it was routine in Connecticut in the 1950s, and it was not regarded as particularly autocratic. Someone had to make those decisions, had to dispose of troublesome bills that the state didn't really need. That was what a leader was there for.

When he was not there, it was sometimes difficult for the legislature to accomplish anything. In 1955, for example, the two chambers considered a proposal to open up the political system by instituting primaries for state office. Bailey was against it. His friend and ally, Democratic Gov. Abraham Ribicoff, wanted to position himself above the battle and ordered the chairman to stay away from the Capitol during the debate. That strategy, however, proved unworkable. The Democrats in the state Senate refused to meet without

Bailey's being present. Bailey returned to the corridor outside the chamber, chose not to fight the issue, and the primary bill became law.

Perhaps the most remarkable quality of Connecticut's political system was its willingness to start the process of reforming itself out of business. The primary law of 1955 was one example. It was not a dramatic change; party committees still made the crucial nomination choices for the legislature and other state offices. All the law did was provide that any candidate who could muster 20 percent support at the party caucus could challenge the caucus choice in a primary. Still, it was a blow against the personal authority built so successfully by Roraback in the Republican party and perpetuated by Bailey on the Democratic side.

More immediate in their effects were the political reforms enacted by the legislature in 1959, the year Ribicoff began his second term as governor and the Democrats gained control of both chambers of the legislature, having won the House, despite its malapportionment, for the first time since 1876. In that year of unprecedented Democratic power, Bailey, Ribicoff, and the party loyalists in the legislature eliminated 102 state trial justice courts and 66 municipal judgeships, all rich sources of patronage, and replaced them with 44 new circuit judges, divided equally between the two political parties. It was not a change that most Democrats in the legislature particularly liked, but they accepted it. The Democratic party had decided to position itself on the side of reform. They did their duty and voted in favor.

That same legislature abolished county government in Connecticut, dismantling a system that had been in place since 1666 but had come under persistent reformist attack as antiquated, wasteful, and corrupt. Each of the state's eight counties had three commissioners, a treasurer, and a scaler of weights and measures. The proposal was to eliminate this whole structure and turn its duties over to state agencies. Once again the rank-and-file Democratic legislators wondered why it was necessary, why it fell to them to break up a political structure they had grown up with and understood. Once again John Bailey told them that neither his personal feelings nor theirs were important. It was reform, it was part of the governor's program, it was politically appealing, it was going to pass, and they were going to vote for it. And they did, all 29 Democrats in the Senate and 141 in the House.

Connecticut politics in the 1950s was no advertisement for the democratic process. It was in most important respects a closed system. Yet the governmental product it produced, with Ribicoff as Bailey's handpicked governor and a collection of senators and representatives willing to be led around like sheep, compares favorably with what was being accomplished in other states whose legislators were beginning to feel the stirrings of personal independence. The same legislature that abolished county commissioners and municipal judges passed a housing discrimination bill and created an office of consumer protection. "This bill is a must," Bailey told legislators nervous about open housing. "If this is not passed, you will suffer in the next election and so will the party. . . . The liberals have to be satisfied."

The lesson of this history is not that what every state needs in the 1990s is an old-fashioned political boss. The lesson is that the cause of decent government is served by the existence of some mechanism that forces legislators to do things they are not individually eager to do. In Connecticut, in the 1950s, the Democratic party chairman provided that mechanism by reminding legislators uncomfortable with reform that they might face a prospect more uncomfortable—the loss of precious patronage and even renomination itself.

It is not possible for a modern leader to raise those issues to a legislator who is uninterested in patronage and has built his own secure base for reelection. Nor is it effective, most of the time, to remind him that the party as a whole might suffer from weak governmental performance and that he would not be spared. Legislators can now run away from their party in Connecticut, just as they can everywhere in the country. The final vestige of straight-ticket voting, the lever that allowed people to vote the entire Democratic or Republican ticket with one flick of the finger, was abolished in 1986. Connecticut was the last state in the country to abandon it.

The balance of power changed again in Connecticut in the 1960s. Democrats became the clear majority party: They held the governorship and the state Senate throughout the decade, and after 1965, when a constitutional convention redrew legislative districts and put an end to overrepresentation of Republican small towns, Democrats won a majority of the state House as well.

By the end of the decade, though, the closed political system was clearly breaking up. John Bailey could not control the legislature anymore; he could not even control the Democratic membership. The problem was not Bailey's age, or staleness in the job, or even his prolonged absences from the state during eight years as Democratic national chairman. The problem was the Vietnam War, and the climate of political restlessness that it inaugurated, and that has been a fact of life ever since.

Vietnam is an important part of the chronicle of political change in this book, and its impact can be found at all levels of the political system. In Sioux Falls it helped generate the skepticism about local authority that unseated an effective mayor and ushered in fifteen years of electoral confusion. In Wisconsin it brought a generation of liberal Democratic talent into the political process and thus determined the leadership of the state in the 1980s. In Connecticut its effects were felt very early. The feuds and passions of the Vietnam debate tore the Democratic party in half and all but destroyed the climate of deference and discipline that had governed state politics since the days of J. Henry Roraback.

Much of this anger was played out at the 1968 Democratic National Convention in Chicago, where Bailey orchestrated the procedures for Lyndon Johnson and Hubert Humphrey, Ribicoff placed Sen. George McGovern's name in nomination as an anti-Johnson protest, and antiwar delegates from Connecticut loyal to Sen. Eugene McCarthy fought for a peace plank in the national platform. Earlier that summer 225 antiwar Democrats had walked out of the state Democratic convention as a protest against what they thought was unfair treatment by Bailey.

More startling was the effect that all this dissension had on the legislature when it met the following January. Democrats who had felt abused by Bailey on the Vietnam issue no longer saw any reason to follow his leadership on legislative matters. They voted for annual sessions and a new joint committee to manage the legislature's business, taking over many of the functions the party chairmen used to provide, especially in matters of patronage. Bailey opposed both measures but couldn't stop them. House Democrats endorsed a state income tax; when Bailey told them it was a terrible idea, they locked him out of their caucus sessions. Ten years after he had persuaded every last Democratic legislator to vote for a series of reform measures few of them liked, Connecticut's last political boss was barred even from talking to them about a new set of reforms he considered suicidal.

Bailey served as Democratic chairman for six more years, the final six years of his life, and he succeeded in regaining a certain amount of influence over his party. In 1974 he helped direct the election of his protégée Ella Grasso as Connecticut's first woman governor. Bailey returned to the corridors of the Capitol during legislative sessions, and to the good graces of the Democratic caucus. But it was not the same thing. Joseph I. Lieberman, Bailey's biographer and a state senator in the 1970s (and a U.S. senator today), thought Bailey adjusted as well as possible to the restricted role that the altered political climate forced upon him. "He recognized the change," Lieberman wrote, "in the self-image of the legislature and its leaders. He gave them the deference they felt they deserved."

One of the Democrats who challenged John Bailey and the entire system of closely held power was Irving Stolberg. Thirty-three years old in 1968, a geography professor trained at Yale and teaching at Southern Connecticut College, he went into politics that year to stop the war. He enlisted in the McCarthy presidential campaign. Two years later he won a seat in the Connecticut House from a New Haven district, the first real antiwar activist, as he remembers it, to make it into Bailey's legislature. The first legislation he introduced was a resolution declaring the Vietnam War unconstitutional. But more significant in the long run than Stolberg's views on war and peace were his ideas about serving in a legislature. He was perhaps the most articulate and self-confident of a whole new cadre of legislators who made it impossible for Bailey to function in the traditional way in the 1970s. "The juncture of Vietnam and civil rights," Stolberg says, "produced people who wouldn't accept the way things were done."

Stolberg's skepticism about leadership was the most obvious feature of his early years as a legislator. In 1972, in his first term, he attended the Democratic National Convention as a McGovern delegate and engaged in a shoving match on the convention floor with the majority leader of the state Senate. Three years later, given the chairmanship of the House Committee on Human Services, he resigned it in a public protest against levels of social spending that he considered too low. Later, when Democrat James Kennelly was

Speaker, he sided against the leadership and with the Republicans on a key procedural vote because he felt Kennelly wasn't keeping rank-and-file members well enough informed of the legislative schedule. Even in the more tolerant atmosphere of the 1970s, breaking ranks on procedure was something Democrats were not expected to do.

But this was a decade in which talent was coming to count for more than loyalty, and Stolberg's ultimate rise to influence was inevitable. Unflappable in debate, utterly confident of his views and his ability to express them, he was an obvious leader. He treated legislative work as a full-time job at a time when few others outside the leadership were willing to do so. He knew the intricacies of every public-policy question and developed an instinct for the politics of the institution. He made up his mind he wanted to be Speaker of the House and wasn't deterred by two losing campaigns. When the job became vacant for a third time at the start of the 1983 session, Stolberg outorganized every possible opponent and won it.

It was an important job, yet it was a frustrating one. The Speaker was now charged with running the Connecticut House, to the extent that anyone ran it. There was no longer a John Bailey in the corridor outside the chamber; the state Democratic chairman had become more or less irrelevant in legislative affairs. Nor was the governor much interested in telling the legislature what to do. William A. O'Neill, the Democrat who had succeeded to the office just before Grasso's death in 1981, was content to assume a low profile most of the time. The Speaker of the Connecticut House could proceed without much interference from above. The interference all came from below, from the rank-and-file members who, like Stolberg himself only a few years earlier, did not believe they had been sent to Hartford to follow the whims of a legislative leader. It was no longer either socially acceptable or politically productive to twist legislators' arms to get them to vote in a desired way.

For one thing, there was very little to threaten them with. The number of patronage jobs available at the state level had declined substantially since Bailey's day, and besides, most of the members weren't especially interested in patronage. Nor was it feasible much of the time to pressure them by going to their local Democratic committees and raising the issue of renomination. The town committees, like the state party, had begun to atrophy. In most communities in Connecticut, the town committee had come to depend more on the legislator than vice versa.

In the legislature of the 1980s, the exercise of power in the traditional way had become obsolete. Still, Stolberg was determined to exercise it somehow. He may have begun his career rebelling against his leaders, but he believed in strong leadership. He wanted to accomplish things. He didn't intend to preside over a participatory democracy. "I questioned authority my whole life," Stolberg said later. "When in authority, I felt it had to be utilized. I couldn't just step back and let things occur."

The House Speaker in Connecticut, like his counterparts in most states, still possessed some significant tools of influence even in the absence of any ability to twist arms. Most important, he could appoint the chairmen and the Democratic members of all the committees. He could use that authority to see that the choice positions were distributed evenly among all the factions and interests in the Democratic caucus, or he could use it to pursue his own agenda.

For Stolberg, it wasn't a close question. In 1983, after six terms in the legislature, he was as committed as ever to the agenda he had brought to Hartford in 1971: a progressive tax system, more spending for social services, and support for abortion, women's rights, and the other social causes endorsed by most liberal Connecticut Democrats of his generation. Stolberg made it clear from the beginning that he planned to use the powers he had—committee appointment, procedure, and scheduling—to advance his ideological goals. He also thrust himself into the electoral process. If there was no longer much latitude for a Speaker to influence members' votes, there was a surprising opportunity to help determine who came to be members in the first place. Many of the things John Bailey had done—recruiting candidates, raising money, helping with strategy—were no longer being done by anyone in a position of authority in the Democratic party. Stolberg took up the slack. "I stepped into a vacuum," he said.

In 1984, and again in 1986, Stolberg spent months on the road looking for people to run for the legislature in open districts and against vulnerable Republican incumbents. He wanted Democrats who could win, but he also wanted Democrats who thought the way he did, who were "progressives," in the language of Connecticut politics in the 1980s. He worked closely with the environmentalists, consumer advocates, and nuclear freeze supporters who had become major players as the traditional party structure had decayed in the years since Bailey's death. He was happy to visit any town to make his sales pitch to anybody who sounded like a good prospect. That was how he came to be in Norwich in 1986, recruiting Shaun McNally: liberal Democrat, experienced campaigner, Peace Corps veteran, social welfare employee. McNally was Stolberg's kind of Democrat, and he got the full treatment. "Irving would tell you," McNally recalls, "that you would be the greatest legislator on earth." McNally, like many of the others, didn't need much convincing. He wanted badly to run.

The results of Stolberg's political effort were very clear. He couldn't prevent Republicans from winning a majority in the legislature in 1984, amid the Reagan reelection landslide, but he did help keep the Democratic losses smaller than they would have been, and to bring in some impressive Democratic talent well matched to his own politics and agenda. In 1986 he started earlier, orchestrated his grass-roots liberal network more effectively, and contributed more than any other single person to the voting that restored Democratic majorities in both House and Senate and reinstalled him in the Speaker's office after two years in the minority.

As he picked up the Speaker's gavel again in January of 1987, Irving Stolberg had a great deal to be proud of. His national reputation was growing: He had just begun a term as president of the National Conference of State Legislatures. In his first two years as Speaker, he had demonstrated a competence and a level of knowledge unquestioned in either party. He had brought the legislature itself closer to a status of equality with the governor and the state executive branch than it had ever been. Meanwhile, he had led Democrats back into control of the House and subtly moved the chamber as a whole a few steps closer to the left, toward his own ideological position. He was, it appeared, the most powerful party leader the state had seen since John Bailey.

It was a dangerous position to be in.

Compared with that of a Roraback or even a Bailey, Stolberg's use of power was really quite modest. He didn't tell legislators how to vote; he didn't threaten to end their political careers; he didn't manipulate patronage jobs their constituents depended on.

But as he settled into his second term as Speaker, an increasing number of members who respected Stolberg's ability began to feel less than comfortable with his leadership. The House ran on the schedule that he established for it. When he met with his lieutenants in the leadership, it was not to consult them about strategy but to tell them what the strategy was going to be. And while he didn't tell people how to vote on the floor, he certainly didn't mind telling chairmen what legislation to move and when to move it. After all, they owed their chairmanships to him, and they were there to help with an agenda—the "progressive" agenda supported by Stolberg and the activist groups that had helped place the Democrats back in control. "I knew where I was on everything," Stolberg says. "I did not stand back and say, 'You guys get together and decide, and anything you decide is fine.' I did not do that."

As an indictment for abuse of power, it is a little thin. But it was an increasingly common view, even among Stolberg's admirers, that he used his position in a manner more appropriate to an earlier time. "Irving misread the spirit of the legislature," says Ronald Smoko, who was House majority leader. "They don't want all power centered in the leadership." That feeling extended down to many of the Democrats whose election Stolberg had helped bring about in the previous few years. "We were a new generation of professional legislators," says Jonathan Pelto, who came in as a Stolberg ally in 1984, at age twenty-three. "We had our own staff, our own offices. And there was Irving clamping down on everything. There was a sense among the younger generation that Irving was just not allowing any upward mobility."

Most troubling of all was what Stolberg wanted to do to the screening committee. It wasn't an official committee of the legislature, just an informal offshoot of the Democratic caucus. But it was a sort of procedural traffic cop, with a mandate to recommend to the Speaker how and when legislation should be brought to the floor. Most important, it was a vehicle for the more conservative faction of House Democrats. It functioned as a brake on what they saw as some of the more exotic legislative ideas of Stolberg and his activist allies.

Stolberg was not happy with the way the committee operated. He wanted to restrict the authority of its chairman, Richard Balducci, and install on it a staff person who would report directly to the Speaker. Then the Speaker would make the decisions. It wasn't exactly a tyrannical move; managing the flow of legislation was, after all, the Speaker's job. But it struck much of the Democratic membership as one move too many. "Irving was taking all the power bit by bit," said a veteran lobbyist who watched these events unfold. "Back in the sixties that would have been all right. That was what you expected from these people."

In November 1988, as George Bush was carrying Connecticut in the presidential contest, Democrats were sweeping to another term of comfortable majorities in the legislature, thanks in part to Stolberg's planning, recruiting, and fund-raising. Shortly after that the Democrats met and nominated Stolberg for another term as Speaker. There was a little bit of controversy: Nobody had ever served more than two terms as Speaker before. But the two-term limit was informal, and, besides, it was commonly understood to mean two *consecutive* terms. Stolberg's tenure had been interrupted by the brief period of Republican control in 1985 and 1986.

There was no formal opposition when the Democrats renominated Stolberg in November. It was nearly two months later that he found out what was actually going on. The Democrats who didn't like him were quiet in the November caucus because they had something entirely different in mind. They were planning to join forces with the Republican minority and defeat him on the floor of the House in January. The plan was a well-kept secret, and it remained a secret to Stolberg until the day before it took place. When the House met on January 12, he had no choice but to watch as thirty-one Democrats voted alongside sixty-three Republicans to strip him of the speakership and its power. The new Speaker was a Democrat, but one who promised to play down ideology and govern by consensus: Richard Balducci.

The real shock was not so much that a Speaker had been removed—those things happen in all legislatures from time to time, and they had happened before in Connecticut. What was shocking was that Democrats had crossed party lines to do it. Through all the modern history of the legislature, all the years of Roraback and Bailey and the years after, that was one form of mischief no group of dissidents had dared to try. One did not allow the minority party to determine who the leader would be. It was not proper; it smacked of disorder—even, to some, of anarchy. But in the legislature of the 1980s, those ideas no longer constituted a taboo. It was feasible, and it was done.

"It was an immense thing that happened," said Janet Polinsky, one of Stolberg's allies. "It was an immense thing, going to the

Republicans and saying, 'Let's have an unholy alliance.' It was very emotional. Balducci cried. It was so against Connecticut politics."

In choosing Richard Balducci as its instrument of rebellion, the anti-Stolberg majority in the Connecticut House knew exactly the sort of Speaker it would be getting. A fourteen-year veteran of the House at age forty-six, Balducci had been an influential member throughout the 1980s without demonstrating many of his predecessor's obvious gifts for leadership. Balducci had brought to politics the same skills that had made him a successful businessman in his hometown, Newington. A friendly and unpretentious man, he was in no way Stolberg's equal as a parliamentarian, political strategist, or expert on policy questions. But he had a feeling for the desires and sensitivities of the modern legislature that Stolberg, for all his brilliance, had somehow lost. "We're going through a transition from leadership to openness," he said after taking over the speakership. "You have to be a good listener to lead. That's what our job is—to be a good listener."

He came into leadership at a very difficult moment. After nearly a full decade of prosperity and generous budget growth, Connecticut in 1989 was feeling the recessionary effects that were plaguing the rest of New England. A decline in the overheated real estate market had led the entire economy into a prolonged period of sluggishness. Without an income tax to rely on for revenue—the legislature had enacted one over Bailey's objections in 1971 but repealed it amid public protest a month later—Connecticut relied on an awkward combination of consumption taxes that in turn depended on robust consumer demand. In 1989 that demand had fallen off, and the state budget was nearly a billion dollars out of balance.

Every proposed solution seemed to carry fatal political flaws. The liberal Democrats in the legislature called for an income tax, as they had been doing for years, but Governor O'Neill said he would veto one. O'Neill suggested a utility tax, but it found no constituency in the legislature. The idea of a tax on insurance premiums came up, but the insurance industry was quickly able to shoot it down. The only answer was to take the existing hodgepodge of taxes, including the sales tax, and nudge all of them up just enough to cover the deficit.

The finance and appropriations committees charged with writing that legislation in the House were unable to do it—they could not produce the votes. So the chairmen of those committees had to draw up a bill themselves, give it to Balducci, and ask him to sell it to the membership. Which was exactly what Balducci did. There were eighty-eight Democrats in the House, and he had to negotiate personally with all of them. "He couldn't yell at people, and he couldn't scream at them," said Patrick Sullivan, who watched it all closely as a lobbyist. "He was their friend and mentor. He pleaded with them, he told them how important it was for the state."

The Republicans, who had been glad to help Balducci unseat Stolberg, had no intention of helping him pass a budget. So he needed seventy-six Democratic votes to get a tax bill through the House. He got eighty of them, eighty out of eighty-eight, including most of the diehard Stolberg supporters. It wasn't exactly unity by the standards of Bailey or Roraback, but it prevented political or governmental chaos for at least one year. "We spent innumerable time in caucus, batting the budget back and forth," the new Speaker said afterward. "We talked and talked and talked."

Balducci's experience serves as a graphic demonstration of the way Connecticut's legislature, like many others, is coming to do business. It is not a mass democracy. It is not a town meeting. The 151 members do not gather en masse and decide what the state budget will be. The leaders get to write the budget. But then, unlike Bailey or Roraback, they have to sell it. They have to begin the tedious process of persuading a majority of the members not to exercise the personal vetoes they believe they are empowered to cast. In that sense politics in the Connecticut House is something like politics in a community such as Greenville or Sioux Falls. Many people have acquired the right to say no to things. It is very difficult for anyone— even someone with the title of leader—to say yes to something and make it stick.

Shaun McNally was one of the people who made Balducci's life difficult in those frustrating weeks of 1989. So were many other Democrats of his generation. At one point in the negotiation process, the leadership worked hard to get the votes of John Wayne Fox, a young Democrat from Stamford. Balducci lobbied him for twenty minutes one morning. This was after a ten-minute pep talk from Governor O'Neill the night before. Afterward, Fox made it clear who was boss. "They know they can't tell me 'Vote for this or

Stamford will never get another penny,' " Fox said, "because I'll tell them to stick it in their ear."

The legislature had reached the point where most of its members would not tolerate any relationship with their leaders except equality. Stolberg did not realize that, or refused to accept it. Balducci did. "I consider everybody an equal," he said at the end of 1989.

That was also the message of John Larson, the youthful Democrat on the other side of the Capitol who had the less arduous but still frustrating job of Senate president. Larson had only twenty other Democrats to lead, instead of eighty-seven. But it was a difference of degree rather than kind. The condition of equality, Larson said, was not something that the legislature had thought up for itself. It was something that had been imposed on it by the society, by the values that its younger members had brought with them. Janet Polinsky, nearly twenty years older than Larson and a legislator considerably longer, a deputy Speaker and a longtime Appropriations chairman, thought exactly the same thing. "It's a little like the breakdown in families," she said. "Mom and Dad don't matter too much."

The leadership of both houses of the Connecticut legislature is by historical standards very young. Most of those in positions of power were born after World War II. Balducci, the oldest of them, was born in 1942; Larson, in 1948. Some of the key members are much younger. Jonathan Pelto, for example, was twenty-one when he became the Democratic town chairman in Storrs; twenty-three when he first won his seat in the House; twenty-five when he masterminded Governor O'Neill's successful reelection campaign in 1986; and twenty-seven when Balducci, looking to build bridges to the more liberal Democrats, selected him to be the new chairman of the House Steering Committee. Pelto was thus a leader long before his thirtieth birthday.

And many of those he was helping to lead were about his age. In 1971 there were 213 members of the legislature altogether, and 3 of them were less than thirty years old. In 1990 the size of the legislature was down to 187, but nearly 30 members were under age thirty. Close to a majority were born after World War II. As the 1990s began, Connecticut was well on the way to being a baby boom legislature. "The driving force behind the baby boom generation is egalitarianism," John Larson says. "The mainstream of America is moving in an egalitarian fashion. We are going to have more leaders who define public policy in egalitarian terms."

There are more than a few observers, of course, who are perfectly comfortable with an egalitarian approach to public policy but wonder whether it is any way to run a legislature. Irving Stolberg, not surprisingly, is one of them. When he talks about all the ways the institution has changed in the twenty years since he joined it, he sounds genuinely ambivalent. "All in all," he says, "we have a better product." He believes in democracy and in accepting the periodic disorder that democracy is bound to include. Still, he thinks real leadership, even in a democracy, has to involve more than listening, polling, and cajoling. He thinks someone has to make the rules. And like almost everybody else around the institution, he agrees that the younger members don't want that. "I don't think they can be led," he complained a year after he had been deposed. "They get a bang out of the process. The problem is there's no direction, no agenda."

By the end of the 1980s, there was a curious ambivalence about the Connecticut legislature: an unshakable commitment to its newfound democratic ways, but also a growing realization that those ways were not producing a very good product. The legislators were reluctant to pay for all the government they had generated, for they found it politically more expedient not to vote for the levels of taxation these programs required. No party chairman could make them cast those votes, no governor of recent times had been willing to try, and the clear message of Stolberg's removal as Speaker had been that legislative leaders would be well advised not to try, either.

"We are paralyzed," Jonathan Pelto complained in 1989, "by an inability to deal with the tax structure. There are all these people who can say no, and nobody to sit them down at a table to get it done. The legislators are convinced they can't be reelected with an income tax, and there's no leadership to tell them they have to do it. I'd love to say how wonderful all this democracy is, but what we really need is some strong leadership. Otherwise we're just going to wallow in absurdity."

It is only in that context that one can explain the ironies of what Connecticut did in the election of 1990. The voters completed the humiliation of what had once been the nation's most deeply rooted two-party system by rejecting both parties and electing an independent gubernatorial candidate who told them that partisanship was

obsolete. In choosing Lowell P. Weicker, Jr., the Connecticut electorate endorsed a man who had spent two decades in Congress as an
individualist renegade, refusing to defer to his own Republican leadership and alienating colleagues of both parties who saw him as
bombastic, headstrong, and unreliable. What Shaun McNally was to
the Connecticut House, Weicker had been to the U.S. Senate for
three terms.

But if Weicker attracted votes on the strength of his independence from leadership, he attracted even more by promising to provide it. He presented himself as the one man big enough, loud
enough, and strong enough to make the legislature cast the politically difficult votes that would bring the economic impasse to an end.
And he turned out to be an easy winner.

It was an odd thing to do: elect Lowell Weicker as governor to
make a whole legislature full of Lowell Weickers behave themselves.
On the other hand, more traditional politicians were not succeeding
at this task. To most of the state's electorate, it seemed worth a try.
Weicker's election was a vote of no-confidence in political arrangements that seemed to stretch back to Bailey and Roraback; it was
also a confused searching for some of the authority that had disappeared with them. It remained to be seen how much of that authority
the state's new leader would try to recapture, and how, given the
obsolescence of party loyalty and party organization, he would go
about doing it. It also remained to be shown just how much leadership the modern political system would, in the end, be willing to
accept.

9

A Quiet Revolution

Most of the stories we have been following have been stories of individual ambition. The people who have transformed politics in Concord and Sioux Falls, the ones who run the legislature in Wisconsin, have entered the process and made their way in it largely on their own. The group support they have been able to command has been support they themselves have generated. Alabama's story is different. In that state interest-group politics is alive and well. Most candidates still run as allies of political organizations, factions, and coalitions. Legislative work is focused on the balancing of those competing interests. In Alabama groups matter.

But they do not matter in the same way they did a generation ago. In the 1950s in Alabama, an alliance of large landowners made the decisions that controlled the legislature and often the governor as well. They held that power not because they had any natural flair for politics but because they were the state's traditional governing class. They were the symbol of authority. It was a closed system, and they were the ones who had been inside when the gate was shut.

Landowners still compete for power in Alabama politics, but the operative word is *compete*. Sometimes they get what they want; sometimes they lose. The state's political system has opened itself up to a whole new array of interests that collide with each other in the quest for support at the polls and votes in the legislature. There is no voice of authority. The only way to win is to traffic in the commodities that make a difference in any open political system at any level—talent, enthusiasm, and time.

In 1982, unnoticed by the rest of the country, a revolution occurred in Alabama. Power in the legislature—the real power to control the state—passed to a liberal alliance that local politicians know simply as The Coalition: teachers, blacks, trial lawyers, and unions. Four years later the coalition was defeated by an alliance known equally simply as The Conservatives: the traditional landowners were part of this coalition, but corporate business was a more important part; so were insurance companies and organized medicine.

Voters cast the ballots that created all this change, but they were not the initiators. There is no evidence that Alabama citizens demanded more liberal government in 1982, or that they were eager to repudiate it in 1986. The 1982 revolution was a triumph of organization and strategy by the liberal forces—the only forces that understood the politics of the time well enough to operate comfortably in it. They were the ones with the impressive candidates, the volunteer support, and the polling data that showed them where to spend their money. The reward for their professionalism was political power. The 1986 counterrevolution occurred because the conservatives learned to play the game by the rules that had unseated them four years earlier. Wounded by a decisive and unexpected defeat, they converted what had been an informal alliance into a professional political organization of their own.

Control is sure to swing back and forth in the years ahead. The one permanent change is in the level of sophistication needed to operate successfully in the state's political system. Alabama may still be one of the nation's most backward states, but its campaigns will never again be the casual enterprise they were for most of the twentieth century. The winners will be those who invest the time and energy it takes to cultivate the needed talent. That applies to interest groups as surely as it does to individuals.

State legislatures have not been popular institutions in many parts of the country in modern times, but the Alabama legislature has long had an image problem far worse than most. In 1971 a Ford Foundation study ranked the Alabama legislature last among the fifty states in independence, last in accountability to the public, and forty-eighth in overall ability to function. Shortly after that a touring journalist described the physical setting of the legislature as "the shoddiest I have seen anywhere in the United States." Lacking any office space, the legislators were reduced during evening sessions to sending out for food and eating dinner at their desks in the chamber.

Until the early 1940s the legislators met in regular session for exactly fifty days once every four years, and that session took place just as the new governor was settling into office. By the time he figured out what his program was, they were on their way home, and he could get them back only by calling a special session. In 1939 the constitution was amended to provide for biennial legislative sessions, but this made little difference, for a thicket of constitutional provisions blocked the legislators from doing anything very significant, especially if it involved raising money. The wealthy Alabama landowners who wrote the 1901 constitution did not want their taxes to go up, and they elevated that desire into a constitutional principle.

So Alabama politics evolved over the twentieth century into a two-track system in which gubernatorial elections aroused the passions of the citizens but the leaders chosen in those elections found they could do little with the office. Governors who did not know how the system worked found out very quickly once they took office. James E. Folsom, Sr., won two campaigns for the statehouse (in 1946 and 1954) on a platform that included new taxes for education, old-age pensions, and highway construction, and reapportionment of the legislature itself. Hardly any of his program was enacted. Alabama's closely held political system did not permit it.

The same system confronted George C. Wallace when he became governor in 1963, assuming the office he was to dominate for eighteen of the next twenty-four years. During his heyday in the 1960s, it is true, the legislature generally gave Wallace what he asked for. He forced upon it more special sessions, more workdays, than members were accustomed to, and he frequently managed to cajole them into passing the bills he requested. Wallace was determined, for example, to create an extensive junior college system, and by the 1970s Alabama had one that was huge, not to say swollen.

But Wallace, like nearly all the Alabama governors before him, knew what he was allowed to ask for. None of the Alabama politicians who were around during the early years of his governorship confused Wallace's tactical control with any real power to change the government of the state. In the words of Bradley Moody, a political scientist at Auburn University in Montgomery: "The big mules were always able to say, 'Wallace, beyond this point you shall not go.' They were afraid to confront him openly, but they could control him on the issues that mattered to them."

For decades all the literature on Alabama cited the governor as the dominant political force and the legislature as passive, and, within the confines of the system, that was true. The legislature, perpetually absent and lacking any staff or resources, was inert. Any new ideas had to come from the governor. But the legislature, through its constitutional inertia, possessed what amounted to a veto over any significant gubernatorial initiative. For the rural forces that controlled the legislature, and therefore ultimately the state, the exercise of power was not a strenuous activity. The provisions of the Alabama constitution and the apportionment of legislative seats gave them an enormous advantage, and preserving it did not require any particular political skills or enthusiasm for government. All they really had to do was find their seats in Montgomery each odd-numbered year and see that no action was taken in the few weeks of legislative business to upset the system that made their lives comfortable.

This political system was built, as similar ones were built all over the South in those years, on malapportionment. Every county, regardless of how small, was guaranteed at least one seat in the Alabama House. The larger cities were all but disenfranchised. Birmingham, as its metropolitan area grew to include nearly a quarter of the state's population, was limited to 7 of 105 House seats for more than sixty years. The rural counties in the southwest quadrant of the state elected the leaders who went to Montgomery decade after decade and saw to it that very little changed. Of the interests that operated this self-perpetuating system of rural political power, two were pivotal: the Alabama Farm Bureau and the timber industry.

The Farm Bureau, as in other states, operated in Alabama through the extension system of the U.S. Department of Agriculture. The department's agents in each of the state's sixty-seven counties were in effect recruiting agents for the Farm Bureau. The farm bureau boards in each county represented a roster of the local rural power structure—not only farmers but bankers and farm implement dealers. For decades these boards possessed the ability to speak for and influence rural Alabama as a whole. And what they said loudest of all was that property taxes—taxes on farmland—must not be increased. Before 1965 it was commonly estimated that the Farm Bureau controlled the votes of about 40 percent of the legislators in the 105-member House and 35-member Senate.

The timber industry did not have as efficient an instrument as the Farm Bureau to present its case, but it has always owned enormous amounts of land in Alabama, a legacy of the sawmill entrepreneurs who first cut down the state's piney woods at the end of the nineteenth century. The leadership of the legislature has traditionally included a disproportionate number of people with intimate timber connections. In the late 1940s, when Folsom proposed increasing the property tax, he was foiled by state Senate leaders who were not only rural conservatives but sawmill owners themselves.

What finally started the process of change in Alabama as elsewhere was *Baker v. Carr,* the 1962 Supreme Court decision that made malapportionment unconstitutional. Three years later, reapportioned and redistricted in accordance with the Court's requirements, the Alabama legislature looked considerably different. Birmingham suddenly found itself with twenty seats in the state House instead of seven. But reapportionment did not guarantee immediate political change. Rural conservative power proved remarkably resilient. The larger counties continued to elect legislators on an at-large basis, and a majority of those elected came from affluent, generally conservative areas. They saw little reason not to defer to the rural leaders, leaders to whom the exercise of power was still natural and effortless. While cities began to squeeze out a larger share of state funding, the traditional arrangements remained in place when it came to overall control of state government.

A reapportionment with more striking consequences took effect in 1974, establishing single-member districts all over the state. That change made it impossible to dilute black votes by concealing them in at-large constituencies in the cities. Before 1974 there was one black member of the state House; after the election that year there were thirteen, seven of them from Birmingham. The turnover in the legislature's membership was enormous. More than 70 percent of the people who made up the 1975 legislature had not been members of the previous one.

Still, when it came to political control, the new legislature bore a remarkable resemblance to the old. The man chosen House Speaker in 1975, Joe McCorquodale, was as good a symbol of old-fashioned Alabama politics as anybody in the state. He was in the timber business himself, and he made no secret of where his sympathies lay. "The timber industry knew," says Roy Johnson, who entered the House that year, "that as long as McCorquodale was Speaker, nothing abhorrent to them was going to pass. And they didn't have to work at it. McCorquodale had a pine-tree mentality."

It seemed to many in Alabama politics in 1975 that only the names and the district boundaries had changed. The old interests were in charge. There were two men, though, who saw something different—a political system ready to be taken apart. One of those men was Joe Reed; the other was Paul Hubbert.

The 1901 constitution had been written in large part to prevent blacks from voting in Alabama, and it had succeeded. Among other consequences this permitted the legislature to be dominated by white conservatives from overwhelmingly black counties. Through much of the 1940s and 1950s, the premier legislator was Roland Cooper of Wilcox County, a parliamentary wizard known as "the wily fox from Wilcox." Cooper represented a district that was roughly 80 percent black, but he had no political reason to work his parliamentary wiles in behalf of his district's majority because they could not vote. In the 1940s, 5,706 whites were effectively the county's whole constituency.

The federal Voting Rights Act of 1965 did not change any of this overnight. But it did lead to the growth of the all-black Alabama Democratic Conference, which took the lead in promoting a significant black presence at the 1968 Democratic National Convention. Joe Reed, the head of Alabama's black teachers' organization, was a delegate to that convention. In 1970 he became chairman of the Alabama Democratic Conference. That year the ADC began requiring Democratic candidates for statewide office to make a personal appearance before the group in order to receive its endorsement.

George Wallace, running for governor, not only refused to appear but based much of his campaign on the need for whites to fight against the "bloc vote" in Alabama, by which he meant the black vote, especially Reed and the ADC. Reed was already distributing what he called "guide ballots" throughout black areas of Alabama, urging newly registered black voters to go to the polls and vote only for those whites who had been willing to talk to the ADC. Wallace managed to resuscitate his career by running against the black vote in 1970, but Howell Heflin, running for the state supreme court, and Bill Baxley, a candidate for attorney general, both went to talk to the ADC, received its endorsement, and won.

Joe Reed spent the 1970s perfecting the strategy of using the courts to bolster black political strength. He got a court order requiring that polling place officials reflect the composition of the local electorate. He fought to place deputy registrars in every precinct, empowered to enroll new voters any time during the year. By 1980, when the U.S. census determined Alabama's population to be 26 percent black, Reed had built an organization and a strategy capable of using those numbers to political effect.

Candidates who did not get the ADC endorsement learned that there was no real point campaigning in the black community. Larry Dixon, running for the state Senate in Montgomery one year in a Democratic primary against a Reed-backed opponent, spent heavily on advertisements in the city's black neighborhoods yet lost them by 15 to 1. "If you want to know what real anxiety is," Dixon said afterward, "spend $8,000 and months campaigning in a district, and then walk into the polling place on election day and see thousands of people standing around with cards telling them to vote for your opponent."

Meanwhile, Paul Hubbert was discovering that teachers, like blacks, possessed latent political strength in Alabama. In the 1960s Hubbert had been a classroom teacher himself, in Fayette County, in rural north Alabama, but he left to get a doctorate at the state university in Tuscaloosa, then became superintendent in Troy, a small town 50 miles from Montgomery. He was always political, even as an administrator. His dissertation had been about the passage of education bills in the Alabama legislature. And he was constantly looking for ways to take some political advantage of the sheer numbers the teachers possessed—even in the 1960s there were nearly 40,000 of them in the state. In 1969 Hubbert moved to Montgomery to take over the office of the Alabama Education Association.

The AEA had never been much of a force in state politics; it was an easygoing, nonpolitical service club for teachers, with school superintendents making most of the important decisions. Hubbert changed that very quickly. In the first few months after he took his new job, he was faced with a political challenge, and he decided to experiment.

Governor Wallace was under federal court order in 1971 to improve conditions in the state's mental hospitals. There were not many options for raising the money, and the Wallace administration decided the least painful choice was to shift the money from the teachers' retirement fund into mental health. Wallace was not an easy force to contend with in those days, but Hubbert did what he could to mobilize his members all over the state, and the result shocked him as much as it shocked everyone else. The teachers won big. The governor ended up getting only nine votes on the House floor. That vote was the beginning of organized education as a colossus in Alabama.

Hubbert saw what any intelligent political strategist might have seen—that on the basis of numbers alone, teachers represented a potentially important pool of votes and campaign contributions. But he realized something else that was less obvious and, in the long run, more important: that there was a manpower shortage in Alabama politics, and teachers were perfectly placed to fill it, as organizers, campaign workers, and candidates.

The Alabama legislature had always been dominated by lawyers. In the first state Senate that met under the 1901 constitution, lawyers cast 71.5 percent of the votes. Forty years later they still constituted 45.5 percent of the membership. In some sessions it was considerably more. "In a thirty-five-member Senate," recalls Bob Ingram, who began covering the legislature as a reporter in the 1950s, "it was not unusual to have twenty-five lawyers. They dominated the place." At the same time teacher-legislators were virtually nonexistent. In the first four decades of the century, only 3.2 percent of the members of the state legislature listed any form of teaching as their occupation.

But as the 1970s proceeded, the reign of the lawyers had to end. It was simply becoming too difficult to practice law and politics at the same time. By the mid-1960s the system of biennial legislative sessions was proving inadequate, as George Wallace found himself calling special sessions to deal with budget problems nearly every year. In 1974 annual sessions became a fact of Alabama political life. Some lawyers in full-time practice did not mind downgrading their work to part-time status and placing the bulk of their attention on politics. But most did not want to do so. Others had no choice: The state ethics rules adopted in 1973 required a lawyer-legislator not only to disclose his personal clients but to provide information about the income and client base of his firm. Quite a few of the larger firms did not want to release such information and found it preferable simply to discourage their lawyers from running for office.

In the old legislature many of the seats that were not held by lawyers were occupied by small-town merchants and businessmen. As late as 1976, 27 percent of Alabama legislators listed themselves as lawyers, 19 percent as business owners, and 10 percent as real estate agents. In the words of Bob Ingram: "It was the successful lawyer, businessman, farmer. It was an honor. You'd be called senator for the rest of your life, after you were out of office." But in the 1970s the small-town businessmen began making the same decisions the lawyers were making: Service in the legislature was not worth the sacrifice—in time, salary, and privacy.

Teachers were not in that position. They did not have businesses to run, or clients to protect, and while legislative service was not exactly lucrative (total annual compensation reached the $25,000 mark only in the mid-1980s), it paid about as well as most teaching jobs. Moreover, many teachers possessed exactly the right set of skills for political work. They were highly verbal, accustomed to speaking in public, and comfortable at persuasion.

Perhaps it was only a matter of time before somebody in Alabama education realized what was out there for the taking. In any case, by the end of the 1970s teachers were everywhere in Alabama politics, lobbying, campaigning, and getting elected to office. "There was a power vacuum," says political scientist Bradley Moody, "and the Alabama Education Association took advantage of it."

Some explain what happened in more personal terms. "Paul Hubbert took the AEA from a ladies' tea-sipping organization," says one veteran Alabama journalist, "and built it into the most potent political force in Alabama." He didn't do that by issuing orders from his office at the foot of Goat Hill in Montgomery. Hubbert spent a great deal of the 1970s driving the back roads of Alabama looking for talent. Wherever there was a district that seemed winnable, and a teacher rumored to be good at politics, Hubbert went recruiting. It wasn't the most enjoyable way to spend those hundreds of evenings and weekends, but Hubbert felt the prize was well worth the effort.

A decade later the results spoke for themselves. By the time the

House and Senate met for their 1985 session, the membership included 40 active or retired teachers out of a total of 140. There were 22 lawyers, barely half the proportion there had been a decade before. The House had only 9 lawyers out of 105 members, and only one lawyer who had been there as long as three years. By 1987 the number of teachers in the legislature had increased further. The Alabama ethics commission reported that 58 of 140 were teachers, former teachers, or spouses of teachers.

Every two years since Hubbert began his recruiting, organized education has come up with a plentiful supply of candidates and campaign workers with a sense of how to win elections and a willingness to spend their time doing so. Teachers who make it to the legislature normally find that someone back home is more than willing to fill in for them in the classroom so they can spend as much time as they need on politics. "If you are in education, your job will be taken care of," says Bob Ingram. "There's a support system back home that no other professional has."

By the late 1970s Paul Hubbert and Joe Reed were well on their way to transforming the Alabama legislature. But they were even further along on another of their chosen tasks: transforming the state Democratic party. In most states in the recent past, it has not mattered to many people who served on the executive committee of the Democratic party. But during much of the Wallace period in Alabama, it mattered significantly who held those positions. The governor's opponents wanted to bring Alabama into compliance with the desegregated Democratic politics of the national party; Wallace wanted a party loyal to his own views and saw any competition as an effort to embarrass him in national political affairs.

In the early 1970s the state Democratic chairman was Robert Vance, a Birmingham lawyer committed to fighting Wallace and maintaining a more liberal "loyalist" party in Alabama. Vance was up for reelection as chairman in 1974, and it was not clear that he had a majority of the 105 votes that would be cast in the executive committee. So Vance did what any beleaguered party official might have done under the circumstances. He stacked the committee. It was legal, and it was easy. Three new seats for Joe Reed's black organization, three for organized labor, three for the women's federation, and three for the Young Democrats. All the new people were loyalists, and Vance was reelected easily.

A decade later that event was largely forgotten in Alabama politics. But the newcomers it had brought in, nearly all allies of Reed and Hubbert, stayed on to take control of party affairs. By 1984 the executive committee had been packed again and again to reinforce the control of teachers and blacks. There was a formal requirement that 25 percent of the seats on the executive committee be reserved for blacks. At that point there were more than 250 members on the committee, and the liberal forces had an unshakable majority. "They just took over the executive committee lock, stock, and barrel," says Bob Ingram. "Nobody else cared."

By then, conservative Democrats realized that they had ceded a base of real power to their opponents. But there was little they could do about it. "The executive committee was a low-key, insignificant position," says Rick Manley, a leader of conservative rural Democrats in the legislature. "It was at the bottom of the primary ballot. Lots of people didn't even vote on it. Someone saw that they could seize control by getting candidates to run for it—frequently uncontested."

Like so many positions of importance in American politics in the last generation, control of the Alabama Democratic party passed to a new set of interests for a very simple reason: They wanted it more than anybody else did. It was not immediately apparent to many people in Alabama politics why serving on the Democratic executive committee would be worth the time and effort it took to seek the position and attend the meetings. In that respect, Paul Hubbert and Joe Reed were able to see the future much more clearly than the establishment they were challenging. They saw how important control of the state's party machinery might ultimately prove.

By 1982 it was an open secret that Hubbert and Reed were the new kingmakers in the state Democratic party. Reed's Alabama Democratic Conference and Hubbert's Alabama Education Association were the crucial factors in contests for the legislature and for statewide office. And they were, in political terms, one organization. After Alabama schools were desegregated in 1969, Reed's black teachers' group merged with the white teachers' association headed by Hubbert. Reed, while remaining in charge of his black political movement, went to work full-time for Hubbert in the AEA offices on Dexter Street in Montgomery, just below the state Capitol. More than half the blacks elected to the legislature in the 1980s were connected with education in one way or another. It was difficult to tell exactly where black power ended and teacher power began.

Nobody in Alabama understood this transformation better than George Wallace. The governor had not regained his health during four years of retirement after 1978, but he wanted to return to the statehouse, and the opportunity existed because Fob James, the politically inexperienced businessman who had replaced him, had decided that one term was enough.

But it was not clear just how, at the age of sixty-three and in chronically bad health, Wallace was to achieve his comeback. No candidate was going to be elected governor in the 1980s as a segregationist. Nor could Wallace count on profiting very much from the sympathy that had made him unbeatable after the attempt on his life in 1972. Ten years is too long to sustain a sympathy vote. The Farm Bureau/timber coalition had never liked Wallace very much; it had learned to live with him in the 1960s because of his political strength.

It was in this political climate, in the years of his retirement, that Wallace began seeking out Paul Hubbert, calling him at home, getting together on weekends, wanting to talk about Alabama politics. To Hubbert, Wallace seemed genuinely sorry for some of the things that had happened in the 1960s. "George Wallace had a lot of time to ponder his place in history," said Hubbert. "He wanted one more shot at the governor's chair to show that he was not a bigot. He wanted a chance to redeem himself."

Others believe that guilt had nothing to do with it—that Wallace made his peace with the state's liberal forces because there was no other practical way for him to return to office. In any case, though, he did it. Wallace clearly was not the favorite of the AEA and ADC when he launched his 1982 campaign, but by the fall, when he faced a potentially difficult contest against Republican Emory Folmar, the mayor of Montgomery, Hubbert and Reed were among Wallace's most enthusiastic supporters. And Wallace went after the black vote—which he had scorned only a decade earlier as the "bloc vote"—with every means at his disposal. He admitted he had been wrong about segregation. There were ads on black radio stations that fall combining a Wallace campaign speech with choruses of "Amazing Grace."

When Wallace won the governorship by an impressive 200,000 votes, it was clear that the liberals had been responsible, if not for the result, then for the lopsided margin. It was widely assumed that they would soon be collecting their reward. And it turned out to be handsome indeed. An incoming governor traditionally chose the Speaker of the Alabama House, and after his 1982 election Wallace selected Tom Drake, a onetime wrestling champion who had gotten his start in politics by staging wrestling shows for Wallace campaigns in the 1950s. One Sunday after the election, Wallace called Joe Reed over to his house in Montgomery. Then he summoned Drake to talk about committee assignments in the new legislature. "You just give Joe what he wants on these assignments," Wallace ordered.

The legislature that convened in 1983 was something new in Alabama politics. Business did not control a single committee. Blacks held key chairmanships. Labor loyalists dominated the Business and Labor Committee in both the Senate and the House; in each case the chairman was a member of the Communications Workers of America. The *Montgomery Advertiser* reported that "the interests which languished in the wilderness during the McCorquodale years—teachers, blacks and labor—are now the powers."

The Alabama House and Senate had drawn new districts for themselves in 1982, to comply with the now universal requirement of one person, one vote. But Alabama is one of the states included in the "pre-clearance" provisions of the Voting Rights Act, which means the U.S. Justice Department has to give its approval to any changes the state makes. Before the 1982 primaries could be held, the Justice Department objected to the new district lines on the ground that they would effectively dilute black voting strength in six districts in the rural Black Belt and one in Birmingham. The legislature revised the lines, and the state held its elections without any further ruling. Then, shortly before Christmas, the Justice Department declared the second set of lines as discriminatory as the first and ruled that still another set would have to be drawn. What was more, another election would have to be held within one year.

By the spring of 1983 the entire issue was in the hands of the U.S. Court of Appeals for the Fifth Circuit, the same court whose desegregation rulings had been the prime target of Wallace's campaigns in the 1960s. From a variety of new district maps submitted to it, the court chose one personally drafted by Joe Reed. And Reed was far from modest in talking about the importance of what he had accomplished. "I got the whole turnip," he was quoted as saying.

What followed was one of the boldest demonstrations of raw political power any state had seen in recent times. Because the balloting under the third set of district lines would be in a special election, there was no requirement that either party hold a primary. The Republicans did hold one, but the Democrats, Alabama's overwhelming majority party, left the nomination of their special election candidates entirely up to the party's executive committee. In practical terms, that meant two people would be making the decisions: Paul Hubbert and Joe Reed. As Bob Ingram describes it: "Paul and Joe sat up in a hotel room and puffed their cigars and picked the legislature."

What they possessed was the simple power to preserve the careers of allies and end the careers of enemies. In seventeen House districts the new map pitted one incumbent against another. Hubbert and Reed simply chose the one they preferred. It was not always an obvious choice. Rick Manley, who had been in the House for seventeen years and served as Speaker pro tempore, was thrown in with a freshman. The freshman was a Hubbert-Reed loyalist; Manley had been the floor leader for McCorquodale and the Farm Bureau/timber alliance. The freshman was chosen. Manley was forced out of office. In five cases conservative Democrats faced no incumbent opposition in their districts, but the executive committee chose to dump them anyway, on the ground that they had used their legislative seats to work against Democratic party priorities.

It was, from any perspective, an ironic episode. The goal that Hubbert and Reed were seeking was the overthrow of the old closed political system, and the empowerment of people and interests that system had essentially ignored. But the method they employed was more autocratic than anything even the most dictatorial planter or timber baron of the previous generation could have conceived. As far as Hubbert and Reed were concerned, that was nothing to worry about. If landowners could manipulate the system for a century for the benefit of the affluent, they told each other, then surely they could manipulate it once for the dispossessed. It was only fair.

Not everyone in Alabama politics, however, chose to see it that way. The Hubbert-Reed move shocked Democrats all along the spectrum who felt legislators were entitled to use the label of their party without passing a loyalty test. Some of the closest allies of blacks and teachers still believe the move was a huge mistake. "It was terribly unfair," says John Teague, a liberal who was Senate president pro tempore in 1983. "People all over the state felt it was unfair. It left a sour taste in everyone's mouth."

Still, it worked. A few conservative Democrats challenged the decision, ran as independents against the "handpicking," and won. One state senator ran as a write-in candidate and defeated the Hubbert-Reed nominee. But in most districts the fallout was minimal. The voters did not care. The choice most of them faced in the fall was between a Hubbert-Reed Democrat and a Republican, and Republicans still do not win elections to the legislature in most parts of Alabama.

The liberal coalition, already strong in the legislature, became that much stronger in the wake of the 1983 special election. The House moved five or six seats further in a liberal direction. There were six new black House members, bringing black membership in that body to nineteen, and two new black state senators. One could now drive west from Montgomery all the way to the Mississippi border without crossing a single precinct represented by a white state legislator. When the new House and Senate convened in 1984, it was no longer possible to deny the obvious. The Alabama legislature, bulwark of the status quo since 1901, had fallen into liberal hands. What had the conservatives done to let this happen?

What they had done, in the opinion of both sides, was nothing. "We were sitting on the sidelines," says Tom Coker, who took over after the 1983 debacle as the business community's chief political strategist. "Alabama is basically conservative. Those liberals filled a vacuum. We gave them power on a silver platter." Alabama elections in the 1980s had come to be won on the basis of organization and turnout. Blacks had the numbers—a quarter of the state's population—and Reed's "guide ballot" system had made it possible to deliver a large chunk of those votes. The teachers had the ability to generate talent, organize a campaign, and make it effective. Business had none of these advantages.

Business did have money. PROGRESSPAC, the business political action committee hastily organized for the 1983 election, put $200,000 into campaigns for the legislature to try to hold back the liberal tide. But it was not a sophisticated operation. "We were giving money," says Coker, "without any research to show where to give." Nor, contrary to popular belief, was the business community a very effective lobbying force within the legislature. Members from most districts had traditionally sided with timber and the Farm Bureau in the belief that it was politically imprudent to do anything else. In previous years they had no doubt been right. But by the 1980s these and other business interests were essentially living off their reputations. They expected to be able to wield political power without expending much time or effort, and without building much professionalism among those who spoke for them. "The business lobby when I first got here was abysmal," says Jim Campbell, a business-oriented Democrat who arrived as a member of the House in 1978. "They had people lobbying here who couldn't find the bathroom."

In the aftermath of the twin election shocks of 1982 and 1983, the situation began to change. The Associated Industries of Alabama, which had traditionally represented the "big mule" corporate interests of Birmingham, merged with the Chamber of Commerce, which spoke for small business and small-town conservatism. The new organization, the Business Council of Alabama, began conducting political polls and research to see how their one weapon—money—might be most effectively deployed. By 1985, as the next general election approached, business was showing signs that it was ready to operate in the changed political environment, one which required it to reach down to the local level and compete if it was going to regain its influence.

But to win back the legislature and the leverage it had lost in Alabama politics, business needed more than an operational face-lift. It needed an issue to use against the opposition. There happened to be one available: the pernicious influence of lawyers in Alabama politics.

There was an irony in that focus. For nearly a century lawyers ran Alabama politics, and hardly anyone seemed to complain. Now, as their presence in state government was declining steadily, they were being singled out as villains.

The lawyers who ran the Alabama legislature in earlier years were not very different from the other elements of the small-town elite. "They are for the most part," political scientist Hallie Farmer wrote in 1948, "lawyers whose clients are the business interests in the state. They are attorneys for lumbermen, mine owners, public utilities, banks and other corporations." But the lawyers who became a business community target in the 1980s were not the ones who had been politically influential in the old days. They were a new group, and they were specialists—trial attorneys who sued corporations and insurance companies in cases of workmen's compensation, personal injury, and medical malpractice.

These trial lawyers had moved into politics in an organized way in the 1970s, not as candidates but as contributors to the teacher-labor-black coalition. This move was in part a calculated assessment of where they could do themselves the most good. Unlike teachers or blacks, the trial lawyers offered neither campaign manpower nor a significant bloc of votes. But they did have money, at a time when the liberal coalition badly needed it. They also had some clear legislative interests. The state supreme court had ruled in the late 1970s that an employee could sue his superior or any co-worker for negligence in Alabama. This ruling proved a bonanza not only for those suing but for the lawyers representing them as well. The business community was determined to nullify it by referendum and got it on a statewide ballot. But the trial lawyers, joining forces with labor and the rest of the liberal coalition, defeated the referendum. From that point on, the trial lawyers were identified in the public mind as a central element in the liberal coalition.

There was more to the lawyers' presence in that alliance than financial self-interest. The Alabama Trial Lawyers Association was run by people who had spent their professional lives arguing in court against the greed of employers and the corporate community. They not only said it, they believed it. Their work turned them into populists. They came to see themselves as protectors of helpless working people who had been victimized by a small-minded corporate establishment. "It's the liberal nature of the trial lawyer that puts him in the coalition," says Kenneth Mendelsohn, a prominent trial lawyer in Montgomery. "Many of our clients are black. We tend to defend the rights of blacks. If we represent these people in court, we attempt to represent them in the legislature."

But as genuine as the populism of trial lawyers may have been, it did not define their image among the electorate at large. Lawyers, laws, and litigation had become objects of ridicule all over the country in the 1980s, and Alabama was no exception. The trial lawyers were ripe for attack on the ground that they were not protecting the helpless but making themselves rich at the expense of the consumer.

The specific issue was tort reform. Alabama's leading corporations, insurance companies, and medical establishment formed an umbrella organization, the Civil Justice Reform Committee, to seek limits on the amount a plaintiff could collect in malpractice and personal injury cases. As in other states, juries in Alabama had awarded multimillion-dollar judgments in such cases. The business community argued that these verdicts were forcing up the costs of insurance to consumers and, in some cases, denying them medical care at any price.

The tort reform issue was to overwhelm everything else in Alabama politics through the 1986 election year and on into the legislative session that followed. It was the business community's ultimate weapon, not only against the trial lawyers but against the entire statewide liberal alliance. "It's hard to get businesspeople excited unless there's a danger you can point to," says Tom Coker. "We blew up tort reform into the biggest issue the state had ever seen. We had every horror case we could find." At one point Coker's allies found a pregnant woman who had had to drive 100 miles to deliver her baby because the local doctors in her rural community had been unable to get medical malpractice insurance. All of this, the business group insisted, was the fault of the selfish lawyers in Montgomery and the liberal power brokers who backed them. All over Alabama candidates armed with the funding and the research help of the Business Council ran for the legislature in Democratic primaries warning of the need to save the state from the cabal of liberal special interests that had been running it since 1982.

What exactly had this cabal been doing to Alabama during its four years in power? The truth was, not very much. Some of the more important changes had actually worked in a conservative direction. The co-employee rule, allowing workers to sue their supervisors for damages, had been eliminated by the legislature in 1985, to the displeasure of trial lawyers and the general satisfaction of business, which had been fighting it for nearly a decade. Labor-dominated though it may have been, the legislature went along with arguments that the co-employee rule was hurting the state's business climate.

The liberal legislature did impose about $350 million worth of new taxes during the 1982–1986 period, mostly business taxes, but the property tax, the age-old symbol of conservative Alabama economics, was left undisturbed. There were unsuccessful efforts by labor to pass a prevailing wage bill, aimed at establishing union pay scales on state construction projects, and by lawyers to change the state's contributory negligence laws to make suits easier. But few of the controversial items on the liberal wish list passed.

Teachers, of course, did very well in the four years under liberal control. By 1986 it was widely believed around the Alabama legislature that Paul Hubbert could determine the course of votes simply by giving a thumbs-up or thumbs-down signal to his loyalists on the floor. Hubbert insists that he never once did that, not only because it would have been presumptuous but because it would have been unnecessary. But Hubbert did get a lot of what he wanted from the legislature between 1982 and 1986. Teachers received back-to-back 15 percent pay increases, raising the salaries of some senior teachers to $40,000 and lifting Alabama to twenty-seventh in the nation in teacher pay, even though the state was languishing at forty-eighth in overall spending per pupil. In the long run Hubbert was also interested in pumping a great deal of money into the educational process itself, but such a massive change would have to await the building of a coalition broader than any he had yet put together. Of more immediate political importance, Hubbert persuaded the legislature to approve a "negative dues check-off" for members of the Alabama Education Association. Money from each teacher's paycheck would be transferred to the AEA political action committee unless the teacher specified otherwise in writing, thereby guaranteeing substantial funding for AEA-backed candidates throughout the state each election year.

Business had the money to match them in 1986. But more important, the Business Council found people to do the hard work Hubbert had done in the 1970s. They took to the road and found candidates. The results were remarkable. The Business Council involved itself in eighty-two House elections and twenty-five Senate elections in 1986, and won a combined total of ninety-four. Before the 1986 election, business forces controlled no more than 40 of 105 votes in the Alabama House, and an embarrassing 10 of 35 in the Senate. Immediately after the election, those figures were more like 60 in the House and 20 in the Senate.

Most of those shifts occurred in the Democratic primary, with the defeat of Hubbert-Reed Democrats by business-backed challengers. But the most dramatic single event occurred after the primary was over. Lieutenant Governor Bill Baxley, a Hubbert-Reed ally unable to win a majority in the Democratic primary for governor, found himself in a runoff with Attorney General Charles Graddick, who held office as a Democrat but whose political alliances were mostly on the Republican side. Graddick's campaign echoed the "special interest" theme of the Business Council, which had promised him a $300,000 contribution the day he made the runoff. Some 30,000 Alabama voters had cast Republican ballots in the initial gubernatorial primary, and Graddick went after them for the runoff, urging them to cross over to the Democratic side and vote for him over the liberal Baxley.

It was a smart strategy, and it worked. On runoff day, Graddick upset Baxley by fewer than 10,000 votes, and there was no question that the Republican crossovers had made the difference. The only problem with Graddick's strategy was this: It was illegal. Democratic party rules forbade such crossovers in a runoff and barred any candidate from seeking crossover votes. Graddick had not only sought them but used the powers of his office as attorney general to discourage election officials from enforcing the law. When Baxley took the issue to federal court, the judges reached the reasonable conclusion that the result was invalid and ordered the party either to hold a new primary or to declare that Baxley, having received the most legal votes, was the winner. Hubbert, Reed, and the other Democratic party brokers opted to skip the primary and give Baxley the nomination.

Meanwhile, the Republicans had nominated Guy Hunt, a former probate judge and Amway soap salesman who had been the nominee against Wallace in 1978 and had barely managed a quarter of the vote. Hunt was seen as a sacrificial candidate in 1986, just as he had been eight years earlier; no one expected him to come close, even against Baxley, even with the Business Council stirring up statewide resentment toward the liberal coalition. No Republican had drawn even 40 percent in an Alabama gubernatorial election in this century.

But 1986 was different. Bolstered by the resources of the Business Council, the hostility to liberal "special interests," and the second "smoke-filled room" nomination process in the Democratic party in three years, Hunt defeated Baxley and became the state's first Republican governor since Reconstruction.

And when the legislature convened again in 1987, the liberals found themselves evicted from power in every important office. The Senate was presided over by Lt. Gov. Jim Folsom, Jr., who had received a Business Council commitment for $200,000 in contributions the day Graddick got his $300,000. Tom Drake was forced to give up his bid for another term as House Speaker and was replaced by Jimmy Clark, a wealthy real estate investor who said he envisioned the legislature "freeing itself from the AEA and the trial lawyers." Clark declared, "I'm hell on lawyers," as he rounded up the votes for Speaker. "There's too much suing and we've got too many lawyers." The revolution, such as it was, seemed to be over.

Clark quickly proved that he meant business. All the liberal committee chairmen of the past four years were removed. There had been four black chairmen in the previous legislature; now there were only two. "It's ridiculous, insulting, a throwback to the days of McCorquodale," said one black House member. Joe Reed's Alabama Democratic Coalition held a protest march to accuse Clark of racism, but it had little effect. Power had shifted.

The one political certainty in Alabama in 1987 was that tort reform would become law. What few people realized was how much drama could be extracted from a contest whose outcome was no longer in doubt. After all, tort reform bills had been enacted in more than twenty states during the 1980s, and in none of them had the subject taken on the characteristics of theater. For Alabama conservatives, though, a little more emotion on tort reform was nothing to be afraid of. It promised to underscore the message about who was running the show, and that, after all, was what the election of 1986 had been all about.

So the great debate began with volleys of rhetoric about life and death. "This is killing people," said Speaker Jimmy Clark. "Those who say there's nothing wrong with the tort system, I'm going to let them keep the blood on their hands." To counter statements like those, the trial lawyers brought to the statehouse a brain-damaged nineteen-year-old girl whose affliction they attributed to medical incompetence. All other action ceased in the Alabama House when a package of eleven tort reform bills reached the floor. Ten of them passed in a midnight vote.

Eventually the legislature sent Governor Hunt a package that placed a $1 million cap on wrongful-death awards against doctors and a $400,000 cap on damages for pain and suffering. In July, Hunt signed the bills, predicting that they would "tear away some of the shackles that bound Alabama's vitality in the past." A few days later Hunt ran an ad in the *Wall Street Journal* announcing the state's new pro-business psychology. The president of the American Tort Reform Association said exactly what the Alabama corporate community wanted to hear. "If I had a business in Mississippi," he said, "I'd think about moving it to Alabama."

That summer, in the immediate aftermath of the tort reform triumph, it was hard to escape the idea that conservatives would be running Alabama for the foreseeable future. Hardly anyone realized just how vulnerable they were, or how quickly the balance of power could change again.

One wing of the conservative alliance consisted of the forces that had ruled the legislature virtually unchallenged for decades before 1983: timber companies, textile manufacturers, large-scale southwest Alabama landowners, and the Farm Bureau. They wanted exactly the things they had been getting from the system for years: low taxes, especially on land, low labor costs, and as minimal a state government as possible.

The other component of the alliance was a set of far more cosmopolitan business interests, many of them based in Birmingham, most of them operating in other places besides Alabama. Among its leaders were Winton M. Blount, a multimillionaire contractor and onetime U.S. postmaster general; Joseph Farley, president of Alabama Power Co.; and John Woods, chairman of Birmingham's AmSouth Bank. These men wanted to launch a crusade for economic development, and they wanted state government to play a major role in it. They were not particularly concerned with labor costs; they wanted an environment that would attract new employers and high-paying jobs. They wanted to improve the educational system, and they were willing to raise taxes to do it.

These were the interests that dominated the Alabama Business Council, and they were the ones Jimmy Clark listened to. The president of the council, Clark Richardson, was the Speaker's nephew. So it need not have come as a shock to many Alabama politicians when Clark, flush from his impressive victory on tort reform, announced that his next priority was a new law that would make it easier for local governments to raise property taxes. Nevertheless, it tore the conservative coalition apart.

Among those who felt betrayed by Clark was Guy Hunt. During the 1986 campaign Hunt had talked about the liberal cabal in the same menacing tones Clark had. Now, as governor, he wanted to take aim at the heart of the cabal, the Alabama Education Association. Hunt sought to eliminate a $41 million shortfall in the state operating budget by diverting money from education. Then he began talking about removing school principals from the tenure protection system, giving more power over education to the state finance director. The businessmen Jimmy Clark listened to would have no part of it. They thought that if Alabama wanted to be competitive economically in the years to come, it needed to spend more on education, not less.

It was at that point that the Speaker began hearing from an old political adversary, a man he had once described as "the worst thing that ever happened to Alabama." This man told Clark that if he believed in economic development, and if he thought that required a better educational system and a round of tax increases, and if some of his old conservative allies were too dense to understand, then there was an established statewide political organization that did understand, and wanted to help. Moreover, it was an organization that knew something about rounding up votes. Its initials were AEA. "I didn't drive any wedge," Paul Hubbert said afterward. "I just moved into the vacuum that was created. Clark had more need of us than he thought he would have."

A few months later Clark's property tax bill passed the Alabama House, with the AEA, in Hubbert's words, "putting the muscle behind it." The bill later fell victim to a Senate filibuster, but what mattered politically was that the teachers were no longer relegated to the sidelines. They were back in the government of Alabama. Before long Clark was making statements far different from the ones he had made in the 1986 campaign. "There will be no bashing of teachers in Alabama," he announced, "during the next four years."

When the next legislative session opened, Clark gave up on the property tax and decided to try for a 0.5 percent increase in the state income tax. Once again he failed. But the teachers were with him all the way. And he was with them: When Hunt submitted a budget limiting teachers' salary increases to 2.5 percent, and called for the creation of new state and local citizens' committees to monitor the performance of the school systems, Clark was opposed. And they went nowhere.

The year 1988 was not a pretty one for the Alabama legislature. The House and Senate failed to agree on a general fund budget before the scheduled adjournment in April, so they had to come back for a special session in August and, when that proved fruitless, still another session at the end of September. On many budget issues there were no stable majorities; often Clark seemed to be losing his grip on the House.

But as the special sessions wore on, with legislators shouting and arguing with each other late into the night, Paul Hubbert had the luxury of sitting quietly in the gallery, never needing to use his famous thumb, if in fact he had ever used it. The budget he cared about, the education budget, had passed unanimously, with teachers' raises three times larger than the ones the governor had proposed. Hunt's "accountability program" had been ignored. And Hunt himself had gone on television a few days later and proclaimed Hubbert the "czar" of the legislature.

At the end of the year there was another purge in the Alabama House of Representatives, one that very nearly reversed the moves Clark had made upon taking over. Many of the conservative Democrats who had been the beneficiaries of the first purge were now ousted from positions of responsibility. Backers of the liberal coalition were restored to chairmanships and the official good graces of the leadership. Governor Hunt even issued a press release calling attention to the event. "The gang of Hubbert," he said, "has taken over again in Montgomery."

It was a stunning ending to the drama of 1986. Yet in retrospect it made perfect sense. It had been unrealistic to think that Paul Hubbert and his allies could be out of power for very long. In the course of more than a decade, teachers had become the strongest single presence in Alabama politics, and they remained the strongest, notwithstanding the 1986 result. Early in 1989 Paul Hubbert decided to test that strength in a different sort of way. Newly recovered from a liver transplant that had restored him to good health, Hubbert let it be known that he wanted more out of politics than a reputation as a back-room strategist. He announced that he was running for governor in 1990.

In the end, that gubernatorial campaign did not succeed. It did take Hubbert and his coalition further than even most supporters thought possible at the start. The executive vice-president of the Alabama Education Association, a man who had never run for any office in his life, was nominated over some of the state's most visible and prominent Democrats, and then drew 48 percent in the fall against an incumbent who had dedicated four years to the avoidance of controversy and the single-minded pursuit of reelection.

One could look at the results of the 1990 election and conclude that very little had changed in Alabama. There would be another conservative administration in Montgomery; the massive investment in education and all-around government activism that Hubbert had promised, and that had come to most southern states in the 1980s, would not come to Alabama until 1994, at the earliest.

But as he pondered his narrow defeat, Paul Hubbert could also look back upon two decades of remarkable change in Alabama, change that he had in large part generated and that had brought him influence beyond anything he had ever envisioned. During the 1970s and 1980s, Hubbert taught the two principal factions in his state the most important lessons of modern American politics. He taught the liberals that the political power long denied them was there for the taking, provided they could summon up the ambition to take it. He taught the conservatives that their self-image as Alabama's governing party no longer guaranteed them majority support in the legislature or at the polls. If they wanted to govern, they would have to become professionals.

Over the course of a decade, a rough sort of equilibrium had come to exist. Hubbert's side won clear victories in 1982 and 1983; the conservatives won an equally clear victory in 1986. The 1990 campaign produced more of a standoff. It is impossible to say who will win the next rounds of competition and govern Alabama in the coming years. But it is safe to say how that side will win: by approaching politics Hubbert's way, committing the talent, enthusiasm, and time for which there is no longer any real substitute.

10

Cycles of Change

The currencies of modern political success are constantly changing hands. A concentration of talent turns up where it had never appeared before, as with teachers in Alabama in the 1970s. Enthusiasts can emerge, win impressive victories, and then grow disillusioned and withdraw. Meanwhile, as the day-to-day life of a political institution becomes more complex, time becomes more crucial. People who have large amounts of it to spend become more influential.

Any of these things can happen in any place. In Colorado, over the past generation, all of them have happened. Power has passed from a small rural elite, working at politics casually and part-time, to an equally small cadre of ideological enthusiasts, and now, very gradually, is shifting to a new set of politicians whose crucial political asset is the number of hours they are willing to devote to the work.

An Alabama state senator of the 1950s, transplanted suddenly to the Colorado legislature in Denver, would have had a reasonable chance to understand it. The consuming passion of race was absent, of course, but the principle of political power was the same: Agricultural interests ruled, protected by malapportionment. Three decades ago rural Colorado had barely 40 percent of the state's population, but it claimed nearly 60 percent of the legislative seats. A typical session in the Colorado House included roughly twenty-five legislators from the Denver area and forty from the outlying areas of the state. It was not very difficult for the forty to rule, and they ruled blatantly in their own favor. Denver didn't get the highway money its population entitled it to. It wasn't allowed to tax railroads at the same high rate the rural counties were.

Even more than in Alabama, the wishes of the legislature determined the public policy of the state. Colorado has never really had a strong governorship. The governor submits a budget every year, but the legislature has the right to ignore it, and it nearly always does. As far back as anyone in Colorado politics can remember, the Joint Budget Committee of the legislature has written the budget and set the state's economic priorities. "The governor of Colorado has the responsibility to run the state," Gov. Richard Lamm was to say in the late 1970s, "but he does not have the authority." This was even more true in the 1950s. The legislature was the government.

The common perception about the legislature in those days before reapportionment is that it was, pure and simple, a cowboys' club. In strict numerical terms, that was not really true: No more than a quarter of the members at any one time ever listed farming or ranching as their occupation. What it indisputably was, however, was a small-town legislature, populated by men who had grown up with agriculture and its values. Prominent among its values, as in Alabama, was a belief in modest government financed by minimal taxes. The Colorado legislators of that generation wanted the state to do everything it could to protect and expand the supply of scarce western water available to agriculture. Otherwise they brought with them to politics a visceral distrust of legislative activism.

Legislative sessions were short. As soon as the days started warming up on the eastern plains and on the western slope of the Rockies, there was mounting pressure to adjourn and head home for spring planting. The average session, starting in January, lasted just over ninety days. While these legislators were meeting, though, they stayed in Denver. It was not possible for most of them to return home to the plains or the western slope at night, or even on weekends. The Denver contingent went home each evening, but they constituted only about a third of the membership, and, by choosing to be commuters, the small urban bloc further isolated themselves from power, dealing themselves out of the decisions that were routinely made late at night over drinks at a few downtown hotels and bars.

If the legislature was not a cowboys' club per se, it was definitely an outstate men's club, and those who wanted to have any influence at all had to accommodate themselves to it one way or another. That was true of the urbanites and suburbanites, and it was true of the few women who managed to make it to the legislature in those days. Ruth Clark won a seat in the Colorado House from Fort Collins in 1956, making her one of seven women in the institution when she took her seat there the next January. Fort Collins was beyond commuting distance, so for the three months of the legislative session she took a room at the Shirley Savoy Hotel, informal headquarters of the legislature's male leadership. One night Clark returned to her room after dinner and found a live pig, placed there by Doc Lamb, the representative from Morgan County. It wasn't just a sexist prank. It was a statement about who governed. Anybody else who wished to participate was obliged to defer.

Why did the cowboys who ran Colorado politics pursue public office in the first place? What motivated them to drop what they were doing for three or four months every year and serve in the legislature? Was it fascination with the governmental process, or the desire to enact an agenda? Neither. The small-town politicians of the 1950s, in Colorado as almost everywhere in America, thought of government as a necessary evil rather than a subject of abstract interest. Other than protect rural water rights, there wasn't much they wanted government to do. The best way to explain their presence in office is to say that they were members of a small-town governing class, and that running for the legislature was one of their responsibilities. In Doc Lamb's Morgan County, as in rural counties throughout much of the country, political influence and economic influence were pretty much the same. The farmers, ranchers, bankers, and insurance agents who were the leading citizens of those counties served on the Chamber of Commerce, the county boards, and the school boards. And because there were seats in the legislature to fill, they went to Denver in January. This governing class was Republican in some areas of the state, Democratic in others—Democrats actually controlled the legislature through much of the late 1950s and early 1960s—but it was conservative no matter which party was in charge.

It was a structure of power that any of the leading Alabama legislators of this period would have grasped in a moment. The legislature was the logical extension of community life and community power back home. The one question difficult for these people to answer about themselves would have been the question of motivation. They didn't need to be motivated. They governed because they were supposed to.

In the 1970s motivation began to matter. As reapportionment dissolved the built-in rural advantage, as political office and political power in the communities themselves began to be dispersed, as service in the legislature became more demanding and more time consuming, those who weren't sure why they were there ceased to be the majority.

For a brief time in the early 1970s, the crucial motivation in Colorado politics seemed to be environmentalism. Concern about overdevelopment and pollution along the populous East Front of the Rockies led to a revolt against plans to hold the 1976 Olympics in Denver and brought into office a new cadre of environmentalist Democrats. By 1972 they had taken over the party structure from the rural conservatives who had dominated it during most of the years since World War II. In 1974 the enthusiasm of the environmental activists and popular revulsion over Watergate gave the Democrats control of the Colorado House for the first time in a decade. But that flame burned itself out rather quickly. The enthusiasm that turned out to be crucial in Colorado politics over the next decade came from a different direction. It came from the right.

During the latter half of the 1970s, Colorado generated a supply of conservative talent far out of proportion to its size. Some of it was simply a reaction to the brief period of environmentalist control that peaked in 1974; some of it reflected the presence of the Joseph R. Coors Brewing Company and the willingness of the Coors family to finance conservative campaigns for the legislature. To a great extent it was a marriage of circumstance and personal ambition. The state had attracted a generation of educated, articulate professional people who saw Colorado and the West in general as a refuge from the big-government decadence of the East, and who saw a political career as a means of fighting the moral and economic failures of liberalism.

Some of these transplants became political activists. Growing up in a Democratic family in the Chicago suburbs, Ken Kramer had dreamed of a career in politics. But nothing worked out for him. He tried to get a patronage job with the Cook County Democratic organization but was turned down. He ran for the student senate at the University of Illinois and lost. "I've never been the kind of person who was naturally popular," he was to say later on.

But when he left the army in 1970 and took a job as a deputy district attorney in Colorado Springs, he began to see Colorado and conservatism as an antidote to all his frustrations and failures farther east. By 1972 he was running a Republican campaign for the legislature; in September of the following year, less than three years after his arrival in the state, he was appointed to the legislature himself. He wasn't just enthusiastic about taking his seat there—he was fanatical about it. He hand-carried his certificate of election to the secretary of state because he said he didn't trust the post office to deliver it.

Once in office Kramer seemed to attract attention with every move he made. He introduced an antipornography bill and warned that its defeat would mean "inviting live sexual shows with people and animals" to operate under state sanction. He warned that the way things were going, "within the not-too-distant future, we will all live under socialism." Kramer's style struck even some of his conservative colleagues as extreme. But his overall outlook fit in comfortably with the conservative enthusiasm that was coming to dominate the legislature during his years there.

The year after Kramer went to the legislature, Steve Durham was elected to represent a nearby district in Colorado Springs. On a personal level Durham wasn't much like Kramer at all. He was a homegrown Colorado product, he hadn't been fascinated by politics all his life, and he wasn't much interested in legislating on morals and pornography. But he shared with Kramer an instinctive dislike for liberalism and government regulation, and for the Democrats who had seized control of the Colorado House in 1974.

In 1976 all the forces of conservative enthusiasm came together: moralists like Kramer, libertarians like Durham, money from the Coors network, and help from the business community in general, which was frightened at the prospect of a long-term Democratic legislative majority. Conservative talent seemed to emerge everywhere that year. "We produced some great candidates in 1976," Durham recalled a decade later. "It was the best crop of candidates we've ever produced. We kicked the hell out of the Democrats with them."

Going into 1976 Democrats held a big advantage in the Colorado House—thirty-nine of sixty-five seats. But it disappeared overnight that November, replaced by a new chamber with a five-seat Republican majority. Meanwhile the GOP had held on to its slim majority in the state Senate. It was clear that the architects of the reversal were conservatives who agreed, one way or another, with people like Ken Kramer and Steve Durham. Soon after the 1977 session began, the conservative enthusiasts in the legislature began to acquire a new media nickname. They were called the Crazies.

Despite their name the Crazies were not a fringe group by any means. With a solid bloc of fifteen to twenty votes in the House Republican Caucus, and an equally loyal core of support in the smaller Senate, they had the numerical strength to impose a veto on crucial budget decisions in the Republican majority caucuses, where real power resided. More important still, though, was their intensity. The enthusiasm of the Crazies simply overwhelmed the casual political approach of those legislative leaders still hanging on from the cowboy days. "Some of the Crazies literally wanted to close the government down," recalls Bill Artist, a more moderate Republican legislator who served with them in the 1970s. "But they were powerful because they were locked in step."

Kramer never succeeded with his antipornography bill, or with any other initiatives like it. Where the conservative enthusiasm left a profound impact on Colorado was in economics, the subject that gave moralists such as Kramer and libertarians such as Durham a large piece of common ground. In the early 1970s, despite the heritage of cowboy control, Colorado was becoming a relatively high-tax state. For a brief period it ranked tenth among the fifty states in taxation per capita. It was sixth in per capita expenditures for education, fifth in expenditures for welfare.

After 1976, prodded by the Crazies and their preeminent role in the Republican caucuses, the legislature imposed a 7 percent annual limit on increases in state expenditures, regardless of what the inflation rate might be in a given year. It imposed across-the-board reductions in the state income tax and indexed the state tax rate to inflation, so that tax payments would not automatically go up just because the cost of living went up. It was a Reagan-style economic revolution well in advance of Ronald Reagan's arrival in Washington and far beyond anything he had attempted in California. Democrat Richard Lamm sat in the governor's mansion during these years, but there was nothing he could do to stop it. The Republicans in the legislature had the votes. Five years after the pivotal 1976 election, Colorado ranked in the bottom half of the states in per capita taxation.

In assessing that fundamental change, we need to pay appropriate respects to the tax-cut fever that swept most of the country in the closing years of the 1970s. While the Crazies were rewriting the economic rules in Colorado, Howard Jarvis and Paul Gann were preparing Proposition 13, the property tax limitation passed by initiative in California in June 1978. Within months similar measures were being approved at the state and local levels in places as different as Michigan, Massachusetts, and Maryland.

None of that, however, quite explains Colorado. Arguably, at least, it altered the economic basis of its government more dramatically and with more permanent effect than any of the other states that experienced a tax revolt during this period. Colorado went further than California, further than Michigan. And it did so without the public clamor or controversy that surrounds a statewide initiative vote. It moved much more quietly, in a series of relatively routine legislative enactments.

The reason Colorado's legislature went as far as it did toward scaling back taxes and government was not that the voters pushed it that far. The voters acquiesced, even approved. But the engine for drastic economic change was the conservative talent that had injected itself into the state political process over the preceding five years. The critical factor was not what the electorate demanded but what the Republican right had been able to supply. The critical decisions were the career choices made by the Ken Kramers and the Steve Durhams in the early years of the decade. It is hard to find another state where conservative enthusiasm so altered the makeup of a legislature. That is why it is so hard to find one that acted so drastically as the tax reduction issue made its way across the country.

However, the enthusiasm that revamped Colorado government did not long survive its own success. The 1980 election was kind to the Republicans, enabling them to consolidate their hold on the state Senate as well as the state House, but soon after that the Crazies began to break up. Ironically, the Reagan administration contributed to the breakup by hiring many of them.

Robert Burford, who had been the Crazies' successful candidate for House Speaker in 1979, went to Washington to head the

Bureau of Land Management. Anne Gorsuch, his ideological ally and longtime personal companion, went to Washington as well. In Colorado, Gorsuch had established herself as a leader of the Crazies' faction by heading the fight to close down the state women's commission. In Washington, as Anne Burford, she lasted two years as head of the Environmental Protection Administration before resigning in a cloud of controversy over the mismanagement of EPA funds and the seriousness of her efforts to fight pollution. Even Steve Durham, the scourge of regulation and intrusive government in the Colorado House, became a federal appointee. He accepted Anne Burford's offer to be the EPA's regional administrator in Denver. By the end of 1981 it almost seemed as if there were as many Colorado Crazies in the Reagan administration as there were in the legislature.

Ken Kramer was not in the Reagan administration, but he had left Denver for Washington all the same. An open seat had come up in 1978 in the Colorado U.S. House delegation, and he had taken it, defeating a moderate Republican in a bitter primary, then coasting to victory over a Democrat in the fall.

But promotion to Washington was only a small factor in the Crazies' decline. More fundamentally, they did not believe in government enough to maintain their enthusiasm for it once the frustrations that launched their political careers had been largely relieved. The enthusiasms that drove Kramer and Durham into politics in the early 1970s weren't duplicated among many of their ideological soul mates who came along later.

Bill Owens was one of the few exceptions. Considerably younger than Kramer or Durham, Owens was a true "movement conservative," a leader in Young Americans for Freedom in college, and he had gotten himself elected to the legislature in 1982, only seven years after graduation. Six years later he hadn't lost his enthusiasm. He was moving to the state Senate and thinking about an eventual campaign for Congress. But he was part of a dwindling band. "There aren't many movement conservatives coming in here now," Owens conceded in 1988. "The balloon has deflated. We have a conservative spending policy in this state, and a Republican legislature. There isn't a lot of interest in making it any more conservative."

Steve Durham says the same thing. He left the EPA when Burford resigned in 1983 and returned to take a seat in the Colorado Senate. In 1988, the year he turned forty, he was one of the last of the original Crazies left in the legislature, and he was getting ready to leave it himself for a private business career. "It's virtually impossible to find good candidates," he says. "There's no real conservative motivation now. There's no greater enemy to a political movement than success."

The departure of the conservative enthusiasts opened the way to still another shift in the makeup of the Colorado legislature, one that gathered momentum gradually in the 1980s, promising to be more permanent and, in the long run, even more far-reaching. It has not been a change in ideology, or in partisan balance. It has been a change in gender.

There is no longer anything very startling about the combination of women and political power in America. A woman sits on the Supreme Court. The Democratic party has nominated a woman for vice-president of the United States. Texas, Kansas, and Oregon all have female governors. Still, those are individual achievements. What women have not done at the national level, in the past twenty years of organized feminism, is push their way into political office in numbers approaching their presence in the society. They hold barely 5 percent of the seats in the U.S. House, and only two out of one hundred places in the Senate. Even at the state legislative level, progress in the 1980s turned out to be slower than many expected. As of 1988 the proportion of women in state legislatures had risen only to 15 percent.

But none of those frustrations apply to Colorado. When the Colorado House convened for its regular session in 1987, women held twenty-five of its sixty-five seats—a higher percentage than in any legislative chamber in the country. More important, the proportion of women in the Republican majority caucus—the organization controlling the business of the House—was eighteen out of forty. It was stamped on the consciousness of everybody doing business in the Colorado House that women were not that many votes away from a majority. It is very possible that those votes will come in the 1990s.

"In the next four to eight years," one male legislator predicted in 1988, "we're going to have a woman Speaker and a woman president of the Senate. In the meantime, the male leadership is going to have to adjust." In their more candid moments, the women legislators of Colorado like to tell the current leaders that the handwriting is on the wall. "One of these days we're going to be a majority around here," state Rep. Dorothy Wham told Speaker Carl Bledsoe one day in 1987. "Then we'll see which way the cabbage is cooked."

It is possible, if one chooses, to explain all this as a product of something that lies deep in the collective psychology of the state. Like other places in the West, Colorado has a tradition of women in public life that dates back to territorial days. Women have held one or more statewide offices for much of the past generation. Colorado was one of the first states to ratify the federal Equal Rights Amendment. And so on. But none of this really explains very much. There are many states with a similar history, and none with a legislative chamber anywhere near 50–50. The best way to understand the feminization of the Colorado House is to return to the question of the job itself—what it requires and what it pays.

Like its neighboring mountain states, Colorado retains some of the deep-seated suspicion about government that characterized it in the days of rural control. It has never really abandoned the appealing notion of the citizen legislature—the public-spirited collection of farmers, businesspeople, and other hardworking folk who leave their jobs and communities for a short time each year to transact the business of the state.

The Colorado legislature bears many of the physical trappings of the amateurism its citizens consider a virtue. The members do not have private offices, and they do not have any permanent staff. A bill was introduced in 1988 to give each member one paid staff member, but it was denounced on the floor and had to be withdrawn. "I see us taking a step in the direction that California has gone," a veteran senator warned. "You get one staff member and pretty soon you get another one. Then you need a secretary to direct the staff."

Colorado has never abandoned the theory of the citizen legislature. What it has abandoned is the practice. With a population of more than 3 million and a metropolitan Denver complex that confronts all the problems and complexities of urban America, Colorado is a big-time state. The Colorado legislature may be organized as a part-time institution, but it does not operate that way. In the 1980s it met endlessly, prevented its members from holding down any other full-time job, yet failed to pay them a wage they could live on. In some recent years the legislature has been in session more than 200 days—nearly seven months. Even under a 1988 constitutional amendment, fixing each year's regular session at 120 days and no more, the job is guaranteed to occupy any legislator from New Year's until the middle of May, assuming there is no special session later in the year—which there was in 1989, the first year the new system was in place.

To be a member of the Colorado legislature is to be one of one hundred people charged with governing a sophisticated, diverse, and challenging state. It is an interesting job. But at $17,500 per year it is no job for a breadwinner. The Colorado legislature is now composed almost entirely of people who can devote most of their time to it without having to worry about holding down a full-time job somewhere else.

Several kinds of people fit into the category of "nonbreadwinner" that has come to dominate legislative life in this state. There are some who are independently wealthy. There are retired military officers collecting comfortable pensions, and aging ranchers who have left management of their property to their children. There are a few lawyers and oil company executives whose firms understand the power of the legislature and don't mind subsidizing an employee who is absent for months at a time. There are men whose wives are highly paid professionals and who can live with $17,500 a year as a second income. Most of all, however, there are women—highly educated, affluent suburban women.

Few of Colorado's female legislators maintain any illusions about why their numbers have grown so large. "At seventeen thousand dollars a year," says Rep. Margie Masson, "most men aren't interested in the job. If we had a seventy-thousand-dollar-a-year legislature, I don't think the numbers would be the same."

The dramatic changes in its legislative life have coincided with equally important changes in the demographics of Colorado. If the most important shift of the past twenty-five years has been the transfer of representation and power out of rural hands, then the second most important has been the transfer from city to suburb.

In 1955, when metropolitan Denver had twenty-five of the sixty-five seats in the Colorado House, seventeen of those were within the city. Today the city of Denver actually sends fewer legislators to the state Capitol than it did in the 1950s. The growth has all been in the suburbs, and the legislative numbers reflect that. Of the thirty-five legislators in 1987 who came from the metropolitan Denver area, twenty-four were from the four suburban counties—Adams, Arapahoe, Jefferson, and Boulder. A majority of those were women. This electoral result speaks volumes not only about current Colorado politics but about modern suburban culture in America. Over the past generation, in postwar bedroom communities across the country, women have become the central figures in public life.

In these suburbs it has not been possible for men to control political decisions by controlling economic decisions, the way they traditionally did at the small-town level. The suburbs, until very recently, had no large-scale economic life of their own. They employed few people and produced relatively few goods and services. The men who might have been political leaders focused their attention not on their hometowns but on the downtowns where they earned their livelihoods. "The banker who lives in the suburbs hasn't been there politically," says Bill Owens, who is part of the male minority representing suburban Denver in the Colorado legislature. "That banker works for United Bank downtown. His focus is the Denver Chamber of Commerce, not the Arvada Chamber of Commerce."

But affluent postwar suburbia had to have a public life, whether its male breadwinners paid much attention to local issues or not. Parks and schools had to be built, charity had to be financed, organizations needed to be created to make some semblance of community possible. And women, whether or not they held elective office in the formal sense, did the organizational work that established a suburban public life. In so doing they prepared themselves, sometimes inadvertently, for the wide-open politics that emerged in fast-growing states like Colorado. And they developed an enthusiasm not only for the work they were doing, and the excitement of the process, but for the government they were creating. "They get active in the PTA," says Owens. "Their goal is to get more money for their school. Then they want to get a crosswalk for the homeowners' association. They are socialized in a process of using government for positive means. They see government as a friend."

Carol Taylor-Little is a good example. In her twenties and thirties she was a housewife, an ice skating teacher, and a real estate broker in Arvada, an affluent suburb northwest of Denver. She had three children, divorced, and remarried a man with three children of his own. Her work as an activist in the Arvada PTA led her into Republican politics as a self-described "block worker and phone caller." She was a member of the Colorado Commission on Women. In 1982, when Arvada's House seat opened up, she eagerly went after it. "I had been lusting after the seat for years," she remembers.

The skills it took to win that election were the same ones Taylor-Little had honed over the years as a volunteer for the PTA and other civic organizations. There is no way to advertise on television or radio in a district like hers. The campaign consists mostly of making telephone calls and ringing doorbells. Taylor-Little knew more about that sort of work than any other candidate, and she wanted the job more than anyone else. She was a comfortable winner.

For four terms, until she chose to retire in 1990, Taylor-Little kept her district safely in Republican hands and contributed one more vote to the already massive GOP advantage in the Colorado House. It could not be said, though, that she did anything to make the place more conservative. "I happen to be a feminist," she says. "I am a moderate Republican female feminist." When the House voted along party lines in a debate over labor or taxation, she was comfortable enough sticking with the traditional GOP position. But when the debate shifted from "pure" economics to education or health care or senior citizens, she was nearly always among those advocating more government attention to solving the problem.

Jeanne Faatz's story is a little different. Her district is within the Denver city limits, and less safely Republican than Taylor-Little's district a few miles away. But it, too, is in a comfortably middle-class residential area. Faatz has been teaching in the metropolitan Denver public schools much of her adult life. Like Taylor-Little, Faatz married early, raised two children, divorced, and immersed herself in local volunteer work. She was president of the local YWCA and a volunteer for UNICEF. She learned how to organize a campaign—a campaign for charity rather than elective office, but a campaign nevertheless.

Faatz's district, like the one in Arvada, does not lend itself to media blitzes from candidates for the legislature. But it is a good place to use direct mail, and by the time Faatz ran for the Colorado House in 1978, she knew how to employ it effectively. She sent out brochures featuring herself on her parents' front porch at age three, playing the violin at age seven, then cooking at home, with her children hanging on to her apron. Faatz won that election with 55 percent of the vote, and she has never had a serious challenger since. "The fact that I do a lot of campaigning all year discourages them," she says. "I've never felt like taking a chance. So I campaign every time as if it were the first time. As long as I'm going to run I want to win."

Claire Traylor never really needed a job in private life. She was twenty-three when she married Frank Traylor, and his income as a surgeon was always more than enough to support a comfortable house and a family of four children in Wheat Ridge, just south of Arvada. From the time her first child was born, in 1957, to the year she won election to the Colorado House, in 1978, she was not employed full-time.

But she was preparing for a political career, whether she knew it or not. She was a leader in the Junior League. She ran the drive to enact a tax increase to finance drainage improvements. She was in charge of Call for Action, a sort of early ombudsman–hot line program. "I was well known in the community," she says. "I was a professional volunteer. . . . It's a door-to-door district. That's kind of fun." Traylor was elected to the Colorado House in 1978, the same year as Jeanne Faatz. She replaced her husband, who decided after two terms that he did not have time to do the job. Four years later she moved on to the state Senate.

To run for the Colorado legislature is to participate in a remarkably fluid process. In the spring of every election year, the parties hold caucuses at the precinct level. In nearly every case the choice of the caucuses becomes the overwhelming favorite to be nominated in the September primary. It is possible to skip the caucuses and head straight for the primary, but few do so successfully.

Not many people bother to go to the precinct caucuses; in most places attendance is less than 10 percent of those eligible. The candidate who knows how to organize the few committed participants is the one who wins. It would be a perfect situation for an old-fashioned party boss, except that there is no one remotely like that in Colorado. Caucuses are open to talent, and in the Denver suburbs the way to use that talent is to establish a reputation in local public life and make sure your friends show up in the right place at the right time, and stay for the whole evening. Neither sex has a monopoly on those abilities, but in suburban Denver, at least in recent years, they have been displayed best by people like Carol Taylor-Little, Jeanne Faatz, and Claire Traylor, people who have been practicing them for years in other kinds of public pursuits. As Taylor-Little says, "There is a way to develop political skills as a volunteer that you don't get as a business executive."

To trace the lives and careers of these women is to begin to understand one of the more interesting facts of recent political life in Colorado—the fact that the Republicans have established unshakable legislative majorities. Colorado has had a Democratic governor for the past fifteen years. Four of its last seven campaigns for the U.S. Senate have resulted in the election of the Democratic candidate. But when it comes to the state legislature, Democratic control is only a dim memory. In the past quarter-century the Colorado House has been Democratic only once, for the two-year interlude generated by Watergate and the environmental enthusiasm of 1974. The Colorado Senate has not had a Democratic majority since 1962.

The Republican party has controlled the legislature by winning in the suburbs, where nearly half the vote in the state is now concentrated. It wins there because it finds candidates who thrive in the suburban political environment—candidates who have the right combination of qualities to appeal to an affluent, sophisticated electorate and the willingness to immerse themselves in a job that requires long hours of grueling work and does not pay a breadwinner's wage.

The conditions that prevail in Colorado are the same ones that have crippled the Republican party at the polls in many states and cities around the country. It is not easy to find conservatives willing year after year to put up with long hours and low pay for the privilege of being part of a government they essentially distrust. But in Colorado the Republican party has not needed to find conservatives to win. Most of the women who thrived as Republicans in the Colorado legislature in the 1980s had little in common with Ronald Reagan or the national GOP agenda. They joined the GOP because that was the way to win elections in the places they represent. The Colorado Republican party, like the Democratic party in the Deep South a generation ago, has been so successful for so long that it has become a vehicle for ambitious people who don't really agree with much of what the party has been saying in recent years on the national level.

Seen from a distance, Colorado government does not appear to have changed dramatically with the arrival of so many women legislators. The politics of the 1980s was shaped by the antitax, antigovernment mood of the late 1970s, and to a great extent the decisions of that era still control the work the legislature does. The statutory 7 percent annual lid on the growth of state spending has locked into place a low-tax, low-service style of government. Those who favor a heavy investment in social services—and that includes most women legislators of both parties—have been on the losing end of most budget decisions in recent years.

Moreover, the top leadership positions all remained in male hands through the 1980s. Carl Bledsoe, the House Speaker until his retirement in 1990, was an eastern Colorado rancher who would have felt perfectly at home in the institution of the 1950s. The Senate president, Ted Strickland, was a two-time gubernatorial nominee who worked for an oil company. The Democrats elected a female House minority leader, Ruth Wright, but her opportunity to achieve real power depends on a change in party control, whose chances appear slight. Still, there is a great deal more to the life of a legislative body than budget decisions and leadership elections. One does not have to spend much time in the corridors of the Colorado state Capitol to discover that the agenda of the legislature has changed. Women have changed it.

In every recent session of the Colorado House, child support has been a major legislative issue. In 1986 the legislature established a statewide formula recalculating child-support payments to match the income of the supporting parent. The next year those entitled to support were given the clear right to request garnishment of the wages of an ex-spouse who holds back payments. By 1988 the debate had moved further—the issue was whether garnishment ought to be mandatory in child-support cases, with or without evidence of neglect. On this last issue the most intense arguments were not between women and men, or even between married and divorced women, but between divorced women who had remarried and those who had remained single. The remarried bloc felt that mandatory garnishment was demeaning to their current husbands, most of whom were divorced themselves.

While the garnishment issue was being thrashed out in a conference committee, the House itself was discussing a related issue—whether the divorced wives of military officers were entitled to part of their husbands' pensions upon their retirement. A Colorado court had recently reversed precedent by ruling that they were, setting up a showdown in the House between the two fastest-growing blocs of members: women and retired military personnel. The military bloc—three retired lieutenant colonels entered the House in 1987 alone—controlled the sizable delegation from Colorado Springs, home of Fort Carson and the U.S. Air Force Academy. When the legislature finally acted on the issue, the two sides fought to a virtual draw. Legislation was passed effectively declaring that divorced women were not entitled to their husbands' military pension money as alimony. But an amendment specified that the money could be used for child support.

In 1987 Colorado became the first state in the country to authorize dental hygienists to set up shop independent of dentists. Republican Bill Owens, who sponsored that bill, saw it primarily as a free-enterprise issue. That perspective alone, though, would not have taken it very far. Dentists are a significant pressure group in Colorado, and they opposed it. Hygienists are not an organized political force. But Owens's bill took on the status of a women's issue, and it eventually became law. "If I had tried to deregulate taxicabs," he said afterward, "I would have had to beg, borrow, and plead to get votes, especially women's votes. But the hygienists were all women, and they complained about how they were being kept in servitude by the dentists."

Not all the feminist projects in the Colorado House have involved much tension and controversy. Some have barely been noticed. Dorothy Wham and Bonnie Allison sponsored a House bill allowing the Colorado Health Department to spend private money running a breast cancer screening program. Somebody else might have thought of that, but Wham and Allison were more likely to— both of them had had breast cancer. It was the sort of modest bill the Colorado House passes now that it tended not to bother with in the old days. "We don't think of it as a feminist agenda," Wham said. "It's just that the influence is there."

The Colorado legislature has thus evolved over forty years from an institution preoccupied with water rights to one that spends part of every year arguing over child support. It has been a remarkable transformation, and it is one that can best be understood by focusing on the office and its requirements—the ones that prevailed in the 1950s and the ones that will prevail in the 1990s.

Talent was important then, as it is now. But not in the same sense. When the legislators of the 1950s described a colleague as possessing political talent, they were talking about an instinct for the legislative process, for the strategy and negotiation that allowed a member to deliver for his district or for whatever economic interest he had chosen to represent. It was a skill that was exercised quietly in the committee rooms of the Capitol and over drinks at the Shirley Savoy at night. A member who had that ability eventually acquired a reputation at home, among the elites that mattered at election time, as someone who was "doing a good job in Denver." That reputation helped keep him in office as long as he wanted to stay there.

Today when legislators mention the idea of political talent, they may be talking about the same sorts of instincts. But they may be talking about something else altogether. Winning election to the legislature has come to require its own set of skills and instincts, pretty much separate from those that govern the legislative process itself. Unlike in the old days, there is a common feeling that the sort of talent that gets someone elected to the legislature does not automatically generate success within it.

This is, in fact, the major source of tension between men and women in the Colorado legislature: the underlying complaint of the men that the women have become master politicians without becoming legislators. "These women have the perfect skills for getting reelected," Christopher Paulson, then the House majority leader, said one day in 1988, in the middle of his second year in the job. "They go home at night and write notes to thank the people that helped them get elected. Those are sure votes. But they don't have the right skills for legislating. They don't have any business experience. They don't have any experience making decisions. They don't understand why everything cannot be done." One can dismiss this tirade as the sexism of an Air Force officer—which Paulson once was—or, more charitably, as the complaint of a harassed and overworked legislative leader at the end of a long day. The fact is, though, it reflects a tension that has increased dramatically throughout the political system in recent years. It is not really a matter of gender. It is a tension between the politics of campaigning and the politics of legislating.

The more campaigning becomes a science unto itself, the more public offices and rewards flow to people who have mastered its details. This is not only true of state legislatures; it is true of city councils and of the presidential nominating process. The ability to canvass for votes in Iowa or New Hampshire does not have much to do with the qualities that make a successful president. But it has come to be a virtual prerequisite for anyone who wants the job.

The talent that counted most in Colorado politics in the 1950s was the talent to influence decisions in small private groups. Those who displayed it in their communities more often than not had the opportunity to display it in the legislature, if they so chose. Today those abilities still influence legislative decisions. But they do not, in very many cases, determine who serves. The makeup of the legislature is determined much more by the talents that Carol Taylor-Little, Jeanne Faatz, and Claire Traylor cultivated in the Denver area: canvassing door-to-door, organizing caucuses, putting together a persuasive piece of direct mail. They are the talents of public communication. They are the talents of an open political system, not a small private circle.

And those are the talents that are going to win elections and determine the makeup of American legislatures for the remainder of this century and beyond. They are not the monopoly of either party, or either gender. But they are exercised effectively by those who can sustain a long-term enthusiasm for the effort, and especially by those willing to translate that enthusiasm into the commitment of huge blocs of time.

To say that the notion of time has become crucial to the process is to address a question broader than whether sessions take four months or six months. Colorado's 1988 constitutional amendment limiting regular legislative sessions to 120 days is not going to have much effect on the supply of political talent in the long run. What matters more is the time consumed by an open political system as practiced in Colorado and in states like it across the country. Colorado legislators need to commit the time it takes to provide the constituent service that has come to be expected, to meet with the local pressure groups that did not exist twenty years ago, and to solicit the campaign funds that frighten away serious opposition at election season. Those are the ingredients of full-time work, whether the legislature is actually in session for 90 days, 120, or 200.

Closed government, of the sort that existed in Colorado in the 1950s, is relatively efficient. Meetings don't have to take forever; decisions can be made quickly, and results don't have to be explained in public over and over again. Once government moves into the sunshine, the process stretches out—not just legislative sessions but the entire apparatus of government that surrounds a legislature such as Colorado's. And time takes its place alongside talent and enthusiasm as a critical commodity. Those who are willing to invest it come to occupy positions of elected influence. Those who are unwilling must figure out a way to influence the process from the outside.

11

The Natural Majority

The higher we climb in the American political system, the more urgent it becomes to explain the central contradiction of that system over the last twenty years: the fact that the voters' clear preference for Republican presidential candidates has done nothing to make the GOP the majority party in the country as a whole.

When we consider Congress, that contradiction presents itself in its most provocative and challenging form. It may not strike everyone as odd that the presidential victories of Richard Nixon, Ronald Reagan, and George Bush have failed to guarantee Republican control of the Concord city council or the Alabama legislature; state and local politics, it is possible to argue, may simply operate under a different set of rules. Congress, however, is national politics. It ought to operate by the same rules. It debates national issues and produces most of the people who run for president. If Republicans are so good at electing presidents, why are they so bad at electing people to the Senate and the House?

Election history, like any other form of history, can be seen from a multitude of perspectives. So it is possible—and relatively easy—to interpret the last twenty years of congressional election results as a reflection of shifting moods and preferences among the electorate. This is, in fact, the conventional wisdom, and it can be reasonably summarized as follows:

Richard Nixon's presidential victory of 1968 presented the Republican party with an excellent opportunity to become the nation's majority party, but they squandered it. They made little headway in 1970 because the economy was in mild recession; they performed even more disappointingly in 1972 as Nixon focused on his own reelection and provided his party's candidates almost literally no help; then they were all but wiped out in 1974 by voter disgust at Watergate, falling back to fewer than forty seats in the Senate and barely one-third in the House. Jimmy Carter's emergence on the presidential scene in 1976 represented a further delay in Republican hopes to build a congressional majority, temporarily reattaching to the Democratic party the loyalties of rural white southerners who would be a crucial ingredient in any future Republican control.

The election of Ronald Reagan in 1980 appeared to present a new opportunity for Republicans (the argument continues), but by then the critical momentum had been lost. Voters had grown accustomed to divided government, and Democratic officeholders in the South and in other conservative areas had become adept at presenting themselves to the electorate in ways that did not seem ideologically threatening. Besides, Democratic legislatures had drawn congressional districts in most of the large states in ways that penalized Republicans, and the numerous financial and organizational perquisites of congressional office made incumbents extremely difficult to beat, working to the benefit of Democrats as the party already holding most of the seats.

This, as I say, is roughly the conventional wisdom. I would not try to argue that it lacks any validity. Obviously Watergate was a devastating setback to Republicans in Congress, one from which they did not quickly recover. What I do propose is that we leave these familiar arguments aside, and try a modest experiment. Let us see how much of the last twenty years of congressional history we can explain by telling a story in which the main characters are the people who chose to offer themselves for Congress, rather than the people who chose to vote for them.

The overriding issue in 1970 and 1972, the two national elections of the Nixon years, was Vietnam. There were aspirants for Congress in those days reflecting the whole spectrum of opinion on the subject.

There were candidates who wanted all U.S. forces sent home from Indochina at once, and candidates who felt that such views constituted surrender to the forces of international communism. There were candidates who saw the antiwar movement as the heir to two centuries of principled American dissent, and others who thought it amounted to treason.

The antiwar movement continued to make a vast segment of the American electorate uneasy. It was in 1970 that a group of construction workers in Manhattan, noticing that an American flag on a downtown office building had been lowered to half-mast by antiwar protesters, mounted the building's scaffold, raised the flag again, and roughed up some of the protesters, apparently with the approval of most passersby. Those hard hats were members of the "silent majority" that Nixon was including in his blueprint for Republican dominance in the decade to come.

But the important fact about silent majorities is that they tend to be silent. It is a safe bet that none of the hard hats who raised the flag that day ran for office in 1970, or anytime thereafter, and a reasonably safe bet that few of them enlisted as volunteers to help elect anybody of their persuasion to public office. Support for the Vietnam War, defense of the American flag, and loyalty to traditional American values were voting issues in the 1970s, and they provoked some arguments in the streets. But they did not propel many people into political careers. The antiwar movement did. Vietnam was an issue that moved candidates and won elections, and the benefits were nearly all on the antiwar side.

In 1970 "participatory democracy" was a popular slogan, and some of the nation's most prestigious liberal arts colleges allowed their students time off from coursework to participate in the congressional campaigns that spring and fall. Organizations with names like Referendum '70 and Congressional Action Fund raised money and rang doorbells in districts all over the country. Students who supported the Nixon Vietnam policies were as free to participate as their antiwar counterparts, but there was little evidence of their presence. The 1970 congressional campaigns, like the Eugene McCarthy presidential campaign of 1968, offered thousands of liberal young people a chance to sample the personal rewards of political activism. Many of them enjoyed it, and stayed with it.

Perhaps the best-publicized primary for the House that year

was in the suburbs of Boston, where Robert F. Drinan—Jesuit priest, law school dean, and author of the book *Vietnam and Armageddon*—ran as an antiwar candidate against Philip J. Philbin, a seventy-two-year-old back-bench Democrat who had never opposed the war and had little to say about it. Drinan's campaign attracted a horde of volunteers from Harvard, Tufts, Brandeis, and Wellesley, targeted sympathetic voters in a more systematic way than had been done for years in a Boston-area district, and ousted Philbin by more than 6,000 votes. Drinan's election was a national story, and a symbol of what the antiwar movement could accomplish with the right skills in the right place at the right time. More important in the long run, though, were events and career decisions under way in 1970 that were impossible to notice at the time.

Tom Harkin wasn't running for anything in 1970: He was in law school in Washington, D.C. But he had returned from five years as a Navy pilot in Vietnam with a disgust for the war, and during his spare time in law school he got a job with the House Select Committee on U.S. Involvement in Southeast Asia. He went back to Vietnam to investigate prisoner-of-war conditions, and found and publicized the "tiger cages" in which soldiers captured by the South Vietnamese were being kept. He became a national director of the Committee for a Sane Nuclear Policy. Those were the experiences that led him to return to Iowa, run for Congress, and succeed on his second try in 1974.

Steve Solarz was a candidate in the 1970 campaign, but not for Congress. He was running for his second term in the New York Assembly. Three years earlier, fresh from Columbia, where he had gotten a master's degree in public administration, he had returned home to Brooklyn to manage the antiwar congressional campaign of a local businessman challenging the Democratic organization. That campaign failed, but by the time it was over Solarz had the contacts and the experience to run for office on his own. A vacant Assembly seat turned up, and he went for it and got it. In 1974 he found his congressional opportunity with the bribery indictment of the congressman he had started out fighting in 1967. Running for Congress in his own name this time, Solarz was an easy winner.

Vietnam has long faded as an issue in American politics. But by the mid-1980s Harkin and Solarz were senior members of Congress and, when it came to legislative influence, very much in their prime. Harkin was a member of the Senate Appropriations Committee. Solarz was chairman of the House Subcommittee on Asian and Pacific Affairs.

It would be foolish to insist that people like Harkin and Solarz wouldn't be in office now if it had not been for the Vietnam War. Harkin had worked in an Iowa Senate campaign while he was in college; Solarz had been a student council president long before he became an antiwar campaign manager. No political issue, no matter how emotional, is sufficient to make a skillful candidate out of somebody with no aptitude for politics. But for many people in their generation who did have that aptitude, antiwar politics offered an outlet for public expression, a training ground for nuts-and-bolts skills, and a perfect bridge from postadolescent protest activity into a meaningful adult career. Thousands of people dabble in politics as students and then drift off into careers they see as more lucrative or more respectable. In the Vietnam years a larger number of these people than usual stayed in the game. And the consequences for the Democratic party and the political system have been great.

One might say the same about another event that shook Congress and the country just as Vietnam was beginning to fade. It seems odd to talk about Watergate as a source of inspiration for political candidates; it is treated far more often as an explanation for continued political apathy on the part of the electorate. In 1974, though, Watergate was a powerful recruitment tool for the Democratic party.

Not all the Democratic political figures who hark back to Watergate as their sudden springboard to political activism should be taken at face value. There were more than a few Democrats in 1974 who simply adopted the rhetoric of Watergate-inspired altruism as an effective campaign tool. But large numbers of Watergate-generation Democrats were convincing in their insistence that the scandal led them into political ventures they otherwise would not have made. Many of them gradually shed even the veneer of amateurism and became hardened, successful politicians.

Robert W. Edgar was one. When the Watergate cover-up became public knowledge in 1973, he was a Methodist minister, the Protestant chaplain at Drexel University in Philadelphia. Most of his work there, such as his establishment of a "Hassles and Hangups Counseling Center," had a distinct 1960s liberal flavor. Still, Edgar had never done anything in politics. "Until a year before the election," he continued saying for years, "I had never been to a political meeting."

Edgar turned political on the night in 1973 when President Nixon fired Archibald Cox, the Watergate special prosecutor. He chose to run for Congress as a Democrat in suburban Philadelphia's Seventh District, a Republican stronghold, and in the fall of 1974, at the height of the furor over the impeachment hearings, Nixon's resignation, and Ford's pardon, he won. Edgar held that seat, against the most determined and well-financed Republican opposition, five times. In 1986 he failed in a try for the Senate and left public office. By then, however, he had established a record in the House that included the chairmanship of an influential caucus of industrial-state members and successful agitation for changes in the way federal public works projects are financed. It made a difference to public policy that Edgar had been there those twelve years.

One reason Edgar was able to leave behind those accomplishments—one thing he had in common with Solarz, Harkin, and the Vietnam generation—was his belief in government as a positive social force. "The man in the street," he said in his first campaign, "has not taken an altogether cynical view of government. He's just looking for someone he can trust to articulate his views accurately and to represent him more honestly." Edgar was fond of describing himself as a nonpolitician. But he was never an antipolitician. He saw nothing inherently corrupt about the political process, the welfare state, or the notion of government as the ultimate equalizer of benefits in American life. Once he got into office—once he "became a politician"—he was eager to use government that way. And like many Democrats of his generation, the more skillful he grew at using government, the better a politician he became.

As activists, drawn into politics by causes, people like Bob Edgar, Steve Solarz, and Tom Harkin had little in common with the officeholders who dominated the House of Representatives as late as the 1960s. Those incumbents of the previous generation embarked on political careers for a variety of reasons—desire for personal advancement, feelings of obligation to a community elite, recruitment by a patronage machine—but causes and issues rarely had much to do with it. Harkin, Solarz, and Edgar had far more in common with the people who were coming into political power at the same time in state and local government. They were part of a political culture not too different from the one in which Steve Weir was operating in Concord, California, and David Clarenbach in the Wisconsin legislature. It was a culture in which causes and issues could be made to serve personal ambition without sacrificing honesty in any significant degree. It was perfectly possible to serve an honest cause and practice a profession at the same time.

No doubt there were a few Republicans in the early 1970s who were drawn into politics by the Vietnam War as a cause on the conservative side. They believed in the war effort, or found the peace movement appalling, and immersed themselves in a campaign for Congress. But they were very few indeed. The least popular war in American history was not the sort of cause on which political careers were built.

Watergate is an even clearer case. Perhaps, at the height of the controversy in 1974, someone, somewhere in America, was motivated to run for office because he felt the president and the president's party were being mistreated. But if he exists, I have not heard about him. For the GOP, Watergate was pure disincentive. It caused Republican voters not to vote (a major reason Democrats gained more than forty House seats in 1974), it caused Republican politicians not to seek higher office, and it caused young people of conservative sympathies to avoid public office altogether, not just in 1974 but for years after. The third of these results is the least notorious, but in the long run it has been the most devastating.

The mid-1970s marked a modern low point for the Republican party in its ability to frame issues and generate talent. There were Republicans who entered Congress in 1974 and 1976, but for the most part they were simply veteran officeholders following the internal logic of careers begun long before. There was scarcely any of the enthusiasm around which new careers and successful campaigns are built. By the end of the decade, though, the situation had changed. The Republican party did find a voice, and it recruited some talent. It did so in what might seem a bizarre way—by trumpeting its disgust at the very government it was asking people to join.

In 1978 Republican candidates all over the country ran for Congress on the same issue, the massive Kemp-Roth tax cut aimed at stimulating the American economy by turning back billions of dollars from government to the private sector. This was the first national introduction to the doctrines of supply-side economics.

Kemp-Roth was a very attractive idea, not just because it tapped into the obvious national resentment against high taxation but because it gave Republicans the feeling that they were sounding positive and upbeat for the first time in a generation. "Republicans have always played the role of spoilsports," said Sen. Richard G. Lugar of Indiana. "Kemp-Roth has given us a new argument and a new style, and it's delightful." A skeptic might have asked, even then, whether opposition to taxes and government constituted a "positive" program for the long run, but few Republicans were worried about that issue. Kemp-Roth was a breath of fresh air.

Not that 1978 produced any massive gains for the GOP at the congressional level. Republicans picked up three seats in the Senate and fifteen in the House. But the campaigns that year brought in a bright crop of enthusiastic freshmen, the equivalent, one might say, of the Vietnam and Watergate generation for the Democrats. These people made it clear that their disgust at government had brought them into politics, and they left no doubts about what their agenda as congressmen would be.

"I came here with a goal in mind," said freshman Rep. Phil Gramm of Texas (then a Democrat by formal affiliation, but already a Republican by ideology), "of reversing a thirty-year trend toward government power." Ken Kramer of Colorado, a leader of the Crazies in the state legislature, was also elected to Congress in 1978. He sounded distraught about the level to which things had degenerated. "We are strangled by government red tape," Kramer said, "and drained by government regulations administered by an ever-growing, insensitive, unaccountable bureaucracy." When the new Congress convened in 1979, Republican leaders found they had acquired a corps of political strategists, conservatives whose antigovernment enthusiasm translated into practical interest in working toward eventual GOP majorities. It all portended good things for 1980, and those things happened. Republicans achieved control of the Senate that year for the first time in nearly three decades. They lifted their House strength back to 192 seats—the level they had held before the 1974 election. The antigovernment enthusiasm and the failings of the Carter administration generated strong Republican campaigns all over the country, many of them from first-time candidates who were drawn in by the tax and government issues and by Reagan's presidential effort.

Denny Smith of Oregon was one of them. A newspaper publisher and political novice, he defeated the House Ways and Means chairman, Al Ullman. Smith had no particular fascination with politics or government—a onetime Air Force pilot, he viewed his congressional service as a "combat tour": zoom in, make a quick strike to balance the budget, then escape to resume his business career. Politics was not something he wanted to adopt as a profession. In that respect he was typical of many of the conservative Republicans who were sworn in with him as freshman members of the House of Representatives in 1981.

Victories by Smith and others of similar ideology led to widespread predictions that the Reagan years would see the completion of the Republican realignment that had stalled during the Nixon period. The successes of 1980 would generate more conservative talent, and the popularity of President Reagan would make the voters receptive. The GOP would solidify its majority in the Senate and move closer to an outright majority in the House. But this scenario did not happen.

Democrats, the supposed victims of the 1980s realignment, recovered in 1982 to take back twenty-six House seats, thereby regaining working control of the chamber and forestalling any more conservative legislative triumphs of the sort that defined the first year of the president's term.

There is a conventional wisdom about the 1982 election, and it is a plausible one: The Reagan economic program, passed virtually intact in 1981, was not working. Large areas of the industrial Northeast and Midwest were suffering through the hardest times they had known since the Great Depression. The national unemployment rate rose above 10 percent one month before election day, and that statistic generated a concern bordering on panic. So the first midterm election of the Reagan era turned into a Republican disaster—not the partisan standoff that traditionally occurs at the two-year point in a new president's term.

The conventional wisdom on this subject is not wrong. Republicans did lose seats in 1982 because they were perceived to have generated a recession. But in a crucial way they were victimized as much by their success as by their failure. Conservative anger against government—the anger that drove Ken Kramer, Phil Gramm, and their counterparts of the late 1970s—had begun to abate by 1982. It had to: Ronald Reagan was in office, expressing the same antigovernment sentiments that the party's bright young congressional candidates had been expressing. His program of tax and budget cuts had not been obstructed by the Democratic House majority; it had become law virtually as written in the White House. The Carter years had been a time of extraordinary emotion on the American right, and they had generated some extraordinary personal effort. By 1982 the fire was out. The Reagan victories of the preceding year were sufficient to persuade an entire corps of conservatives hostile to government that their personal presence was not required in the institution that disgusted them. Republicans who might have run for Congress began to choose other sorts of work—much as the conservatives in Colorado chose not to remain in the legislature once it seemed less offensive to them.

Democrats possessed no issue in 1982 that had the recruiting power of Vietnam or Watergate. But they did not need one. By that time they were producing a new generation of superior professional politicians, people who had devoted their lives to the business of campaigning and did not need the fervor of an issue to sustain them. Most of them talked about the federal deficit in 1982. Jim Slattery, running for an open congressional seat in Kansas, even described the deficit problem as "the political equivalent of the Vietnam War." But Slattery, like his fellow Democrats of 1982, had abilities and ambitions that transcended any particular issue.

He had been elected to the Kansas House at age twenty-three, while still in law school. Seven years later he retired—not to concentrate on a career in private life but to devote more of his energy to preparing a campaign against Jim Jeffries, the Republican congressional incumbent in the state's Second District. Slattery was ready for anything. One day in early 1982 a federal court redrew the lines of the district to include, among other places, the small rural enclave of Clay County. The next morning Slattery was in Clay County shaking hands. A few weeks later Jeffries announced his retirement. At age thirty-three Slattery was in perfect position to reap the rewards of his political training. He was an easy winner that fall, and Republicans have not contested the district in any serious way since.

The politics that worked for Jim Slattery in Kansas that year worked equally well for Tim Penny in Minnesota. Penny was a handshaker too. He worked the main streets of 150 towns in his district in 1982, echoing his first campaign for the state Senate, launched in 1976, when he was twenty-four years old and just a year out of graduate school. Penny won the state Senate seat after visiting every household in the district three times, and he won election to Congress the same way, capturing a district that had last chosen a Democrat in a horseback campaign in 1890. Minnesota Republicans were convinced that Penny was a fluke, a lucky winner in a year of economic unrest against a Republican tarnished by personal scandal. "He just borrowed the district from us for two years," the local GOP chairman said. "We'll win it back." But they have never even come close. Penny's district, like Slattery's, is now a solid building block of the House Democratic majority.

The 1982 results did more than reflect a national unrest over economic troubles. They revealed the fallacy in what had been the optimistic Republican blueprint for congressional campaigns in the 1980s. Strategists for the GOP had been convinced—and Democrats had genuinely feared—that the enormous Republican financial advantage and the availability of funds from the business community could create a long-term GOP majority at the House level. The money was there in 1982; the candidates, by and large, were not. The Democrats who reestablished control over the House that year did not do it with sudden infusions of cash, or in most cases with slick television advertising campaigns. They did it with personal skills cultivated over years as professional politicians. Republicans could not match that talent, and they could not buy it.

The importance of sheer talent was underscored in 1982 by the campaign of John Kasich of Ohio, the only Republican challenger in the country to retire a Democratic incumbent that fall. Kasich was the Republican equivalent of a Slattery or a Penny, a man with politics in his blood. He was another handshaker; he had taken a state Senate seat away from a Democratic incumbent in 1978 by visiting every household in the district several times. He re-created that strategy in his campaign for Congress. Kasich didn't win that election on money, or on modern technology; the Democratic incumbent, Bob Shamansky, outspent him. Kasich won the way virtually all elections in this country are still won: the hard way, the physically punishing way. In so doing he demonstrated that Republicans are not immune to the professionalism that breeds electoral success. But it remained to be shown how, as the party skeptical of government in the United States, they were going to generate as much of the right sort of talent as the other side.

. . .

The 1984 congressional elections were notable for the upheaval that did not take place. Reagan was reelected president in a landslide, but the Republican congressional harvest was meager indeed: a gain of fourteen in the House (giving the GOP ten fewer seats than they had after the first Reagan election in 1980) and a net loss of two in the Senate. Of the fourteen seats Republicans gained in the House, ten were in Texas and North Carolina. Elsewhere, the election amounted to a standoff. Republican strategists attributed their disappointingly small improvement in the House to Democratic gerrymandering. But to anybody who followed the progress of the campaigns all year, another problem was visible, and it was simply a more serious version of the problem that had afflicted the GOP in 1982. There were not very many credible Republican candidates in position to take advantage of whatever electoral benefits the Reagan landslide might provide.

By the fall of 1984 this was an accepted fact not only among party strategists but among the business-oriented political action committees once considered a crucial source of Republican strength. The Business-Industry Political Action Committee, unable to find a full menu of challengers that looked attractive, simply cut back its involvement in the campaign. "The challengers this year don't measure up," said Bernadette Budde, the organization's director and probably the most influential PAC strategist in Washington at that time.

There remained one serious indignity left for Republicans to suffer, and they suffered it in 1986: the loss of their tenuous six-year Senate majority. It was an event that nearly everyone who watched congressional elections could see coming. For one thing, it made historical sense. In the entire history of popular Senate elections, the party holding the White House had never lost fewer than four Senate seats at the six-year point in its presidential tenure. The Republicans in 1986 did not have a majority sufficient to withstand even a four-seat loss. The GOP could plausibly claim—and did claim, after the fact—that the loss of the Senate in 1986 was a fate beyond their control.

One can't help wondering, though, what might have happened if the cast of candidates had been different: if the Republicans had been defending their Senate majority with attractive, sophisticated young incumbents capable of presenting an appealing message in an appealing way. What they had was something different. The 1980 landslide had swept in half a dozen weak Republican candidates who could not have won on their own and never quite figured out how to use their first term to guarantee themselves a second. Paula Hawkins, in Florida, never shook off the lightweight reputation she acquired at the start of her term by serving gourmet dishes at a luncheon meeting she had scheduled to denounce food stamp fraud. Jeremiah Denton of Alabama embarrassed some constituents and startled others by casting his crusade for moral regeneration in terms that were sometimes profane and often crude. Mack Mattingly of Georgia, a typewriter salesman who had never run for office before 1980, struck even some of his own party's observers as being in over his head. After five years these senators had not built any semblance of a political organization in their home states. Mattingly, in fact, boasted that he did not need one. He felt ideology and media would accomplish for him what used to be accomplished by the painstaking performance of favors and cultivation of allies. That turned out not to be true.

Perhaps the greatest contrast in talent, though, was in South Dakota, where James Abdnor had ridden to victory in 1980 on a tide of Reagan votes and resentment against his Democratic opponent, Sen. George McGovern. Abdnor was an appealing enough politician by old-fashioned South Dakota standards. He was friendly and unpretentious. It was hard to find a café in the smallest county in the state where he had not turned up for breakfast at least once in a thirty-year political career. But Abdnor, at age sixty-three, was ill-equipped for a modern campaign even in an old-fashioned midwestern state. He was inarticulate and poorly informed on most issues that reached beyond the familiar territory of water and agriculture. He had never played a significant role in the legislative process, either as a senator or during four previous terms in the House. Without the advantage of the Reagan tide that he had enjoyed in 1980, he was not an easy candidate to sell in a tough Senate competition.

Democrat Tom Daschle, by contrast, represented the state of the art. From the day he arrived in Congress in 1979, after a yearlong campaign in which he rang 40,000 doorbells and won by 139 votes, Daschle had shown an uncanny instinct for the issues on which a political base could be built. He became the most conspicuous sponsor of a multibillion-dollar plan to expand credit to farmers. He was a tireless promoter of "gasohol," a gasoline substitute produced from grain grown in South Dakota fields. He became a defender of the cause of Vietnam veterans. And he was a zealot when it came to constituent service.

Abdnor spent time with constituents too; he devoted whole afternoons to conducting personal tours of the Capitol for visitors from South Dakota. But touches like that were no more than a friendly gesture for Abdnor. For Daschle they were a science. For that matter, so was politics. Jim Abdnor was a rancher who had managed without too much strain to get himself elected to a variety of offices over three decades. Tom Daschle was a politician. Winning elections was his job.

Abdnor was well financed in his 1986 campaign effort, and he had expert advice. After his halting performances in a series of debates and forums, his media consultants did what they could to turn his weaknesses into a virtue. "People say I'm not the best talker in the Senate," Abdnor confessed in a beguilingly modest television commercial. "Heck, I'm not a great dancer, either. But I'm a great fighter for South Dakota." It was a good idea, and it won back some of the votes that had been slipping away. In the end, though, Abdnor's confession and his efforts to link Daschle with unpopular liberal causes fell short by nearly 10,000 votes.

It is possible, under the right circumstances, for a party to erase the damage inarticulate candidates do to their own causes. But, given a choice, it is better to have candidates who can talk in the first place. Could a more talented incumbent than Jim Abdnor have pulled out 10,000 extra votes and held the Senate seat in South Dakota? Yes. Could an entire crew of more impressive incumbents have bucked history and kept the Senate in Republican hands in 1986? Perhaps. We will never know.

Ronald Reagan did not create the talent shortage that has made Republicans a long-term minority party in Congress. But in his way he added to it. In the fall of 1986, as the GOP struggled to avoid the Senate debacle that ultimately occurred, Reagan took to the road, investing some of his personal popularity in an effort to prop up shaky Republican senators. The effort was a failure. But the message Reagan delivered that fall offered some clues to the nature of the problem.

In speech after speech Reagan told audiences that the Democrats had made a mess of the country in the years before 1980, and that he and his Republican colleagues were the "cleanup crew" that had straightened it out. After six years as president and six years of Republican Senate control, he was presenting the GOP not as the nation's logical governing party, deserving of continued support, but as a team of watchdogs willing to perform the unpleasant chore of governing the country in order to prevent the Democratic villains from returning to power and making a mess again. After nearly two full terms as head of the American government, Reagan had not lost his desire to ridicule that government, hold himself apart from it, and ask the voters to help him protect them from the absurdities of the political system he had been chosen to lead. The message appealed to the nation's natural skepticism about politics and politicians. But it was not a very good way to argue for a Senate majority. When a house is messy, its residents welcome a cleanup crew. When the place is clean again, they thank the crew, pay them, and let them leave. If the crew wants to stay, it has to offer reasons why it is still needed. The Republicans did not do that in 1986.

For all the shortcomings of the national Democratic party over the last two decades, this much must be said for its candidates: They wanted to be the government. They were not embarrassed about being the government. And so, through the 1970s and 1980s, the Democratic party strengthened itself as the vehicle for people who grew up interested in government and politics and wanted to make a career of them. And the Republican party was forced to compete as the vehicle of those who felt that government was a dirty business and that they were demeaning themselves to take part in it.

As the 102nd Congress takes office in 1991, the U.S. House of Representatives has been controlled by Democrats for thirty-six years without interruption. Republicans held the U.S. Senate from 1980 to 1986 but then lost it decisively and have failed in two attempts to win it back. There are thirty-one state legislatures controlled by Democrats and only five by Republicans (thirteen are split, one is nonpartisan). More than 60 percent of all state legislators sit on the Democratic side of the aisle. All this in an era when Republicans are the clear majority party in presidential elections.

I have already mentioned some of the standard explanations for this state of affairs. There is the argument from gerrymandering— Democrats have been in control during the reapportionment battles at the start of each decade, and they simply drew the districts to perpetuate their advantages in the legislatures and in the U.S. House.

There is the argument from simple incumbency—the self-promotional tools available to the officeholder now make incumbents extraordinarily difficult to dislodge, and the party that holds the majority has been all but frozen into power. There is the separation-of-powers argument—voters deliberately choose Republican presidents and Democratic legislatures because they feel more comfortable when neither party has a monopoly.

Each of these arguments has some plausibility, but each is unsatisfying in its own way. For every state in which a Democratic majority redistricted in a blatantly partisan manner in the 1980s, there is one in which the process was bipartisan, or skewed in favor of incumbents on both sides, or where the requirements of one person, one vote, reined in any temptation for the Democratic party to behave irresponsibly. There is no question that gerrymandering has given Democrats a few extra seats in the U.S. House and in scattered legislatures, but it does not come close to explaining the massive advantage they have maintained in so many diverse places over so many years.

Nor is it sufficient to argue that Democrats have perpetuated their majorities simply by lavishing public relations weapons on their incumbents. Incumbency is a critical force in congressional elections. But if it were the only critical force, the results would be radically different in contests where no incumbent was running. Republicans would start to win a disproportionate number of open seats and gradually make inroads on the majority. In fact, nothing like this has happened. In the four congressional elections of Ronald Reagan's presidency—1982, 1984, 1986, and 1988—a total of sixty-six Democratic seats came open through the departure of an incumbent. Republicans won fewer than a quarter of them: sixteen, to be exact. Meanwhile, Democrats were winning sixteen of the sixty-seven seats left open by Republicans. It amounts to a standoff. Strip away incumbency and you still do not find any consistent pattern of Republican progress.

The separation-of-powers theory is hard to refute. Anybody who wants to believe that the average person walks into the polling booth intent on balancing Republican representation in the White House with Democratic representation at other levels is entitled to believe it. I have never done this myself, and I do not know anybody who has. It seems to me most people do the best they can to make what they consider a sensible choice for each office on the basis of the few relevant scraps of information available to them. The burden of proof on this issue lies with those who insist that some form of subtle electoral calculation is responsible for Democrats winning so many elections. It is hard to think of what the proof might be.

A less radical version of this theory holds that voters balance their tickets more or less inadvertently. It is not that they have any abstract preference for divided government, the theory goes, but that they see presidents and congressmen as serving different purposes. People want presidents to reflect their own instincts and values, and Republicans come closer to doing that for a majority of the electorate. Congressmen, in contrast, are judged by how well they deliver— how good they are at providing federal money for the district and personal service for the constituency. Democrats are the ones who know how to do that, and voters reward them accordingly.

This is the most reasonable of all the arguments so far. But if we take it seriously, it returns us to the issue of candidates and talent. Why, of two candidates running for Congress, would the Democrat have a better sense of how to establish his competence at using the resources of office for the benefit of the voter and the community? Democrats obviously have something going for them. What is it?

It is this: The Democratic party is the party of government in the United States, or, more precisely, the party that believes in government and communicates that belief to nearly everyone who follows politics. As such, it is the obvious magnet for people who think running for office is worth the considerable sacrifice it entails. Those are the sorts of people who get elected at this juncture in American politics. They are the ingredients of a majority.

No one should deny that government bashing can be an effective campaign weapon. But under our current political system, in which the success of any party depends on the steady recruitment of full-time talent, government bashing is no way to build a majority. Even if Reagan's rhetoric had not made careers in politics less appealing to young Republicans, however, the GOP would have a problem winning elections below the national level. Reagan's views merely reinforced a prejudice that already exists among young people who choose to vote Republican.

Consider two bright, glib, personable twenty-five-year-olds with a natural talent for salesmanship. One is a liberal Democrat who sees government as a benevolent instrument of social policy. The other is a conservative Republican who agrees with the national

GOP leadership that government itself is a large part of the problem. Which one is more likely to put his talents to work selling himself to the voters as a candidate for public office? Which one is apt to decide that it is more respectable (as well as more lucrative) to sell insurance or real estate or computers?

This, in simplified form, is the dilemma that confronts Republicans whose job it is to recruit candidates for office. They must persuade people who do not think very highly of government to drop what they are doing and spend months maneuvering for a chance to become part of it. That is not an impossible task, and there are years when it can be done rather well. When there is a liberal Democratic president to arouse conservative resentment all over the country, a decent supply of Republican talent shows up in many places with the zeal and energy to turn the enemy out of office. In 1978 and 1980, years of Democratic control in Washington, Republicans came up with strong congressional candidates in numerous districts they had never to expected to win.

But Democrats are, in general, much less dependent on favorable years and galvanizing issues to bring out candidate talent. It wasn't any resentment or single-issue cause that led Robert Torricelli to run for Congress in New Jersey in 1982, or Jim Jontz in Indiana in 1986. They were doing what they had wanted to do all their lives.

When Torricelli was in his teens, he was working for the Bergen County Democratic organization. In college he ran three campaigns for class president, renting a sound truck to attract voters. After graduate school he went to work for New Jersey's governor, became executive director of the state Democratic party, and got a job on the staff of Vice-President Walter Mondale. Then, when the incumbent in a Bergen County congressional district began to look vulnerable, Torricelli moved in, campaigned door to door for months, and beat him.

Jontz was only a year out of college when he decided he wanted a seat in the Indiana legislature, and he was not deterred by the fact that the Republican incumbent in his district was the House majority leader. He won by two votes. From that day on, through twelve years as a state legislator, Jontz worked at politics full-time and overtime, living contentedly as a bachelor on his legislative salary of less than $20,000 a year. When he ran for Congress in 1986, his Republican opponent liked to say that Jontz was a pro-family candidate and a pro-jobs candidate, but he had never had a family and he had never had a job. It was a clever line, but Jontz won the election.

Anybody is free to object, of course, that there are conservative Republicans just like this in any legislative body—people who love politics even as they distrust government. In the U.S. House, there are Georgia's Newt Gingrich, the long-range electoral strategist and minority whip, and Vin Weber of Minnesota, who has warned conservatives that "you can't govern the country without being political." The point is, though, that Weber and Gingrich are exceptions. Professionals such as Torricelli and Jontz are the norm on the Democratic side; dozens of others fit a similar career pattern. It does not take long to make up a lengthy list of congressional districts like the one Jontz represents, districts that are habitually Republican but have been captured by a superior Democratic talent. It is difficult to come up with even a handful of Democratic districts that talent has placed in the Republican column.

The election that cost Republicans the Senate was the last congressional election of the 1980s that attracted any significant national attention. In 1988, amid the noise and bad feeling of the Bush-Dukakis presidential contest, the Senate and House campaigns were scarcely noticed. When the voting was over, and it turned out that there had been virtually no change in the political makeup of either chamber, it was widely pointed out that the vote had been more than anything else a triumph of incumbency.

Over the next two years, the issues of incumbency and prolonged tenure forced their way into political campaigns to a remarkable extent. The residual American resentment against politics and politicians staged one of its cyclical appearances at the center of national debate. Candidates for Congress and for a host of state and local offices in 1990 based their campaigns on a "throw the bums out" argument. Three states used the initiative process that year to pass laws limiting tenure in legislative office, and one of those laws— Colorado's—was written to apply to Congress as well. In the end, though, the incumbency issue was much more effective at generating media coverage than it was at defeating incumbents. Once again, more than 96 percent of all House members who sought reelection achieved it, and the voters unseated only one U.S. senator, a smaller number than in any election in the past thirty years.

As paradoxical as all this seems, it should not puzzle us very long. A professional who devotes twenty years of his life to politics and reaches its highest levels of success should be able to manipulate the tools of incumbency with sufficient skill to deflect virtually any public issue, even incumbency itself. The term-limitation activists are right in one important respect: given the money and resources any member of Congress now possesses, it is virtually impossible to defeat him unless he is indicted or commits some other unforgivable political blunder.

In other words, the way to win a seat in Congress is to hold one already. The way for a party to control Congress is to offer incumbents in a majority of the districts. But to say this is to ignore the most important questions. How did these incumbents get there in the first place? How did the majority party manage to maneuver itself into that enviable position? Did it succeed by mirroring the ideological sentiments of the voters? By the chicanery of gerrymandering? Was it the innocent beneficiary of a subliminal American preference for divided government? Or did it, as the party that is not embarrassed to govern, install itself in power the hard way: year by year, seat by seat, candidate by candidate, the natural majority by virtue of ambition and talent?

12

Careerists in Action

The professional talent that has built a Democratic majority in Congress over the past twenty years has succeeded equally well at changing the nature of the institution. It has transformed Congress into a place whose members arrive young and independent, make it the consuming passion of their lives in their most productive working years, and leave only when they reach retirement age or feel the temptation to seek some higher office.

Almost every election year, it is true, at least one impressive and ambitious young member of Congress startles his colleagues by announcing that he has had enough. The burden of the job is greater than the reward, and he is going home. For a short time these premature retirees inspire minor media events, and are pursued by newspapers and television reporters eager to document a growing trend of congressional burnout. The typical member under the age of fifty can just about guarantee himself more national media attention by quitting than he ever got by legislating. Taken as a series, these decisions and the accompanying news coverage leave the impression of a relentless congressional life that devours its most talented young people and leaves aging time servers to write the laws that need to be written. It sounds believable.

Until one stops to consider what it is that makes events newsworthy. News is the unusual. If the retirement of young, healthy congressmen finds its way into print and onto television, common sense dictates that it must be a rare occurrence. And it is. In 1988 in a House of Representatives composed of 435 people, there were exactly two voluntary retirements by members under the age of sixty. One of those was by a member who had been hounded for years about misusing his campaign funds; the other was by a member who expected an appointment to state office. In the one-hundred-member Senate, there were also two retirees. Both of them—Paul Trible of Virginia and Lawton Chiles of Florida—ran for governor within two years after going home. They did not leave politics any more than the vast majority of their colleagues who decided to remain in Congress.

This should come as a surprise to nobody. When one considers everything it takes just to win election to Congress these days—the raising of half a million dollars or more, the yearlong disruption of personal and professional time, the indignities of hand-to-hand campaigning—it is obvious that very few people would make such an effort for an office they did not intend to keep a long time. The last two decades have not only brought drastic changes in the working life of the average member of Congress but also served up a generation of members who enjoy that life and are not going to burn out very quickly.

Before 1970 most members found that legislating was not all that difficult a job. It was a relatively cloistered enterprise. Committee meetings were mostly closed to the press and to the public. Many crucial votes in the House were anonymous—no record was kept of how any individual voted. Campaign finance was essentially the member's business; there were no national reporting requirements, and few questions were asked. No significant disclosure of one's personal finances was required.

Perhaps more important, there was no public expectation that a junior member show up at home every couple of weekends to demonstrate how close he was to the voters. If he chose to stay in Washington and keep a relatively low profile back home, chances were he could get away with it. Neither national party worked very hard to turn up vulnerable incumbents on the other side, and the rival party campaign committees did little more than funnel cash to their own incumbents. There were marginal districts, of course.

Some members from competitive areas have always had to fight for reelection. But for the average member before 1970, service in Congress promised not only the likelihood of long tenure but civilized hours and a modest work load as well.

Over the following decade the rules of the game changed. The processes of Congress—and sometimes the members' private lives—were opened up to press and public. Dozens of pressure groups began watching members on a day-to-day basis. Spotting weak incumbents became a full-time job for the parties and for a burgeoning community of political action committees in Washington. Nearly any House member could still get reelected if he dedicated himself to doing so, but there were few free rides left.

The 1970s were a transition period. Many members who started serving in the "easy years" saw the demands multiply and opted for an early exit, helped along by generous pension benefits that took effect in 1972. For a period of several elections ending in the early 1980s, there was a substantial turnover. But that transition is over. Few serious candidates for Congress start out at this point with any illusions about what the job entails. If they do, the campaign itself is enough to disabuse them.

There are thousands of politicians around the country who decide every year that a career in Congress is not for them. But they do not make that decision after two years or four years in office. They make it in advance, knowing what is involved. Congressional burnout still exists. But it isn't a midcareer problem anymore. It happens at the starting gate. The ones who decide to run for Congress in full knowledge of the sacrifices are very much like the people we have been meeting at all other levels of the process. Congress is the object of their ambitions, the focus of their single-minded professionalism. They like running for office, and they like staying in office. The means they have found for staying in office are an important part of the story of congressional change over the past generation in America.

Through the 1980s the U.S. House acquired and came to deserve a reputation as an "incumbent protection society" that organized itself in every possible way to guarantee the reelection of its members every two years. The devices used in this process are no secret: self-promotional newsletters, mailed regularly to thousands of households at taxpayer expense; weekend trips to the district virtually year-round, funded through regular staff allowances; constituent service offices, as many as three or four in some districts, organized to make friends with voters one at a time by tracing their lost social security checks, finding out which sorts of federal loans they qualify for, helping them obtain traffic lights at dangerous corners, and practicing countless other forms of vote-gaining kindness; committee hearings in the district, convened for the nominal purpose of investigating public policy but designed to provide favorable publicity for the member in whose constituency they are held.

The system works. Federal funds provide so many effective ways of cultivating the electorate that hardly anybody with the wits and energy to get elected to Congress once has much reason to fear being defeated thereafter. In the 1980s, as House members were perfecting the various tools of incumbency that had been developed for them over the previous decade, the number of those defeated at the polls dropped virtually to zero. In 1986, out of 391 members seeking reelection, 385 achieved it. In 1988, 408 wanted another term, and 402 were rewarded. Even at the height of the anti-incumbent fervor of 1990, 391 out of 407 incumbents were reelected.

To the Republican dissidents in the House, these numbers have always symbolized a partisan fix: a successful effort by a permanent and arrogant Democratic majority to stifle competition for the seats that maintain it. But the real explanation for the incumbent protection system is not the temptations of partisanship but the psychology of the careerist. The House is the way it is because so many of its individual members need to win. They have made enormous sacrifices to get where they are, and if they lose they have no significant professional lives at home to return to.

Tom Daschle is one of the most successful and talented of the modern congressional careerists. He has spent virtually his entire adult life employed by, running for, and serving in Congress. When he was discharged from the Air Force in 1972, he went to work as an aide to James Abourezk, who was about to become South Dakota's Democratic senator, and he left Abourezk only to run for the House himself six years later. He was open and honest about his careerism; asked in the spring of 1978 to list his occupation, he wrote "full-time candidate."

Daschle's narrow election that fall brought to the House an exuberant thirty-year-old Democrat with enormous talent, energy, and charm, six years of seasoning in the legislative process, and an unabashed ambition to make Congress his home. There was no reason for ambivalence about his job; it was the one form of work he had trained himself to do. His task was to make sure he would be able to stay. And Daschle set about that task with a creativity bordering on genius. When it came to constituent service, he was the state of the art. A fair number of the people who contacted his office asking for help got it in a form they did not expect—not just a letter or a phone call but a personal visit from their boyish congressman, offering to straighten things out or just talk them over. While Daschle was in Washington, his traveling office—a large van with his name painted in big letters on the side—made an endless circuit of his district's 116 towns and villages, stopping in front of each local post office or café.

The results of Daschle's campaign for a second House term must have looked like a misprint to outsiders who saw them in the paper the morning after election day. In the face of the 1980 Republican landslide that gave Ronald Reagan an enormous victory in South Dakota and unseated Democratic Sen. George McGovern, Daschle had defeated his GOP challenger by a margin of nearly 2 to 1. It was as dramatic a demonstration as any in modern times of what incumbency can mean in the hands of a dedicated careerist willing to use it for all it is worth.

It is possible to be an effective careerist politician and an effective legislator at the same time; Tom Daschle proved that, as have countless other members of Congress in his generation. What is difficult is to perform those tasks and maintain the same personal relations with colleagues that marked the Congress of a generation ago.

Most modern members of Congress do not know one another very well. This is a truth that journalists seem never to want to learn. Faced with the task of explaining Congress to readers and viewers, they nearly always fall back on the cliché that it is an institution governed by the easy male camaraderie of an Elks Club or a college fraternity. The Senate is still portrayed regularly in bad newspaper feature stories as the "world's most exclusive men's club." When a member is censured, or humiliated on the floor, it is invariably written that such an act constitutes a dramatic break with the institution's clublike atmosphere.

Whether the Senate ever fit this definition is hard to say. Reading some of the better-informed work of the 1950s, one gets the feeling that it might indeed have been a club. William S. White, perhaps the closest observer of Senate life in those days, wrote that a successful senator had to be "in harmony with the special integrity of the institution—the integrity of its oneness." More persuasive yet is a black-and-white photograph of three Democratic senators in an informal 1954 baseball game—Henry M. Jackson batting, John F. Kennedy catching, and Mike Mansfield umpiring behind the plate.

That picture evokes a close-knit social world, an institution of senators who knew one another well, worked and played together, and thought of politics as a team game. Maybe it was misleading even at the time. But by the 1980s, clearly, it had become a relic of another era. The Senate had evolved into an institution where there was little time to think, close personal relationships were difficult to achieve, and individual rights, not community feeling, constituted the most precious commodity.

Edmund S. Muskie entered the Senate fraternity, such as it was, with the huge Democratic class of 1958. Some of his fellow freshmen of that year became his closest personal friends. But by the time he left the institution, in 1980, he was talking in very unclubby terms. "You don't see the other senators very often," Muskie complained toward the end, "and you rarely get a chance to discuss serious issues with them. Days go by when you don't run into more than one or two senators." Thad Cochran, the Republican from Mississippi, arrived in the Senate just as Muskie was leaving it. He noticed the same thing. "There is very little socializing here," he said during his first term. "If I have any free time I spend it with my staff. You begin to feel introverted and self-centered." When Senate Democrats began scheduling an annual weekend retreat in West Virginia during the 1980s, it was not a reflection of comradeship. It was a reflection of their desperate desire to find some time to talk to one another.

The life of the congressional careerist, House or Senate, is an overscheduled one. It is a life whose working days (and those are most of the days in the year) are governed by the sort of events listed on the 3-by-5-inch file cards that nearly every member receives as he leaves the office the night before: Breakfast at seven-thirty with officials of a trade association who happen to be in Washington that week; an hour in the office starting at nine, signing mail and looking up occasionally to hear what the legislative assistant has to say about the upcoming business in the chamber; three subcommittees meeting simultaneously at ten, impossible for one person to keep track of in any conscientious way; lunch with constituents in the members' dining room, punctuated by sudden departures for roll-call votes two or three times during the meal; a full-committee markup session at two, interrupted by several more roll-call votes; a drop-by at a trade association reception at five, followed by another at a fund-raiser for a colleague. Home, perhaps, at eight.

It is not a life that lends itself to clubbiness, or even to serious conversation. Why have members of Congress chosen to lead that life, and not some other? The answer to this question has to begin outside the halls of Congress. If members feel harassed and overscheduled, preoccupied day after day with the demands and peculiarities of strangers, unable to establish any meaningful community with their true colleagues, then they feel some of the things being felt by people all over the country who have never touched politics. Congress is not a small town anymore; neither are many small towns. Most Americans of middle age feel some nostalgia for a simpler time in which life seemed to involve a manageable number of relationships with familiar people. To that extent, Congress is the societal mirror its defenders have always wanted it to be.

But that is only part of the story. Congressional life has been altered by some developments less traumatic to everyday American life. Predominant among them are jet planes and air-conditioning. Before 1960 most members of Congress arrived on the train every January and went home on the train every summer, when the humidity in Washington became unbearable. In between, most of them did not spend much time in their districts. They lived those six months in Washington together, staying in hotels, eating and drinking together at night, developing the relationships that make the awkward business of legislating more natural and comfortable.

The early 1960s marked a rather abrupt change, as Congress began meeting more or less year-round. This was partly because the government they were creating was in turn creating more work for them. It was partly because air-conditioning had made humidity irrelevant. And it was partly because jet travel had made it possible for them to spend long weekends at home during the legislative season, shortening the week in Washington to three days and forcing it to extend further into the fall.

Members of Congress do not spend most of their weekends playing golf or poker with one another in Washington anymore. They spend them back in the state or district, listening to constituents and trying to explain themselves to the electorate. And three-day Washington workweeks are simply too crowded with detail to permit much of the human social contact that used be crucial to the legislative life. In that respect, what has happened to Congress is not much different from what has happened to the city council in Concord, California. What used to be a close-knit group of people who lived, worked, and socialized with one another has become a corps of individualist professionals focused on their own careers and goals, on their personal legislative agendas and local constituent pressures. The same pressures operate on political careerists at any level of government. Once the commitment is made to holding office as a full-time occupation and preoccupation, camaraderie becomes a luxury.

Senators and representatives have become magnificent responders. The flights that bring them home on weekends guarantee them a full array of constituent problems, complaints, and suggestions. Those same flights bring constituents to the Capitol, precluding any real insulation from constituent pressure even within the halls of Congress. It is sometimes written that members of Congress, blessed as they are with a variety of free privileges and perquisites denied to the rest of us, have lost touch with ordinary experiences. In fact, the opposite is true. Congressmen may not have to pay the full cost of an airplane flight or a restaurant meal, but when it comes to hearing constituent complaints, they are tuned in fifty-two weeks a year.

And they listen. Consider what Gaylord Nelson, the three-term Wisconsin senator, said shortly after he left office in 1981: "Every organization in America that has an interest in legislation—and that's all of them—can get here in four hours. Some days I had somebody from the state in my office every fifteen minutes. Seventy percent of my time, or maybe 80 percent, was spent on nonlegislative matters. Constituents judge their senators on how much crap the senator is sending them. The less legislating and the more campaigning you do the better legislator you are perceived to be." One can contrast that with what William S. White wrote in the 1950s about George Mahon, the veteran congressman and appropriations specialist from Texas. "A Mahon at work in the House," White wrote, "is a thousand miles removed from any partisan political stump."

If there is one word that describes what the Congress of the 1950s had that the current Congress does not have, it is *insulation*. Southern Democrats such as George Mahon in the House, James

Eastland and Harry F. Byrd, Sr., in the Senate, and Republicans such as Sen. Styles Bridges of New Hampshire and Rep. Clarence Brown, Sr., of Ohio all did their legislative work insulated from day-to-day constituent demands. That was not necessarily good; Eastland and Byrd used their insulation to deny even the most modest requests by southern blacks for equal legal treatment. But whatever one may think of the product, it is undeniable that most of the legislators of the 1950s came to Washington to do as they saw fit. Today's legislators do not have that freedom on controversial issues—or at least they do not act as if they have it.

In part, as I have said, this lack of insulation is the consequence of technology. But it is also the consequence of the values that members of Congress bring with them to Washington. The more a seat in Congress means to its occupant—the more of his energy and resources he has had to commit to win it—the more time he is going to spend maneuvering to secure a second term in the job. It is this psychological commitment to remaining in office that accounts for the fund-raisers senators begin holding five years before they are up for reelection, and the $5 million campaign treasuries many of them amass when the voting is still two years away. "The Senate is on a hair trigger," Missouri Republican John Danforth complained one day in the midst of his first campaign for reelection. "There's an absence of a long view. People are running for reelection the day they arrive."

Dale Bumpers, the Arkansas Democrat who arrived in 1974, two years before Danforth, said exactly the same thing. "The Founding Fathers gave senators six-year terms," he said, "so they could be statesmen for at least four years and not respond to every whim and caprice. Now a senator in his first year knows any vote could beat him five years later. So senators behave like House members. They are running constantly."

An investment heavy enough to acquire a seat in Congress is, to put it simply, an investment too heavy to risk squandering through political inattention. So members of Congress do what they must to protect the investment—they respond. They may not be statesmen, but they have refined responsiveness to a high art.

The modern congressional generation has not only practiced responsiveness as a political technique; it has imposed it on the people it selects for leadership. Legislative leaders are required now to defer to their members, the people who elect them. Irving Stolberg learned that lesson the hard way in 1989 in the Connecticut House of Representatives. People with much more famous names have learned it just as painfully in Washington. Robert Byrd, the Senate Democratic leader, may have been thinking about these changes late one summer night in 1980 as he stood on the floor trying desperately to arrange a time the next Monday when the Senate could vote on the following year's budget resolution. One senator after another announced that a particular time would be inconvenient. Byrd was reduced to writing all the preferences on a yellow legal pad, a process that made him look more like a man sending out for sandwiches than the leader of a national deliberative body.

It was a small but appropriate symbol of what Senate leadership was becoming, and of what it has become even more clearly in the years since. The leader has to be elected by the membership. They are his constituents. If he does not please them, he does not remain a leader. Byrd himself had become a leader in the Senate by performing endless small favors for his colleagues: keeping them up to date about when a vote was to take place, for example, or postponing the vote if they could not be there. Those favors were the political basis of his twelve-year career as the leader of Senate Democrats. But they also placed a burden of personal favors on all leaders of both parties who have served since.

Legislative leaders have always performed favors, of course. Lyndon Johnson performed more than his share when he was majority leader of the Senate in the 1950s. But in exchange for those favors, Johnson expected members to defer to him on the decisions he considered important, and nearly all of them did. No one has dominated the Senate like Johnson in the three decades since he gave up his leadership to become vice-president. That is not only because no one of Johnson's ability has emerged; it is because no one would be allowed to dictate to his colleagues as Johnson did. In transferring the reins of leadership to the deferential Mike Mansfield of Montana upon Johnson's departure in 1961, the Senate was foreshadowing the egalitarianism that would come to mark virtually all legislative bodies in America.

House leaders underwent their own trial of responsiveness in more dramatic fashion during the 1970s. The huge new class of

House Democrats brought in by the Watergate landslide of 1974 made immediate demands on their leadership, not so much for personal favors but for influence that newcomers had not had in the institution in earlier years.

The events of late 1974 in the House of Representatives are legendary in modern congressional history: four of the most powerful committee chairmen stripped of their jobs; committees and subcommittees reorganized to give the most junior members more chances to participate; "open meeting" requirements expanded to cover the most delicate aspects of the legislative process. Countless articles and at least one book have been written about those events and the young congressmen who orchestrated them. They took place, of course, in the immediate aftermath of Watergate and the Nixon resignation, and reflected the prevailing national distaste for government secrets and hostility to senior political figures. They were, as has been said so often, a revolt against authority.

But what seems equally important about the rebels of 1974, more than fifteen years later, is that they were young people who had gotten themselves elected to important office, however improbably, and were determined to organize their work in a way that would preserve their good fortune as far as possible into the future. That required, at a minimum, persuading leaders to take an interest in the careers and political needs of junior members whose concerns had never been very important in the institution before. It required responsiveness. And not all the House leaders of the mid-1970s were able or willing to provide it.

The seventy-five new House Democrats who showed up in Washington in December of 1974 insisted on meeting with all the major committee chairmen before agreeing to support their continued tenure in office. All of them came, but septuagenarians W. R. Poage of Agriculture, Wright Patman of Banking, and F. Edward Hebert of Armed Services made a terrible impression: Hebert addressed the newly elected members of the House as "boys and girls." All three were unseated.

In some ways the speakership of the House became a stronger institution during the 1970s and 1980s. The newcomers of the 1970s weakened the senior chairmen who had dominated the legislative agenda in the previous decades, and the Speaker could now control the chairmen on a variety of important issues. At the same time, though, the Speaker had less authority over the junior members themselves. He had to cater to their needs and to deliver for them, both inside and outside the institution.

Carl Albert of Oklahoma, who was Speaker in the mid-1970s, never really understood what was going on. He had spent thirty years learning to operate in a House where the function of leaders was to make decisions within a small and restricted circle of influential colleagues. It had never occurred to him that the rank and file, especially the most junior among them, were his constituents. And they made life miserable for him. Before the 1975 congressional session was over, Albert announced that he would not be running for reelection to the House in 1976. He was going back to Oklahoma, where he was appreciated.

Every House leader since then has known perfectly well what he has to do to remain a leader. He must promote the career goals of the Democrats who placed the gavel in his hand. Tip O'Neill had spent two and a half decades in the same closely held House that Albert knew, but when he assumed the speakership in 1977, it was with the vows of democratization and responsiveness that Albert had never memorized. And he kept them. The House schedule was changed to allow, virtually year-round, the long weekends at home that careerist newcomers found vital to political survival. The legislative activists among the junior Democratic cohort were given prominence as heads of task forces created on an ad hoc basis to press for the passage of important pieces of legislation.

The House was coming to be an institution where leaders knew their place, and, for the most part, accepted it. But in the years after that, an additional demand was imposed on them, and this too had an important effect on the life of the chamber. The leadership not only had to respond to its constituency on the inside; it had to portray itself attractively on the outside. The Speaker had to sell himself to the public as a national figure.

That Tip O'Neill should have been the Speaker to preside over this change ranks as one of the great ironies of modern congressional history. No Speaker was ever a less plausible media celebrity. O'Neill spent nearly a quarter-century in the House actively avoiding any sort of publicity. Inarticulate in public speech and ignorant of the details of legislative business, he rarely spoke to reporters, even on a one-to-one basis. He practiced an insider's politics, talking strategy with close friends over poker, golf, or dinner at a Washington restaurant. His public presence was reserved for his Massachusetts constituents; otherwise, he tried very hard to attract no attention at all. His approach to the media and publicity reflected the suspicions of a Boston ward politician.

That approach changed only a little during the first few years of O'Neill's speakership. When Ronald Reagan was elected president in November 1980, Speaker O'Neill was still anything but a household name in most of America. But Reagan's accession transformed O'Neill's job and with it the nature of modern House leadership. Because Reagan's victory had given the Republicans control of the Senate, O'Neill was the one remaining symbol of Democratic power to the Washington media, which needed such a presence to present "the other side" in simple terms. If he had not gone public, there would have been nobody to tell the Democratic story. So O'Neill told it. He began not only giving interviews but issuing statements on Reagan policy timed for the nightly news, and even reciting pungent one-liners drafted for him by a new press secretary whose explicit job it was to take the Speaker public.

The members themselves had begun to view the Speaker's national image as one more element in their electoral careers. That had never been true before. Members of the previous generation had worried about reelection too, but the popularity of Speaker Rayburn, or Speaker McCormack, did not enter into their calculations. They were not national figures. O'Neill was. As O'Neill prepared to retire in 1986, the House Democrats of the 1980s began looking at his heir apparent, Jim Wright of Texas, and asking a similar question: How is his reputation going to affect us? "We've got to polish Jim Wright up," one of them said a little nervously on the eve of O'Neill's retirement. "We want an important, persuasive national figure."

That was what they wanted. What they needed, however, or felt they needed, was something so basic it did not have to be said: They needed a Speaker of the House who did not embarrass them, one whose mistakes and weaknesses would not hurt them at home every election year. This was the standard that Wright failed to meet, and the result was his unprecedented retirement as Speaker and departure from the House in the spring of 1989, only two years after he had assumed the job.

The Washington journalism of that season was dominated by accounts of Wright's ethical conduct in office: the questionable marketing of his book to lobbyists in lieu of asking them for campaign contributions; the employment of his wife in a lucrative, less-than-onerous job by a Fort Worth developer interested in legislation; the intervention by Wright in behalf of his savings-and-loan allies to amend a savings-and-loan bill in ways that will ultimately cost the public billions of dollars. But the unraveling of Wright's House career with such bizarre speed had only a little to do with the details of those charges, or with the action of the House Ethics Committee in filing charges against the Speaker. The issue that sent Wright home to Fort Worth was the virtually unanimous conviction among House Democrats that he would be a political burden they could not bear, or at least did not want to bear, in the 1990 election.

Wright's most loyal defenders admitted that, even if they did not trumpet it about. While the Speaker was still fighting for survival, Rep. Pat Williams of Montana observed that "all politics is local, and local politics will be an influence on how members will vote, and ultimately determine the fate of the Speaker." Minnesota Democrat Tim Penny, less of a Wright loyalist, was considerably more blunt. "The political problem," he said, "is something that won't go away even if the ethics problems are solved. Whether we clear him or not, can we afford to have him presiding or not?"

The answer to that question was never really in doubt, even at the time Penny asked it, several weeks before Wright's resignation. Nor is it an unreasonable question. Congress is a political institution, and the House speakership, if cloaked in the trappings of judicious evenhandedness, is a political office. Those who elect the Speaker have a perfect right to replace him if they feel that is what their party needs.

The fall of Jim Wright marked a climax to fifteen years of changing relations between Congress and its leadership, years in which members by and large ceased to ask what they could do for the leaders and began to ask what the leaders could do for them. Forcing Wright's resignation—whatever merits it may have had as a public policy decision—was the inevitable action of members of Congress whose investment in their political careers, and determination to protect that investment, left them feeling no real choice.

Still, it is hard to look at the political imperative that governs life in Congress without asking, in a somewhat larger sense, Why? The reality, as we have seen, is that incumbents are in almost no jeopardy of defeat. Provided they take reasonable advantage of the many political accoutrements of office that Congress offers them—the free mailings and the trips home and the large staff of caseworkers—they should be all but invulnerable by the time the first reelection campaign comes around. And the overwhelming majority of them are.

Given these circumstances, we might logically expect members of Congress to grow complacent, immersing themselves in Washington life and easing up on the considerable physical burden of year-round responsiveness. In fact, the opposite is true. The young congressman who finds his reelection margins climbing after a term or two toward 70 percent, who no longer attracts credible or decently financed opposition, is not noticeably less obsessed with reelection than his rare colleague who is genuinely vulnerable. It is a remarkable fact of life in Congress that the most secure continue to organize their offices and schedules, to fight for committee assignments, and to evaluate their leadership as if their careers depended on it.

"The reelection issue is omnipresent," said Rep. Ron Wyden, an Oregon Democrat, after he had been reelected to his third term in 1984. "You see members with these cards in their pockets—right after the election—and it will say 2:00 to 5:00 P.M., fund-raising. The average member who gets 70 percent still tends to feel things are pretty volatile in his district."

Where do we look for the source of the political imperative? It is not to be found in the election returns or the mind of the constituency. Neither is it a product of the campaign finance system, the prevalence of television advertising, or the mischief of consultants. We have to look at the minds of the members.

"The reality," Tom Foley said a few years ago, before he succeeded Jim Wright as Speaker, "is that people who couldn't be blasted out of here with a cannon are as skittish about reelection as the rest of us." Foley thought the best way to explain it was to think of the modern congressman as a sort of political athlete, drawn into the competition by temperament, trained to measure his success by his winning percentage, and unable at age forty or forty-five to end his obsession with running even if he no longer needs to run very hard. "It's like the difference," he said, "between sports today and the old days of amateur sports, when gentlemen went out and performed the best they could. Now you have kids trained to swim from six months and practicing six hours a day. There's this terrific drive for performance. It's a little bit like that in Congress now. They have an abundance of ego strength, a certain amount of competitiveness, and a willingness to tolerate pain in order to achieve a goal. It doesn't fall into your lap. They are in that sense more driven than members were in the past."

And they are driven, more than anything else, to reelection. That explains a great deal of modern congressional behavior. But it does not explain everything. The fact is, a talented politician has time and energy for more than one obsession. For the brightest young members of Congress, ambition also works itself out in the drive for influence in the institution, for a say in public policy, for a seat in the important bargaining that is going on. To these people, the political imperative is both a means and an end, a test of performance and an opportunity to buy some free time to work on issues that might not mean much at the polls. It is a chance to write some of their own values and goals into public policy.

Dick Cheney, who served a decade in Congress before becoming defense secretary in 1989, was very much in this mold. As driven as any recent member of Congress, he was determined, from his first months in the House in 1979, to be a national public policy player. As a former White House chief of staff, he had an opportunity to be one. He continued working his Wyoming district far beyond the point of political security precisely because he had policy ambitions. "It's not the fear of losing that motivates me," Cheney said. "It's that the stronger my base is in Wyoming, the more freedom I have in Washington. If I got 70 percent last time, I can go on the Intelligence Committee. I couldn't do that if I got 51 percent. I can serve in the leadership. That requires a lot of time to devote to things that might be difficult politically."

Cheney was not unique. The modern Congress is full of members who maintain what may seem an unnecessary campaign zeal and throw themselves into the legislative process at the same time. It is worth recalling what Gary Hart said when he entered the Senate in 1975 from Colorado, fresh from five years devoted almost exclusively to political organizing and campaigning. It seemed natural to him to want to legislate with the same fanaticism that had marked his campaign work. "To me," he said, "the legislative process is a big kind of smorgasbord. And I don't just want to just eat the desserts or the salad. I want the whole thing."

Or, for a model of the way politics and legislation can coexist as twin obsessions in a single congressional career, one can look at Dan Glickman, a Democratic representative from Kansas. Glickman arrived in the House in 1977 at age thirty-two with what seemed like a tough assignment—holding a conservative Wichita-based district that had gone Democratic for him mainly through the inattention of its previous Republican incumbent. He needed to turn his office into a reelection machine; he also couldn't wait to inject himself into the legislative process at virtually every opportunity.

At the start of his career in the House, Glickman seemed to have amendments to just about every bill that came up. Many of them were transparently designed for political consumption in Wichita. He proposed denying members a hand-bound set of the *Congressional Record* for personal use, and pushed a proposal to remove elevator operators—patronage employees—from the elevators in the Capitol. Many of his amendments were accompanied by a barrage of press releases and local TV sound bites. They succeeded mainly in alienating his colleagues in the House.

That was the Glickman of 1977. The Glickman of 1987 presented an interesting contrast. His district was safe; he had long since discouraged any serious Republican competition. He was still a media hound, visible on Wichita television nearly every night, commenting on world events, discussing his legislative plans, making himself familiar to the statewide audience he needed to cultivate for a Senate campaign later on. "I am never too busy for local TV," he told a reporter. "Not ever. Period." And Glickman was still writing amendments and offering them with the all-purpose intensity he brought to the campaign process. But he wasn't a gadfly anymore: He was a serious and respected legislator. He had used his energy to write much of the federal law on commodity futures trading, to reform government debt collection, to investigate medical malpractice in the military, and to monitor the performance of the air traffic control system.

The evolution of Dan Glickman offers proof that the most frenetic, politically obsessed congressional careerist can become an effective legislator without giving up his political obsession. The two can coexist quite peacefully, and they do for dozens of members of the modern congressional generation.

Moreover, the careerist can find numerous opportunities to legislate in accordance with his own values and instincts without threatening the incumbency that remains first on his priority list. In Chapter 1 we met Glenn English of Oklahoma, the House Democrat who secured his district by agitating for higher wheat prices while carrying out his personal agenda by defending the Freedom of Information Act. His case is not unusual at all. Careerism is not incompatible with ideology; it is not even incompatible with idealism. When it comes to subjects that are not sensitive in the minds of constituents—and there is no shortage of such subjects—plenty of room for creativity exists.

The troubling question is not what the careerist system does to the individual. It is what it does to the institution as a whole, and to the creation of sensible public policy. This is not a question that has a simple answer.

The strongest piece of evidence on the discouraging side is the congressional budget process. In 1974, in an effort to gain some control over federal spending and over the deficit in particular, Congress enacted a complex new legislative procedure that includes separate budget committees in House and Senate and requires passage of an overall budget resolution governing spending and revenue goals for each fiscal year.

It is fair to say that the budget process has attracted the best young talent in both chambers of Congress. Throughout the 1980s the brightest and most articulate young House members fought for places on the Budget Committee. Yet the result of all this concern and good intention is depressingly familiar: A decade after the budget process was put in place, the deficit had ballooned to more than $200 billion, and Congress had enacted a law (Gramm-Rudman-Hollings) empowering the executive branch to lop off billions of dollars in spending across the board to compensate for congressional inability to act. The budget resolutions approved by both chambers each year had turned out to be charades in which the projected deficit was calculated just low enough to draw the requisite majority of votes for passage, regardless of whether those figures bore any relation to the expected economic reality.

It would be foolish to blame this massive failure of nerve solely on the budget committees, or even on the budget process. The enormous deficits of the 1980s resulted in large measure from the refusal of the Reagan and Bush administrations to accept tax increases; Congress could not fairly be expected to vote for a politically difficult tax increase if it was certain to die by presidential veto. Budget committees cannot be expected to vote for deficit reductions that stand no chance of passing on the floor. But to watch the House Budget Committee in action is to confront the failings of the modern

Congress in their most disturbing form: the best professional talent in American politics, publicly committed to solving a serious national problem, unable to make the slightest progress in dealing with it.

However sincere the intentions of their members, the budget committees are markets for the exchange of constituent interests, just as other congressional committees are. There is no culture of self-sacrifice, no set of customs through which members agree to deny their own constituents something in order to make some headway against the national deficit problem. However noble their antideficit rhetoric, Budget Committee members are there to speak up for the people who elect them. And why shouldn't they? Sacrifice, after all, requires a minimal level of confidence that the sacrifice will gain something. To deny one's constituents a tangible federal benefit—a public works project or a weapon built in the district or a cost-of-living increase for the elderly—and then to watch as others refuse to make that sacrifice, and the deficit is barely affected, is to be a chump. And even the smartest, most sincere members of Congress in the 1980s did not devote their lives to politics to turn into chumps at the sight of a large federal deficit. So the deficit did not go down.

One can grow similarly discouraged thinking about U.S. energy policy, and the legislative maneuvering that followed the massive increase in oil prices after 1973. In trying to do something sensible about energy, Congress became the victim of all the important institutional changes that were taking place within it: individualism, hyperresponsiveness of members and leaders, and the desire of virtually everyone for a share in the decision making.

It is not that Congress tried the wrong solution to the energy problems of that era; it tried no solution. Years of intense debate and legislative effort produced no consistent policy, not conservation or strict price controls or reliance on market forces. Any real effort in one of these directions was checked by pressure in behalf of one of the others. The United States, having imported 36 percent of its oil in 1973, was importing just about 50 percent five years later. By 1979 the price of oil had risen to $30 a barrel. The national economy was trying to cope with the frightening inflation rates and interest rates that were the inevitable result. The following year President Carter paid the penalty for this situation as he sought reelection at a moment of genuine national economic panic. Democrats as a whole paid the price as well by losing the Senate in the 1980 Reagan presidential sweep.

There was no energy crisis in the 1980s, and therefore no political agitation surrounding the subject. This had little to do with any public policy decision by Congress or the executive branch; the combination of OPEC's inability to limit its production and the American recession of the early 1980s increased supply and decreased demand to the point where oil prices came down and stayed there for a prolonged period. But for anyone who was around Congress in the worst years of the energy crisis, the prevailing policy confusion still stands as a symbol of modern congressional futility.

As of 1981 there were forty-three House and Senate subcommittees attempting to write national energy policy, with a combined membership of more than half the people serving in both institutions. This awkward profusion reflected the political demand of even the most junior members to be able to tell constituents they were involved in the issue. The job of congressional leaders was more to honor those demands than to broker a solution; the constituency for brokerage was always very small. Leaders operated at the margins of the underlying stalemate.

It was said countless times over those years that congressional inability to act on the energy crisis simply reflected the absence of any consensus in the society on energy issues. America was divided in stark terms between regions that produced energy and regions that consumed it; they wanted and needed different sorts of policies, and there was little basis for common ground. True enough. Still, it was equally true that the modern Congress, just beginning to take shape in the energy crisis years, was not structured to resolve or broker conflict in any way. Even the brightest, most creative members, focused as they were on their own political careers and legislative ambitions, seeing leadership as a support system rather than a voice of authority, were in no position to make much progress against a problem so complex and sensitive.

To write about Congress in those years, to watch a congressional debate on energy or the budget, and to consider the underlying supremacy of local politics and local demands, was to think once again about the insulated Congress of the 1950s, and the value of an institution whose members not only were politically secure but acted as if they realized it. A feeling of security did not guarantee wise

public policy—James Eastland and Harry F. Byrd, Sr., were proof
enough of that—but it did create a setting in which wise public policy
could be made, if those in charge had the judgment and persistence
to make it. Eastland and Byrd were in a position to say yes to the
solution of national problems in a national legislative institution. The
fact that they nearly always said no is not necessarily an argument
in favor of the system we have now.

By the mid-1980s members of Congress were beginning to talk
openly about a sort of paradox of talent, in which the membership
became more and more competent, and the institution more and
more inept. It was easy to find people who echoed the frustrations
of John Spratt, the young Rhodes scholar from South Carolina who
arrived in the House in 1982. "I ought to be able to protect my
constituents," Spratt said one day in his second term, "and the
system as a whole ought to be able to work out all the local self-
interests. But it doesn't."

In the months before Spratt uttered that complaint, Congress
had made its most dramatic confession of incompetence, passing the
Gramm-Rudman-Hollings law that directed the executive branch to
impose on an automatic basis the federal spending reductions that
could not be achieved through the normal legislative process. Never
had the essential problem of the modern Congress seemed clearer:
The changing character of the American political system had generated an unprecedented collection of electoral creativity, ambition,
and talent, and the presence of all that talent had made it impossible
for the institution to accomplish anything significant.

It had become clear that too many of the 535 representatives
and senators had locked themselves into a vicious circle of political
responsiveness. As national problems grew more complex and less
tractable, members of Congress sought to secure themselves in office
by focusing on local interests and demands. However, the more they
pursued this strategy, the further they sank into stalemate on national issues, fostering public disappointment and discontent with
the institution as a whole. The members, growing ever more concerned about their political survival, responded with still further
efforts at local responsiveness, which in turn generated even more
deadlock, seemingly with no end in sight.

The argument that careerism has made statesmanship impossible is a powerful one. Yet it does not explain all that has happened
in Congress since careerism began to take hold.

In the fall of 1986, after more than five years of work, Congress rewrote the federal tax code in a way that not only reduced rates for individuals and corporations but also eliminated a whole generation of deductions, credits, and preferences favorable to myriad interest groups that had contributed heavily to the campaigns of the members. The passage of this bill, however, was not a case of voting for constituent demands over special-interest pressure; every available survey showed that the electorate was profoundly uninterested in the entire question of tax reform. And the pressure groups were profoundly interested; their lobbyists lined the hallways outside the House and Senate committee rooms in which the bill was being drafted.

There are some important particulars that help explain the passage of tax reform. The Reagan administration supported it, whereas Reagan had been, on balance, an obstacle on the deficit issue. And the low rates written into the bill on the Senate side (a maximum of 28 percent for corporations) did defuse some of the corporate opposition. Still, viewed from a few years' distance, the passage of tax reform does not seem to fit the simplistic model of an electorally obsessed Congress. An institution whose members were driven only by careerism and ambition could not have passed it. The case for it was in large measure intellectual, established over nearly five years by Sen. Bill Bradley, the New Jersey Democrat, without the benefit of any major interest-group assistance. Its tortuous passage through the House reflected more than anything the leadership of Dan Rostenkowski, the Ways and Means chairman, and the willingness of that body to accept the leadership he was determined to provide.

When we begin to think about the riddle of tax reform, we are drawn increasingly to the actions Congress took in the latter part of the 1980s that it did not politically "have to take": Enactment in 1986 of a massive immigration bill, one whose drafting and redrafting over five years prevoked the angriest possible confrontations of race, class, and ethnicity. Passage of a bill in 1988 to overhaul the nation's welfare system, despite a long legacy of failure to deal with the ideological cleavages that the issue inevitably created.

When the 100th Congress adjourned late one night at the end of October 1988, House Majority Leader Tom Foley proclaimed it "the most productive Congress in a generation." Perhaps he was exaggerating a bit. It was true, however, that for an assembly of people preoccupied with politics and personal advancement, they had done quite a lot. Besides passing the welfare bill, they had substantially rewritten U.S. trade law and approved catastrophic health insurance for the elderly (although they would repeal the latter within a year). They had approved all the appropriations bills on schedule for the first time in more than a decade. They went home believing that they had something to be proud of: They were legislators after all.

Within a few months, of course, they were casting considerable doubt on that judgment, embarrassing themselves and the institution with prolonged debate over raising their own pay and with the series of disclosures and political calculations that led to the resignations of Jim Wright and Tony Coelho. In the fall of 1990 they made an even worse spectacle of themselves, bickering with the White House over the budget, to the point of forcing a brief shutdown of the entire federal government. In those cases, careerist politics was again in full command.

But this odd combination of events seemed to symbolize the two-sidedness of the modern Congress and the modern congressman. As individuals and as a legislative body, they are capable of hard, disinterested work when they sense that their constituents are not watching too closely and their fortunes are not really on the line. This is the only sensible way I know to explain tax reform: Once it was clear that the electorate did not particularly care, the members surprised even themselves with their ability to write sensible public policy. They are, for the most part, creative people who regard Congress as a worthy place to exercise creative talent.

But they have invested so much in the profession of politics that they lack the self-confidence and the feeling of security that would allow them to exercise their creativity in the public interest with the public watching them. Without that feeling, a great deal of creativity is siphoned off into public relations and the other assorted gimmicks of careerism.

Congress is, more than ever, the product of the ambition and values of the people who have dedicated their lives to getting there. The careerist mentality is their route to success in politics and in life. It is also, for some, an unfortunate obsession and for others, with a genuine interest in solving problems, a confinement.

13

Self-Nomination

When we graduate to the top of the system, to presidential politics, we might reasonably assume that we have finally reached the land of the sovereign voter. The electorate may not know much about the people it is choosing for the Sioux Falls city commission, the Wisconsin legislature, or even the U.S. House of Representatives, but it cannot help hearing quite a bit about candidates for president.

To live through the spring of a presidential election year, in any state in this country, is to be bombarded with images, literal and figurative, of the aspiring nominees. Anybody who comes from a state holding a primary in the month or two after the process begins (and that is about half the states) will be the target of saturation advertising on TV in the days leading up to the vote. Those who live in states that are not part of this early-spring sweepstakes still find it the first item on the evening news, the lead story on the front page of the daily paper, and, at certain moments, the focus of neighborhood gossip.

These aren't state legislative candidates running in an informational vacuum. They are familiar people to us, whether we want them to be or not. We hear about Gary Hart's sex life. We keep seeing George Bush's family. We know about presidential candidates.

But what do we really know about them? Where do they come from? Who sent them? Why this handful of people and not some other handful? These are the critical questions about the presidential nominating process. And once we ask them, we find ourselves returning to the issues of personal ambition and career building in modern American politics. The presidential candidates, like the professionals we have been meeting throughout this book, are the products of self-nomination. They are there because they sent themselves.

It is true, of course, that virtually any serious candidate for president in either party spends an enormous amount of time trying to design a message that will appeal to the voters in the intense atmosphere of a nominating campaign. He looks for a niche to occupy. If nobody is talking tough on national defense, or on the protection of American industry from foreign competition, and polls indicate some untapped support for those positions, then at least one candidate will try to claim it. In that sense a presidential nominating campaign is an attempt to meet a perceived demand.

But to focus on that point, as so much journalistic and scholarly analysis does, is to get it backward. For the most part issues don't generate candidates in presidential politics—candidates generate issues. They talk about defense or trade or civil rights because they have to talk about something. But the issues are not the reason they are there. They do not explain why a certain few politicians choose to spend long days tromping through Iowa and New Hampshire, or why in the end we have to select our presidents from among the few people willing to make that tromp. Those explanations are not ideological in any sense; they are personal.

In the spring of 1988, as Democrats struggled to select a presidential nominee, Rep. Thomas S. Foley of Washington found himself spending a good number of weekends on the road, giving campaign speeches. He was speaking not for himself but for a fellow House Democrat, Richard Gephardt of Missouri. There was something a little odd about this. Foley was at this time fifty-eight years old and the majority leader of the House of Representatives. He had been in Congress twenty-three years. He was no household name in America, but he was probably the single most widely respected member of Congress among colleagues in both chambers. The previous year I had made a point of asking congressional Democrats, whenever I got the chance, whom they would choose as nominee if it were left entirely up to them. I didn't prompt them with any names. Most of them volunteered Foley.

Richard Gephardt was at this time forty-seven years old and had been a member of Congress for eleven years. He was serving as chairman of the House Democratic Caucus, a position Foley had held a decade earlier in his rise up the leadership ladder. Gephardt had been an active legislator. He was a serious and well-liked member of Congress. But had he not decided on his own to become an active candidate for president, it is unlikely that any colleagues would have suggested him as a contender. He was one of dozens of bright young members. He did not stand out among them. And beyond the borders of the Third Congressional District of Missouri, he was not known at all.

Those who make a habit of following presidential campaigns will find nothing remarkable in the fact that Foley was campaigning for Gephardt, and not the other way around. But I think it is rewarding to step back for a moment and ask why the system works the way it does: why age, experience, and preparation might yield in this case to youth, ambition, and sheer brass.

It helps, most of all, to know something about the careers of these two men. It helps to know that Tom Foley never planned or even contemplated a political career: He was working as a congressional aide in 1964 when his employer, Sen. Henry M. Jackson of Washington, urged him to run for Congress from his Spokane-based Fifth District. Democrats were about to win a landslide presidential victory, Jackson said. The Republican incumbent in the Fifth was old and ill. Foley's name was familiar in Spokane; his father was a well-respected judge. It might not take anything more than a modest campaign to sweep Foley into office.

A modest campaign was what Foley conducted. After several efforts to back out of the deal, he managed to arrive at the state election office with his filing money five minutes before the deadline. Jackson and other members of the state congressional delegation took care of his fund-raising for him. He never said a word against the incumbent. On election day the Lyndon Johnson presidential landslide swept him in.

Gephardt's career is a different story. He has been pursuing office all his life. In college he was president of his fraternity and president of the student body. When he returned home to St. Louis from law school, he and his wife began attending Democratic meetings in the city's Fourteenth Ward. He became a precinct captain, then a ward committeeman. As a boyish, well-educated young lawyer, he had virtually nothing in common with the crude clubhouse politicians who dominated the St. Louis Democratic party. But Gephardt saw the opportunities that were there. He used his position as committeeman to campaign successfully for alderman in 1971. In March of 1976 the Democratic congressional incumbent decided to retire. The decision that Foley agonized over for months, Gephardt didn't need to make at all. He had been ready to run for Congress whenever the opening came up. Within a few hours after Leonor Sullivan's retirement announcement, he was in Jefferson City filing his nomination papers. His campaign brochure announced that "Dick Gephardt will be relying on a massive door-to-door effort." In the primary campaign alone Gephardt and his wife and mother rang 40,000 doorbells in the South St. Louis precincts of the Third Congressional District.

It was entirely in character that Gephardt, watching Walter F. Mondale's campaign for president fail badly in 1984, began telling friends that the 1988 nomination would be wide open, and that he could stake as good a claim on it as anybody. And it was very much in character that Foley, informed one day early in 1988 that he was the consensus choice of colleagues as the best-qualified presidential candidate in the party, responded that he valued his privacy too much to be a presidential candidate. He didn't think he wanted "some twenty-two-year-old reporter barging into a hotel room at night and waving a poll in my face and asking me to comment on it." Foley may have wanted to be president, but running for president was simply too great a sacrifice to make.

There is no need to belabor the indignities of the presidential nominating process. We are all familiar with the endurance contest it has become: the "cattle show" public appearances with rival aspirants, the thousands of fund-raising phone calls, the self-aggrandizing courtship of the press. It is no surprise that many people with genuine potential for leading the country would be unwilling to engage in it.

The important point is that the task of running for president is merely a grotesque exaggeration of the job that confronts ambitious politicians at all levels of the system. The expenditure of time and effort required to campaign for president in Iowa and New Hamp-

shire is the logical extension of the door-to-door campaigning required of anyone who wants a seat on the city council in Concord,
California, or any similar community anywhere in the country. What
a presidential candidate does on snowy weekends before the balloting
in Iowa and New Hampshire is the functional equivalent of trudging
up and down the streets of Concord in September in 95-degree heat
reciting an identical message to thousands of voters in the hope that
the smiling face that speaks the message will be the one remembered
in the voting booth on election day.

One might object to this argument by pointing out all the ways
in which presidential campaigns and local campaigns are different.
A serious presidential candidate, to start with the obvious, has spent
millions of dollars on television advertising by the time the first few
primaries are over. Infinitely more people have watched him on the
screen than have met him in person. A candidate for local office in
a suburb like Concord never goes on television. His primary form of
communication with the voter, aside from his thirty-second speech
in the doorway, is the brochure he leaves behind.

But the money that the presidential candidate spends on media
is money he earns the right to spend by subjecting himself to the
physical campaign ordeal. Nobody who has skipped that ordeal in
recent years has been taken seriously as a presidential contender,
regardless of how much money he might have had available to spend
on television advertising. The trudge through Iowa and New Hampshire represents a barrier to entry for presidential candidates in just
the way that a door-to-door campaign represents a barrier for those
who want to sit on the Concord city council or serve in the Wisconsin
legislature. It selects out those people with the requisite skills and
qualities—not just ambition and stamina but a desire intense enough
to keep their campaign going when any candidate of even modest
intelligence is bound to realize just how mindless the whole enterprise can be. Mondale endured a fair amount of ridicule in 1975 when
he declared that he was not going to run for president because he
could not bear the thought of spending an entire year in Holiday
Inns. Serious political leaders are not supposed to say that sort of
thing. But it is not a trivial matter: Mondale was talking about one
of the prerequisites for the presidency in the modern era.

A generation ago, of course, candidates did not win the presidency this way. They ran in primaries, but the primaries played only
a modest role in determining the nomination. The most important

decisions were made, as has become legendary, by small groups of people meeting in private. They were made, one way or another, by an elite. This, too, is a subject that need not detain us long. We all know the significance of the words *smoke-filled room* in presidential campaign history. It is the place where the real leaders of a political party—the leaders of the state delegations—met in the evening hours during the national convention to decide who the nominee would be. If they could not reach a consensus among themselves, the convention droned on, roll call after roll call, until they did. The smoke-filled room that anointed Warren G. Harding for the Republicans in 1920, the deliberations that made Adlai E. Stevenson the Democratic nominee in 1952—these are staples of American political folklore. Novels and plays were written about them, and some continued to be written after the institutions themselves had disappeared from the scene.

But the smoke-filled room, evocative as it may be, is merely a symbolic extension of the system that prevailed at all the rungs of the American political ladder through the mid-twentieth century. Nobody has written any plays about the boys in Kirk's Restaurant in Sioux Falls on weekday mornings in the 1950s, or the coterie of cronies that surrounded whoever happened to be state senator in Greenville, South Carolina, in that era, before civil rights and reapportionment. Still, their deliberations were the political equivalent of the sessions in smoke-filled hotel rooms that determined presidential nominations. They were elites passing judgment on ambitious people who wanted to hold political office. They were the entry barrier. Making it without them, to the Sioux Falls city commission, the South Carolina legislature, or the presidency of the United States, was not impossible, but it was extremely difficult.

One way to explain what has happened in American presidential politics, as in state and local politics, is to say that the barriers have changed. The primary obstacle to nomination is no longer an elite. The obstacle is now a physical one, a personal one. The aspiring candidate no longer needs to worry much about what important people think of him. He needs to worry about whether he has the stamina and desire to make it through the grueling work that lies ahead. These changes in American politics do not entirely explain why we get the presidents we do, but they explain why we get the fields of presidential candidates we do. We are confronted every four years by a crew of people who have proclaimed themselves ready for the rigors of self-nomination.

So it was, in 1988, that Richard Gephardt lifted himself from the middle ranks of the House of Representatives to establish himself as a serious presidential candidate on the strength of his willingness to do over a two-year period in Iowa and New Hampshire what he had done in the neighborhoods of South St. Louis to get himself elected to the Board of Aldermen and to Congress. And so it was that Albert Gore, Jr., thirty-nine years old and three years into a career as junior senator from Tennessee, launched a presidential campaign that kept him in contention until the final weeks of the 1988 nominating season and might, with one or two more early primary victories, have resulted in his nomination.

To be a southern candidate in traditional Democratic presidential politics meant one of two things: It meant running with the blessing of established southern leaders, governors and senators—as did Richard B. Russell of Georgia in 1952 and Lyndon B. Johnson of Texas in 1960—or it meant running explicitly as a challenge to those leaders—as did Estes Kefauver of Tennessee in 1952 and 1956. In the case of Gore, in 1988, it meant no such thing. It merely reflected Gore's own recognition that much of the nominating decision would be made in a cluster of more than a dozen southern primaries held on a single day in March (dubbed Super Tuesday); that these primaries represented a special opportunity for a southern candidate; that no southerner with senior credentials, such as Sen. Sam Nunn of Georgia, was willing to undertake the effort; and that if colleagues were not exactly begging Gore to run for president after three years in the Senate, well, nobody was in a position to tell him not to, either.

One can say roughly the same thing about the man who ultimately became the Democratic presidential nominee in 1988: No one in any decisive position talked Michael Dukakis into running for president; no one talked him out of it, either. It is fair to say of Dukakis in his presidential campaign year that he was a respectable, credible, articulate specimen of liberal Democratic party values in the late 1980s. He believed in the things a Democratic nominee had to believe in—feminism, restored federal funding for social services, a conciliatory foreign policy, and a less costly defense.

But to describe Dukakis, as he made his way toward nomination, as the standard-bearer of any organized interest or faction in the Democratic party is to go much too far. He was a man of ambition and stamina whose public policy views coincided with the consensus in the party's nominating electorate. As such, he survived the game of musical chairs that the nominating process had become. Each time the music stopped, and a rival candidate fell victim to a new round of primaries or caucuses, ousted by a poor showing in New Hampshire or a barrage of negative commercials in the South, Dukakis managed to find himself a chair. Ultimately there was no plausible opposition remaining, and he was nominated. But it is important to remember that even as he stood at the podium in Atlanta, addressing the Democratic National Convention and drawing loud applause from delegates who saw in him a possible means of recapturing the White House, he was still a candidate trying to acquire a constituency. He was not, in anything but the nominal sense, anybody's standard-bearer. That point is underscored by the rapidity with which he lost any national influence in the Democratic party after his defeat in the fall campaign—a campaign in which he did, after all, carry ten states, making a much better showing than three of the previous four Democratic nominees.

I am not trying to say that candidates such as Gephardt, Gore, and Dukakis became credible contenders for president on the basis of ambition, stamina, and nothing else. That cannot be done. Every campaign year brings candidates who offer a respectable résumé, attract a reasonable quantity of attention when they first offer themselves, and then go absolutely nowhere. Gephardt, Gore, and Dukakis each had a considerable amount going for them. They all held significant office, they knew how to raise money, they understood how to deal with the national media, and they conducted themselves impressively in speech and debate. Without those skills and qualities, candidates still do not win presidential nominations.

But these are the skills and qualities that sustain presidential candidacies; they do not generate them. The vote-getting advantages that Dukakis possessed in 1988 help explain why he, and not Sen. Paul Simon of Illinois or former Gov. Bruce Babbitt of Arizona, was the eventual nominee. But they do not explain why he was in the field in the first place, or why other Democratic officeholders with similar qualifications were not. The voters cannot help us with that question. The candidates themselves are the explanation.

.   .   .

To understand the system at its logical extreme, we need to spend some time thinking about a candidate who left the field early in the 1988 nominating process. We need to consider Gary Hart.

When the *Miami Herald* staked out Hart's Washington town house one weekend in May 1987 and found that, contrary to his assurances, he was entertaining a girlfriend, it did more than remove Hart from serious presidential contention. It generated a national debate—still under way—about how far journalists are entitled to go in probing the details of a politician's personal life. That debate is a legitimate one. But what we ought to be paying some attention to is the change in the political system that has made such intrusions seem relevant—even, to many people, necessary.

Gary Hart was the most rootless man to be considered seriously for president in modern times. This was true in both a geographical and an ideological sense. Born in Kansas, educated at Yale, a resident of Washington, D.C., for most of his adult life, he was essentially a stranger to the voters of Colorado when they elected him to the U.S. Senate in 1974. When he campaigned for a second Senate term in 1980, he was still running television ads introducing himself to his constituents. When he began his 1988 presidential maneuvering by talking to reporters in his newly purchased Rocky Mountain cabin, with an elk hide on the wall, he was not returning to his roots. He was trying to create some.

Hart never attempted to persuade anybody that it was a presidential qualification not to have lived anywhere very long. But he did reach national prominence very quickly in his first campaign, in 1984, by stressing that he was a free man, unbound by the strings and commitments that fettered his rival that year, Walter F. Mondale. Hart taunted Mondale from New Hampshire to California as the candidate beholden to grasping labor unions eager to place a tool in the White House. He made an appealing case for himself as someone who was untainted by the interest-group politics that marked not only Mondale but an entire generation of the Democratic party. Hart was the candidate of "new ideas," thoughts rather than commitments, goals rather than interests. It was all woefully unspecific, vulnerable to the "Where's the Beef" criticism that Mondale ultimately managed to run successfully against him in the later stages of the 1984 campaign. But "new ideas" had an undeniable appeal.

Had Hart evaded the *Miami Herald* stakeout and remained a contender in 1988, he would no doubt have found some "beef" to add to his promises of new ideas and generational change. He spent much of the time between his 1984 campaign and the start of his 1988 effort preparing and delivering elaborate position papers designed to refute the charges of insubstantiality that Mondale had leveled against him. But the underlying individualism, the untethered quality of his life, the absence of any fixed address, geographical or ideological—these could not have changed. Hart was the ultimate in self-nomination.

Given this fact, is it any wonder that people were curious what he did with his weekends? When the front-running candidate for the Democratic nomination is a man who speaks largely for himself, comes from nowhere in particular, and reveals very little of his nature in public, it is just about guaranteed that the campaign will be one long series of nosy questions. The *Miami Herald* didn't create the demand for information about Gary Hart—it was trying, however excessively, to meet it.

Some of the same processes had been at work twelve years earlier, when Jimmy Carter ran for president. Unknown and unconnected to any elements of the established political system, Carter spent a full year fending off suggestions that there was something dark in his personal makeup that might disqualify him for leadership. Those episodes have been forgotten because Carter handled them reasonably well and went on to become president. But he was, after all, the candidate who caused a brief sensation by admitting to *Playboy* magazine that he harbored "lust in my heart."

Although a stranger to national politics, Carter was at least rooted in a part of the country and a part of the society. If it was not always clear where he wanted to go as president, it was clear where he had come from. He was a peanut farmer from south Georgia. Hart lacked even that much of a public identity. The fact that reporters found it appropriate to snoop around in Hart's private life should not, therefore, be taken solely as a reflection of changing journalistic customs. It should be taken as a search for evidence that, in an era of self-nomination, has become relevant to the process of presidential choice. The best way to understand this change is to look at some past nominating campaigns in which personal details would have been entirely beside the point.

In 1952 Dwight D. Eisenhower and Robert A. Taft fought to the bitter end for the Republican presidential nomination that ultimately lifted Eisenhower to the White House. It was an angry contest whose intraparty wounds did not heal, in some areas of the country, for the better part of two decades. It was deeply personal in the sense that Taft supporters and Eisenhower supporters disliked each other intensely. But it did not turn in any sense on personal details or revelations. It is ludicrous to imagine reporters of that era launching a weekend stakeout in Eisenhower's or Taft's driveway, and equally ludicrous to think they would have found anything very interesting if they had. But what is more important is that the public had little reason to want the information in the first place. What was going on was a clear-cut collision of political interests. Nobody needed extensive knowledge of the candidates' personal lives in order to decide whom to support.

Taft, the "uncrowned leader of the Senate," in the words of Adlai Stevenson, was the candidate of those Republicans who continued to resist the New Deal at home and an internationalist American policy abroad. His rimless glasses, clipped style of speech, and emphasis on self-discipline and free enterprise were instantly reassuring symbols to the conservative midwestern Republicans who had been the core of the party's support since the nineteenth century.

Eisenhower, by contrast, was not a man of ideology. Through most of his adult life in the military, he had rarely even voted. Until 1948 no one knew which party he favored. When he became a serious contender for the nomination in 1952, he had no platform and no program. But he was the vehicle of an entire wing of the Republican party—the eastern bloc that believed deeply in America's international commitments and thought it folly to try to repeal the New Deal. This was the bloc that had nominated Wendell Willkie in 1940 and Thomas E. Dewey in 1944 and 1948; it was Dewey who orchestrated the tactics leading up to Eisenhower's nomination in Chicago.

Eisenhower himself ran in no primaries that spring. He remained in Europe, as the supreme commander of NATO. It was only when Sen. Henry Cabot Lodge, Jr., of Massachusetts, a charter member of the eastern internationalists, traveled to Paris and persuaded the general not to withdraw his name from the New Hampshire ballot that Eisenhower became a candidate in even the remotest sense. "Under no circumstances," Eisenhower insisted even then, would he "seek nomination to political office" or "participate in the preconvention activities of others who may have such intention with respect to me." All he was willing to concede was that "of course there is no question of the right of American citizens to organize in pursuit of their common convictions." Those last few code words were all it took—by uttering them, Eisenhower was telling his allies to go ahead and nominate him, and they did.

I think we are more than justified in considering those cumbersome phrases of Eisenhowese absurdly disingenuous. Obviously the general wanted to be president; he just didn't want to say so. And we would be silly to pretend that the typical presidential contender of the past was a reluctant dragon, allowing himself to be considered only with the greatest modesty. Taft and Eisenhower were ambitious men. So were Woodrow Wilson, Herbert Hoover, and Franklin Roosevelt. There has always been, in the hesitation of almost anyone urged to run for president, a strong element of disingenuousness. But there is a difference between being an ambitious politician and being a vehicle of that ambition and little else. When the Eisenhowers and the Tafts did run, they were standard-bearers in the true sense of the word. They were the political spokesmen for forces larger than themselves. They spoke for identifiable segments of the society—and were supposed to. There were more important things to know about them than what they did with their Saturday nights.

That was equally true in 1968, when Hubert H. Humphrey, Robert F. Kennedy, and Eugene McCarthy fought for the Democratic nomination. McCarthy was as enigmatic a figure as there has been in presidential politics in modern times. He never even said he wanted to be president—merely that he was "willing" to accept the office. That didn't matter. What mattered was the Vietnam War, and the fact that McCarthy was against it. He went to the convention that year as an antiwar candidate, just as Kennedy would have done had he not been assassinated two months earlier. Humphrey was the candidate of those who, however reluctantly, accepted the American involvement in Vietnam and were unwilling to tolerate a president or a presidential nominee who proclaimed his intention to terminate it.

The era of self-nomination had not begun in the Democratic party in 1968, nor had it really begun four years later, when Humphrey and George McGovern competed for the nomination as the candidates, respectively, of the party's labor-based old guard and its youthful antiwar activists. Humphrey and McGovern were standard-bearers. However intensely either of them may have wanted to be president, they both enlisted their ambitions in the service of forces larger than themselves.

Jimmy Carter, in 1976, was not a standard-bearer. It is more nearly true to say of Carter that he seized upon forces momentarily loose in the body politic—anxiety over Watergate and desire for purity and truthfulness in public officials—and enlisted them in the service of his own ambitions. The constituency that Carter created in 1976 was not a faction or set of interests in the party or the society. It was a temporary instrument.

To argue that the era of the standard-bearer has ended in presidential nominating politics is, of course, to come up against the reality of Ronald Reagan. When he sought and won the Republican nomination in 1980, he was well into his second decade as the national spokesman for a Republican party faction that could be defined in clear ideological terms. Reagan most emphatically did not nominate himself. He carried the message of people who were involved in presidential politics mainly because he was there. But Reagan's success gives us a clue to the sort of standard-bearers who can make the transition to modern presidential politics: those who come from one end of the ideological spectrum and speak for those who feel left out of the regular process. The Republican right felt that way in the society and in the Republican party itself in the 1970s. Under those circumstances, Reagan proved, a standard-bearer can win nomination and election.

The standard Reagan carried, in 1976 and even in 1980, was one of dissidence. His supporters drew much of their strength from the feeling that he was crashing the party from the outside. The sort of discipline and organizational coherence that his forces maintained now seems incongruous anywhere but on the end of the ideological spectrum. The idea of a nomination contest taking place between two well-disciplined factions in the mainstream of a political party, the way it did for Republicans in 1952 and Democrats in 1968, is now difficult even to comprehend. Organizational coherence exists on the fringes of the two parties. The mainstream is the province of individualism and self-nomination.

There was, of course, one genuine standard-bearer on the Democratic side in 1988, and he did well. Jesse Jackson remained in the nominating contest longer than any of Michael Dukakis's other opponents, and he presented the only formal opposition to Dukakis on the convention floor in Atlanta. Jackson's eloquence as a standard-bearer for blacks and for the left in the Democratic party brought him constant attention and made him an important factor in the process all year long. But one cannot honestly say he was a contender for the nomination. It was never possible to construct a reasonable scenario by which he might win the party's endorsement. While he was reaping the rewards of ideological assertiveness, a collection of self-nominees were competing for the real prize.

The crucial task of the self-nominee is to manufacture issues and constituencies. Gary Hart did this very well in 1984. As he campaigned across the country that spring, excoriating Walter Mondale as the candidate of "old arrangements," stale programs, and established power, he tried to argue that he himself represented something. Hart and his advisers suggested that he was the standard-bearer of the "yuppies," the affluent professionals of the baby boom generation whose title has become a cliché in the years since. But Hart wasn't speaking for this constituency; he was merely trying to create it. He was building a campaign around the existence of an enormous cohort of affluent liberals under the age of forty and the assumption that it could be mobilized in the Democratic nominating process. Doing that should not be confused with representation, or with being a standard-bearer in presidential politics.

It did not take a pollster to tell Robert Taft that there were millions of isolationists in the Republican party, and that they wanted to be heard. He already spoke for them; that was why he was a candidate. Nor did anyone have to tell Eugene McCarthy that opposing the Vietnam War might be a good way to become a presidential contender. The interest preceded the campaign. It generated the campaign. In the years since then, though, there have been far more candidates like Hart and Carter than like Taft or McCarthy. The manufacture of issues and constituencies has become the crucial story of the nominating process every four years.

It is the story of George Bush. It is true that when Bush was nominated and elected to the presidency in 1988, he was a standard-bearer of sorts: As Ronald Reagan's two-term vice-president, he was the logical heir to Reagan's conservative constituents, even if they had never been particularly comfortable with him, or he with them. He was the nominal heir apparent, free to cultivate Reagan's supporters in the key primary and caucus states, and if he was not the ideal successor in most of these people's minds, he was adequate, in the absence of any compelling alternative. So he became president.

But the George Bush that we need to think about is not the one who was elected in 1988 but the one who had thrust himself into presidential campaigning a decade earlier. Bush was a man at loose ends in 1978, having returned to private life after years of transient and uneventful service in a succession of jobs: U.S. representative, ambassador to the United Nations, Republican national chairman, envoy to China, director of the CIA. The titles he had held had been impressive enough to make him a familiar figure in government and in Republican politics, but he had not served in any of the jobs long enough to have any significant impact on public policy. Bush was a man with a very good résumé, and lots of free time.

He might have spent the next few years traveling, or writing, or serving as president of a university, or taking over a corporation. He chose instead to spend them in Iowa and New Hampshire, running for president. A voice told him to do that. It wasn't the voice of any set of interests or allies in the Republican party; Bush was a man who had contacts, rather than allies, people who liked him personally but wouldn't have dreamed of urging a national campaign upon him. They wouldn't have known what to tell him to talk about. The voice Bush heard was the same one that spoke to Jimmy Carter, Gary Hart, Richard Gephardt, Michael Dukakis, and Albert Gore. It was the voice of self-nomination. It told him to go to Iowa and New Hampshire, camp out for months on end, generate some issues, create a constituency, and wait and see if lightning might strike.

As a man whose close relationships in politics were personal rather than ideological, Bush was free to aim his message at moderate Republicans and to denounce Ronald Reagan's fiscal views as "voodoo economics." He was equally free to change course in midsummer and abandon those criticisms to accept the vice-presidential nomination. There were no bitter Bush loyalists that summer urging him to hold fast to his principles and his allies. In the course of his campaign for the nomination, Bush had acquired large numbers of friends, votes, and delegates. But he had no constituency to disappoint. He had done what ambitious political professionals now do at all the levels of the political system—city hall, courthouse, statehouse, White House. He had nominated himself.

. . .

Is it possible that this is a good system? Should we feel comfortable leaving the choice of candidates for president to the candidates themselves?

Every election year, much ink is spilled in the effort to defend as sensible the process that exists. Some argue that the presidency is, after all, a physically grueling task, and a politician who tires in Iowa or New Hampshire may not be up to the endless days and impossible burdens of the office itself. Others say roughly the same thing in a more abstract way, insisting that ambition is crucial to success in high public office, and that someone who lacks the fire to compete in strenuous circumstances will lack a crucial component of intensity once installed in the job.

I don't believe either of those propositions. Stamina and intensity are useful qualities in a president, as they are in countless other roles in life, but anybody who thinks about the problem can easily imagine someone who hates campaigning and has never thirsted for public office but would make a superb president. A good nominating system at any level of politics is one in which the traits that make a successful nominee closely match those of a successful officeholder. I don't see how it can be said that we have that. The ability to campaign and the ability to govern do overlap, yes. But not at enough places. The self-nomination system does test a few of the abilities we want in a president. It ignores countless others, ones that can be measured only over the course of a long public career, and by those who have a chance to watch that career close up.

Robert Taft was a terrible campaigner—cold, wooden, and preachy. "I don't like to force myself on people," he admitted in one of his Senate campaigns. Taft was a serious contender for president because his peers—the people he worked with in Congress and the Republican party—decided that he possessed the combination of qualities they desired in a president: intelligence, knowledge, judgment, and character.

In abolishing the deliberative conventions and smoke-filled rooms of generations past, we have essentially eliminated this sort of long-term professional scrutiny. We have taken the decision out of the hands of an elite and given it, in theory, to the electorate. In practice, what we have done is given it to the candidates. They decide what the array of choices will be. The voters are asked merely to make distinctions among the field, to sort out the qualifications of a set of contenders who may not differ very much and whose messages may be almost identical. To expect a Democratic voter in Iowa to know whether Paul Simon or Michael Dukakis would make a better president is to expect a miracle.

This is, of course, what we have done throughout the political system. In allowing people to nominate themselves to any office—city council, legislature, Congress, or the presidency—we have dismantled the structure of peer review, the screening process, that used to guarantee that qualities besides ambition, stamina, glibness, and face-to-face charm would be counted in the selection of leaders.

In the earlier chapters of this book, we have seen that the decline of the screening process has taken its toll on the quality of leadership in some American communities. People promote themselves into office, in a city like Sioux Falls, who never would have made it in the days of the old coffee shop elite. A fair number of them shouldn't be there.

At the local level, though, we can make a claim that the transformation has been worth it. A closed system has been thrown open to all comers. Local politics ought to be, in some sense, a proving ground. Besides, there are limits on the mischief that local officials can do; they cannot, for example, take us into war. Perhaps, at that level, the costs of a wide-open system are costs we should be willing to pay. When it comes to selecting presidents, such an argument is a little harder to sustain. The stakes are much higher, and the benefits of some form of screening process infinitely clearer. Political leaders know things about one another that the voters don't know, and shouldn't be expected to. It doesn't seem unreasonable that that knowledge should be part of the process. In the era of self-nomination, it isn't.

I think the system we have today is impossible to justify on a rational basis. I am not trying to insist that it necessarily produces incompetent presidents, or even ones less competent than those some other system might offer us. At a rate of two or three every decade, we don't get a large enough sample to say anything like that with confidence. Jimmy Carter was the quintessential self-nominated precedent, and there seems to be a rough consensus that he was not a very good one. Warren Harding was the quintessential product of an old-fashioned screening process, and he was totally unfit for the job. The voters of Iowa and New Hampshire who created Jimmy

Carter were well meaning but uninformed. The Republican party leaders who nominated Harding in Chicago in 1920 were well informed but cynical. They liked Harding because they knew he was attractive, weak, and compliant. We are never going to have a system that guarantees good choices.

What can safely be said about the current process, however, is that it is very likely to produce presidents who lack some of the essential tools for governing. It is now possible to become president without a stable constituency or set of allies even in one's own party. It is very difficult to govern effectively that way. To campaign for president as an individualist, as someone who has risen above factions, interest groups, and entangling alliances, is to court eventual frustration in office.

The most common explanation of Carter's failures as president has been that he was incompetent, or, at the very least, so unfamiliar with the ways of Washington that he had no idea how to operate once he got there. This personalizes the problem a little too much. Carter was victimized less by his personality or inexperience than by the way he got himself elected. Without a network of allies in Washington, a firm constituency in the country, a political base to sustain him in hard times, it is difficult to imagine even the cleverest and most experienced politician making much of a record as president.

Jimmy Carter may have been a greenhorn. Gary Hart, who was no greenhorn, would have confronted very similar problems had he been elected in 1984 or 1988. He would have been a prisoner of the national popularity polls. As soon as his casual supporters began to desert him, as they deserted Carter in the fall of 1977, he would have had very little to fall back on. Enacting any sort of a legislative program would have become extremely difficult. Carter proved, and Hart came reasonably close to proving, that it is possible to campaign for president almost entirely alone and do very well. No one has yet proved that it is possible to govern effectively that way.

George Bush, whose ascension in presidential politics was more like Carter's than like Reagan's, has so far escaped the worst of Carter's problems. But the symptoms of self-nomination are present. The single most frequently cited fact about the Bush presidency, that it lacks an agenda, is not only a reflection of the times. It is a reflection of Bush's self-generated campaign in 1980 and his routine promotion eight years later as the man who, having served as Reagan's vice-president, found himself in the appropriate place at the appropriate time.

Agendas are for presidents with constituencies to satisfy and interests to promote. When a self-nominated president offers a detailed legislative program—as Carter tried to do in 1977, sending Congress messages on tax reform, welfare reform, election reform—it all comes off as rather false, like the position papers presidential candidates spew out in great volume mainly because they are expected to. A program doesn't flow naturally out of his campaign or even his career. It is more or less a contrivance. Bush, finding himself in a position not too different from Carter's, solved the problem not by concocting an agenda but by not having one.

In the end, it is not too far off the mark to characterize the presidential nominating process the way Steve Weir described politics in Concord, California, in the 1970s: "It was wide open when I came in here. A guy could walk in from Pleasant Hill, work the city in five years, and get elected."

Those who see the current presidential system as depressingly flawed need to spend more time thinking about all the connections between the way we pick presidents and the way we pick city council members, state legislators, and congressmen. To describe the presidential nominating process as the casualty of rules changes and bad habits acquired during the past two decades, and as fixable by some combination of procedural reforms, is to miss the point. The crucial developments in the process over the last twenty years have roots outside the system, beyond the borders of organized politics. Self-nomination is not the product of rules the political parties have imposed, or of any change in campaign finance, or even of television. Self-nomination has to do with the absence of a screening process, with the end of deference and the departure of figures of authority, in presidential politics as in the politics of Connecticut or Sioux Falls. And to say that authority has eroded is not merely to make a comment on the political process. It is to address much broader questions about American society as it has evolved in the last generation.

14

The End of the Pursuit

There is one event in American politics to which most of the arguments in this book do not really apply, and that is the general election for president. By the early summer of each presidential year, the self-nomination process is over and the nation turns to a campaign in which, for a brief and unique moment, the opinions and values of the electorate really are the decisive factor. However little the voters may know about the vast majority of choices that confront them in American politics, they do have enduring images of what the two major parties are about in presidential politics. And they use those images, for the short time every four years that they are paying attention, to try to understand the two people who have nominated themselves for president as candidates of the major parties.

The Democratic party, over the past two decades, has been burdened in presidential politics with a set of images that makes winning elections very difficult. It is, to the majority of American middle-class voters, the party that wants to tax the many to provide benefits to the few. No matter how poor or deserving those beneficiaries might be, there have not been enough of them to win recent presidential elections. There are no more majority coalitions of the disadvantaged, as there were during the Depression.

That is an oversimplification, of course, but it is the core of the Democrats' presidential problem. It was the issue that drove Richard Nixon's victory over Hubert Humphrey in 1968, and it was the issue that drove George Bush's victory over Michael Dukakis twenty years later. It is the main reason the Democrats have lost five national elections out of the last six, four of them by overwhelming margins. Every four years, in the fall, the voters pay attention and think about the choice being presented to them, and the party whose presentation is unappealing is likely to lose.

The fall campaign for the presidency is our central political event, the one that nearly all of us share, the most intense students of politics and government and the most casual ones, who focus on it for a few days every four years. Its moments of drama become, at least for a while, part of American folklore: Ronald Reagan saying "There you go again" to Jimmy Carter; George Bush saying "Read my lips" in his convention speech; Lloyd Bentsen telling Dan Quayle he is no Jack Kennedy. They are mass experiences. It is understandable enough, therefore, that we would take the familiar elements of the fall presidential campaign and use them in trying to explain the much more diffuse events that characterize the rest of the American political system.

What are presidential campaigns about? They are about television, of course. Presidential candidates do very little once they are nominated other than to stage appearances for one television audience or another. Presidential campaigns are about the polls that help the candidates decide what to say in those appearances, and help them evaluate the success of each appearance the morning after it takes place. Presidential campaigns are about the consultants who read the polls and then shape the candidate's next round of television on the basis of what the polls say. And, most important, presidential campaigns are about messages, simple messages that the candidates want to communicate to the voters about the way they see America and its future. In the past twenty years the Republican party has done much better at this than its opposition.

Most of us who write about politics in this country, and most people who practice it, tend to project the features of the presidential campaign onto all the political events we consider. We describe elections for Congress and for governor as battles of consultants, to be won by the team that produces the most effective commercials. We see the campaigns for these offices as collisions of messages, with the advantage to the side that communicates one as successfully as Ronald Reagan did in 1980, or as George Bush did in 1988. And there are important elections every year that are, in fact, decided this way. A close campaign for the Senate in any of the largest states has become like a small presidential campaign, with candidates dominated by polls, consultants, and television, and the result seeming to hinge on voter opinion and the struggle to frame a simple message that will capture it.

Most of us then go on to make a further assumption. We assume that the continuing competition for majorities in American politics, for control of Congress and the state legislatures, is governed by the same rules as the presidential maneuvering. Republicans never cease to ask themselves what it is about their image, their message, their values that has failed to pry loose Democratic control at the congressional, state, and local levels.

Why do working-class ethnics in the urban North and conservative Democrats in the small-town South fail to vote Republican when the presidency is not at stake? Have Republican strategists not moved far enough in a populist direction? Have they failed to overcome their image as the party of boardroom and country club? Have they talked too much about economics, and not enough about foreign policy and social issues? Or is it the other way around?

Whatever the explanation, the implicit assumption is that the Republicans had a golden opportunity after 1980 to become the nation's top-to-bottom majority party, and that they squandered it by failing somehow to communicate with ordinary people and appeal to them on the issues the way Ronald Reagan did. Republicans have been working on their message for the past twenty years, trying to find the secret ingredient in their presidential campaigning that can be reproduced throughout the political system and harnessed to make majorities at every level. They have not found it yet. A decade from now, I suspect they will still be looking for it.

The reason is that most elections in America do not turn on party or ideology. It does not make very much difference to the outcome of elections for the U.S. House of Representatives, let alone elections to a state legislature or a city council, what either of the two major parties thinks about the vital issues of the day. What matters most, as I have argued throughout this book, is ambition. Political careers are open to ambition now in a way that has not been true in America in most of this century. Those with the desire for office and the ability to manipulate the instruments of the system—the fund-raising, the personal campaigning, the opportunities to express themselves in public—confront very few limits on their capacity to reach the top. The bosses and party leaders who used to pass judgment on political careers have just about all departed the scene. They are no longer a significant barrier to entry.

The real barriers are the burdens that a political career has come to impose on people who pursue it—the burdens of time, physical effort, and financial sacrifice. Politics is a profession now, not just in Congress but in many state legislatures and in countless local governments, where a casual part-time commitment used to suffice. Many people who would be happy to serve in office are unwilling to think of themselves as professionals, or to make the personal sacrifices that a full-time political career requires.

And so political office—political power—passes to those who want the jobs badly enough to dedicate themselves to winning and holding them. As we have seen, they do not come in one standardized model of personality or temperament. I wouldn't argue that, as individuals, they are emotionally healthier or less healthy than those who choose not to run for office. Any attempt to prove this is bound to be spurious. It is possible, of course, to be consumed with politics to the point of pathology. But that is true of any preoccupation in life.

So I don't have any simple generalization to make about the inner workings of the people who have chosen to devote their lives to politics in the last quarter of the twentieth century. They are different people in different places. They are drawn to political careers for different reasons. What stands out, though, is that for most of them the commitment to a political life has been accompanied by a positive attitude toward government itself as an instrument for doing valuable work in American society. There is nothing very remarkable about that. Government is the product that politics produces; hostility toward it is bound to rob many people of their enthusiasm for full-time political work.

The baby boom Democrats who took over Concord, California, in the 1980s; the civil rights and antiwar protesters who eventually became the Democratic leadership in Wisconsin; the teachers who moved in to fill the vacuum of power in Alabama; the skillful professionals who now dominate the U.S. House of Representatives—all of them think positively about government, and that conviction has helped them cultivate the skills for a political career and sustain that career over a number of years.

In some places we met people who were motivated to enter politics more by skepticism about the role of government than by any willingness to expand it. That was true of the fundamentalists at Bob Jones University in Greenville, and the conservative activists who worked a revolution in the Colorado legislature at the end of the 1970s. Still, those are exceptions in the modern American political system. By and large, faith in the possibilities of government to do good has been one of the underlying values of the professionals who have come to dominate that system in the last two decades.

There are others. Equality is a crucial one. The modern political generation believes in equality not just as an abstract social principle but as a way of organizing political institutions. This is the generation that has turned legislative bodies all over the country into egalitarian places in which even the most junior members are entitled to the full privileges of participation, and no one is obliged to defer to the Speakers and presidents pro tempore and committee chairmen who used to be the figures of authority.

Next to equality is individualism—the freedom of the officeholder to go his own way, even when that conflicts with the goals of the caucus or faction or political party to which he nominally belongs. This is the generation of Louis LaPolla, the Utica mayor who says, "I answer to no one, only the electorate," and of Shaun McNally, the Connecticut legislator who says, "It should be possible to be part of the process without being part of the team." It is the generation in which U.S. senators serve entire terms and scarcely know one another, so committed are they to their own projects and schedules in an institution that was once supposed to be like an exclusive men's club.

The third value is openness. Most of the political professionals who have been coming into office and influence in recent years grew up in an atmosphere of closely held political power. They were raised at a time when true political leaders, people like John Bailey in Connecticut and Rufus Elefante in Utica, New York, were frequently unelected and rarely obliged to discuss their decisions with the public or even with the nominal officeholders who were expected to carry them out. When today's politicians came to maturity in the 1970s, they reacted against this system, propelled in large part by

Vietnam, Watergate, and the suspicions of secrecy and power that those events created.

Equality, individualism, and openness are the crucial values of American politics in the 1990s. They are the values of the participants—the people who, having helped to discredit old-fashioned hierarchical leadership, have taken advantage of the absence of that leadership to nominate themselves to office and begin immediately to govern.

The government that these politicians have generated has not always been the government that their constituents would have created had they voted on it by referendum. The diverse array of consumer and environmental programs enacted in Wisconsin in the 1970s and the small-scale welfare state established in the conservative town of Concord, California, in the 1980s reflected the ideas and preferences of the officeholders far more than they did those of the electorate. In the words of Bud Stewart, the city manager in Concord who watched it all happen, "These things weren't imposed on them by any pressure group. This was their own view of right and wrong."

But if the policies of the professionals have often been out of step with the political instincts of the passive electorate—as they were in Concord, where things finally went too far—one has to admit that these people's careers have been consistent with many of the changes taking place in our society beyond the borders of the political process. In building their political lives around the principles of equality, openness, and individualism, the new political leaders have been moving government along the same road that all of our important social institutions have been traveling.

Our political system, top to bottom, needs leadership, discipline, and the willingness of individuals to submerge their personal preferences for the common good. When the system fails consistently to provide these qualities, generating a politics of posturing and stalemate, we conclude that the people we elected have let us down. We ask ourselves why the Utica Common Council has to spend years bickering about the most elementary questions of local governance; why the Connecticut legislature cannot agree on how to tax the state; why Congress lurches from one energy crisis to the next without formulating any national policy at all. Why can't these people get anything done? Who asked for this mess?

None of us did. Yet it will not do simply to pin the blame on those professional politicians whose ambition enabled them to gain elective office. The truth is, we know more than we sometimes think about why government doesn't work. We understand more than we might like to admit about city councils that can't defer to leadership; about state legislatures where every individual is a faction unto himself; about a Congress that lacks any sort of meaningful community among its members. We understand those problems, or should, because they are all around us in American life. For all our ignorance as voters and inattentiveness as citizens, we have a politics that is, in the end, appropriate to its time and place.

Sources and
Acknowledgments

INTRODUCTORY CHAPTERS
(CHAPTERS 1–2)

The analogy between restaurants and American politics is an idea for which I must take full responsibility. For the notion that there is a supply-side aspect to the restaurant business, however, as for other insights large and small, I am indebted to Professor Raymond Wolfinger of the University of California, Berkeley.

The question of how much voters know when they go to the polls is a familiar one in modern political science. The view that they know relatively little has been based largely on the massive data accumulated over the past several decades by the Survey Research Center at the University of Michigan and expressed most influentially in *The American Voter,* by Angus Campbell, Philip E. Converse, Warren E. Miller, and Donald E. Stokes (New York: John Wiley & Sons, 1960). V. O. Key, Jr., offered his response that "voters are not fools" in *The Responsible Electorate* (New York: Vintage, 1966). A more recent treatment of some of these questions is Morris P. Fiorina's *Retrospective Voting in American National Elections* (New Haven: Yale University Press, 1981).

The Walter Lippmann quotations in Chapter 1 are from *The Phantom Public* (New York: Harcourt, Brace, 1925). The comment that "American elections are hardly a classic model of democracy" is taken from *The Political Behavior of the American Electorate,* by

William H. Flanigan and Nancy H. Zingale (Dubuque, Iowa: William C. Brown, 1982).

Divided government in America is as much a riddle to political scientists as it is to practitioners; there is no conventional wisdom about why it exists. There are, however, several convincing refutations of the idea that it is caused simply by gerrymandering or the power of incumbency. One is the essay by Thomas E. Mann in *Elections, American Style* (Washington, D.C.: Brookings Institution, 1987); another is an article by Norman J. Ornstein in *The Public Interest,* no. 100 (Summer 1990). The view that divided government represents a conscious choice by the electorate is associated with Morris P. Fiorina; I appreciated the opportunity to read some of his ideas in prepublication form. Gary Jacobson has been a forceful proponent of the view that divided government results from the different tasks which presidents and members of Congress are expected to perform.

The scholarly literature on the power structure of American communities is enormous and has stoked decades of argument, much of it rancorous. A great deal of the debate centers on three books: *Community Power Structure,* by Floyd Hunter (Durham, N.C.: Duke University Press, 1953); *Who Governs?: Democracy and Power in an American City,* by Robert Dahl (New Haven: Yale University Press, 1961); and *Community Power and Political Theory,* by Nelson W. Polsby (New Haven: Yale University Press, 2nd ed., 1980). Taken together, they offer a short course in where the subject stood a generation ago and where it still stands.

THE COMMUNITIES
(CHAPTERS 3–6)

My chapters on political change in American communities are based mostly on my own interviews with participants in that process, and most of the people are quoted by name. In all four of the cities I studied, however, the written record was a necessary supplement.

Nearly all medium-sized American cities have generated a respectable literature, usually including at least one impressive coffee-table book, on their origins and early development. Rarely do these volumes say anything candid about political conflict in the years since World War II. In some communities the daily press provides a clear view of that conflict; in others, newspapers offer only the bare bones, leaving no clear impression of just who was doing what to whom in the 1950s and 1960s.

The early history and postwar development story of Concord, California, are told in *History of Concord: The Progress and Promise,* by Edna May Andrews (Concord Historical Society, 1986). Two earlier volumes are *Concord: A Better Place in the Sun* (Concord Chamber of Commerce, 1960) and *History of Concord,* by Bethel R. Morris (1954).

Concord does not have a daily newspaper. The *Concord Transcript,* revived in 1987 as a weekly after several years out of operation, did a creditable job of covering the tumultuous 1989 city council campaign, and I found it highly useful. For prior years in the 1980s, the *Contra Costa Times* in neighboring Walnut Creek offers the only reliable coverage, and I was grateful to that newspaper for the opportunity to use its files. The results of the 1989 campaign attracted some national attention: for example, "When Public Art Doesn't Please," by Katherine Bishop, *New York Times,* April 11, 1990.

Two helpful documents on development issues in Concord are *Downtown Concord, Urban Design,* issued by the city council in March 1987, and *Downtown Concord, Redevelopment Area Market Analysis,* prepared for the Concord Redevelopment Agency by Economics Research Associates, San Francisco, 1983.

The most authoritative recent book on Sioux Falls is *Sioux Falls, South Dakota: A Pictorial History,* by Gary D. Olson and Erik L. Olson (Norfolk, Va.: Donning Press, 1985). An earlier work that details some of the relationships between Sioux Falls and the John Morrell Corporation is *The House of Morrell,* by Lawrence O. Cheever (Cedar Rapids, Iowa: Torch Press, 1948).

Managing editor David Kranz and other members of the staff of the *Sioux Falls Argus Leader* were enormously helpful in permitting me access to their files and in answering my questions. In recent years, the *Argus Leader* has produced some impressive analysis of local power and leadership, and I would particularly like to cite "Who Owns Sioux Falls," by Ann Grauvogl, which appeared on August 3, 1986. Two more recent articles deserving of mention are

"Women and Power in South Dakota," published on October 22, 1989, and "Schirmer Years Marked by Visionary Politics," by Jen Deselms, which appeared July 31, 1989.

The story of Greenville, South Carolina, with some of the blemishes included, is told rather well in a recent pictorial history, *Greenville: Woven from the Past,* by Nancy Vance Ashmore (Northridge, Calif.: Windsor Publications, 1986). Another recent volume is A. V. Huff's *Greenville: The Place and People: How We Got This Way,* published by Furman University in 1985. The saga of the Daniel Corporation and its influence on the development of the community is presented in *Charles E. Daniel, His Philosophy and Legacy,* by C. R. "Red" Canup and W. D. Workman, Jr. (Columbia, S.C.: R. L. Bryan, 1981). The business community's point of view is amplified by *Report from Greenville,* a 1987 publication of the Greater Greenville Chamber of Commerce. A useful document with an opposite slant is "It's Good to Be Here in Greenville, But It's Better if You Hate Unions," which appeared in the spring 1979 issue of the journal *Southern Exposure* (vol. 7, no. 1). In Greenville, as in other communities, I am grateful for the opportunity to have examined decades' worth of newspaper clippings; the *Greenville News* was gracious in providing me with this opportunity, as was the local historical society.

For information on the politics of a generation ago in Utica, New York, I am greatly in debt to an obscure but remarkable work, "The Democratic Party in Utica," by Stuart K. Witt (master's thesis, Syracuse University, 1962). It contains information on the values, customs, and finances of the Elefante machine that would be difficult to duplicate by reporting this far after the fact.

The political importance of Utica restaurants has been reliably recalled in three articles: "For Little City Hall, Look Back in Sadness," by Ed Byrne, in the *Utica Observer-Dispatch,* June 14, 1972; "Another City Hall Might Soon Be Only History," by Tim Rice, in the *Observer-Dispatch,* November 6, 1981; and "Pancake House Politicking," by Nicholas Acocella, in *Attenzione,* November 1980.

Utica's alleged ties to the Mafia were the subject of national journalistic attention in the late 1950s and early 1960s. Two representative examples of its notoriety are "Wide Open Town," in *Newsweek,* February 24, 1958, and "Report from Utica," in *Look,* July 8, 1958. The period is recalled from the vantage point of a quarter-century in "Troubled Years in Utica," in the *Observer-Dispatch* of

July 15, 1983. An assessment of the community from the time before the troubles can be found in "Take Utica, for Instance," in the December 1949 issue of *Fortune.*

For many years, coverage of Rufus Elefante in the *Observer-Dispatch* consisted to a great extent of editorials against him. One relatively recent editorial, quoted in this book, is "Machine Politics Wins Recognition but Lacks Respect," published on November 10, 1981. In the twilight of Elefante's career, the *Observer-Dispatch* published a revealing article including a rare interview with him: "The Elefante Saga: Seven Decades of Power, Politics and People," by Marje Patrick, which appeared on September 28, 1986.

The article on Utica's most influential citizens, quoted at the beginning of Chapter 6, is "Movers and Shakers: Inside Area Power Structure," by Tim Rice, in the *Observer-Dispatch* of March 6, 1983. For making it available to me, and for providing me with numerous other articles and various kinds of generous assistance, I am grateful to Tony Vella and George Newman of the *Observer-Dispatch.* The Oneida County Historical Society and its director, Douglas Preston, were also kind enough to allow me to peruse their files.

A general history of the Utica area is *The Upper Mohawk Country: An Illustrated History of Greater Utica,* by David Ellis (Woodland Hills, Calif.: Windsor Publications, 1982). There is further background in *The History of Oneida County,* published by the county government in 1977. The story of Utica's postwar economic transition is usefully recounted in "Economic Developments in the Utica-Rome, New York, Area," an essay by Virgil Crisafulli in *Community Economic Development Efforts: Five Case Studies* (New York: Committee for Economic Development, 1964).

The comments of George Washington Plunkitt in Chapter 6 are from *Plunkitt of Tammany Hall,* by William L. Riordan (New York: E. P. Dutton, 1963).

THE STATES
(CHAPTERS 7–10)

States are the stepchildren of American political studies. Compared with national government at one end and local government at the other, they have attracted far less than their rightful share of either scholarly or journalistic attention. What is true of states in general is even more true of state legislatures; very few people have written about them in a broad or systematic way. So the bulk of what I have to say in this section derives from what I have learned by talking on my own to people who have served in or watched the four legislatures I describe.

It is important, however, to point out a few books that have been helpful to me and that any serious student of state politics should take care to read. For historical background on state politics and power, there is still no work to match John Gunther's *Inside USA* (New York: Harper & Brothers, 1947). Neal Peirce came as close as one reasonably might over the 1970s with his massive series that began with *The Megastates of America* (New York: W. W. Norton, 1972) and continued with eight separate regional volumes. I have found all of them useful over the years. A more recent treatment of twelve states is *The Political Life of the American States,* by Alan Rosenthal and Maureen Moakley (New York: Praeger, 1984), which includes material on Colorado that was particularly relevant to this book. At a higher level of abstraction, Daniel Elazar's *American Federalism: A View from the States* (New York: Thomas Y. Crowell, 1972) is important to anyone who wishes to distinguish state political styles and make sense of them on a regional basis.

On the legislatures themselves, Alan Rosenthal is the preeminent expert, and I have made frequent use of his work, especially *Legislative Life* (New York: Harper & Row, 1981). Equally relevant is Rosenthal's article "A Vanishing Breed," in the November 12, 1989, issue of *State Legislatures* magazine. Dated and forgotten now, but well worth reading for context, is Frank Trippett's diatribe against the legislatures of the 1950s and 1960s, *The States: United They Fell* (Cleveland: World Publishing, 1967).

Very little has been written about the current generation of political leaders in Wisconsin and the values they have brought to the job. Their programs are among those detailed in *Wisconsin Legislative Innovations,* published by the state's Legislative Reference Bureau in 1981. There is a worthwhile profile of David Clarenbach by Betty Brickson in the February 19, 1988, issue of *Isthmus* (vol. 13, no. 8). The quotation comparing the achievements of the Lucey era with those of the La Follette years is from *The Great Lakes States of America,* by Neal Peirce and John Keefe (New York: W. W. Norton, 1980).

The discussion of Connecticut's legislature in the Bailey years draws heavily on *The Legacy* (Hartford, Conn.: Spoonwood Press, 1981), Joseph Lieberman's history of the state's postwar Democratic party. The quotation about Bailey learning to defer to the legislature in his later years is taken from this book. Also useful is *The Power Broker* (Boston: Houghton Mifflin, 1966), Lieberman's earlier biography of Bailey.

Sources on the Roraback years include *New England State Politics*, by Duane Lockard (Princeton: Princeton University Press, 1959), and Neal Peirce's *The New England States of America* (New York: W. W. Norton, 1976). Some of the Roraback story is also brought to life in "An Orderly and Decent Government: The History of the Connecticut General Assembly," an exhibit and pamphlet produced by the Connecticut Humanities Council in 1988.

Some of the operational details of Connecticut legislative affairs are described in *Strengthening the Connecticut Legislature*, by David Ogle (New Brunswick, N.J.: Rutgers University Press, 1969). The same author's reflections on the institution twenty years later can be found in "The General Assembly, 1969–89: Two Decades of Transformation," in the January 1990 issue of *OL Reporter*, published by the Office of Legislative Research of the Connecticut General Assembly. David Ogle and his staff at the Office of Legislative Research were enormously helpful to me during my visit to Hartford and in my preparation of Chapter 8.

It is possible to say with a fair degree of precision who has served in the Alabama legislature in this century; the main reason is the research done over many years by the Bureau of Public Affairs of the University of Alabama in Tuscaloosa. The bureau published Hallie Farmer's 1949 book, *The Legislative Process in Alabama*, with its valuable data on the occupations of all Alabama legislators from 1903 up to World War II. Another useful product of the Bureau of Public Affairs is *City vs. Farm*, by Murray Clark Havens, published in 1957. A recent and comprehensive survey of the details of the state's governmental process is *Alabama Politics and Government*, by James D. Thomas and William H. Stewart (Lincoln: University of Nebraska Press, 1988). Harold Stanley's book, *Senate vs. Governor: Alabama, 1971* (Tuscaloosa: University of Alabama Press, 1975), is an interesting account of one year of legislative life in the middle of the Wallace era. Still relevant and interesting is the chapter on Alabama in V. O. Key's *Southern Politics in State and Nation* (Knoxville: University of Tennessee Press, 2nd ed., 1974).

I was led through some of the byways of Alabama political history by Professor Bradley Moody of Auburn University, Montgomery, and I am grateful to him not only for his personal assistance but for the opportunity to read his paper "Tenure and Turnover in the Alabama Legislature," which was delivered at the annual meeting of the American Political Science Association in Chicago in 1987. Moody also led me to another useful essay, "Alabama Politics, J. Thomas Heflin and the Expulsion Movement of 1929," by J. Mills Thornton III, which appeared in the *Alabama Review* of April 1968.

The doings of the Alabama legislature of the late 1980s were made much more comprehensible for me by Amy Herring, the state capitol reporter of the *Montgomery Advertiser*. I appreciated her time and insights, her introduction to the library of the *Advertiser* newsroom, and her coverage of legislative action. It was especially helpful to read her article on the members of the legislature, "Movers and Shakers," which was written with Peggy Wilhite and appeared in the *Advertiser* on February 4, 1985. Another useful article was "Lobbyists Grease Wheels of Government, Legislation," by Emily Bentley, in the *Advertiser* of March 26, 1989.

The political observer who described the Alabama legislature as "the shoddiest I have seen" is Neal Peirce, as quoted in *The Deep South States of America* (New York: W. W. Norton, 1974).

There is nothing like Hallie Farmer's book available for Colorado, but there is a wealth of statistical information about the postwar Colorado legislature in *The Colorado General Assembly, 1955 to 1977*, published by the Colorado Public Expenditure Council in 1977. Two relevant journal articles covering portions of the same period are "Profiles and Careers of the Colorado State Legislature," by Victor S. Hjelm and Joseph P. Pisciotte, in the *Western Political Quarterly*, and "The Relative Success of Women Representatives in the Colorado Legislature," by Lyn Kathlene, in the October 1986 issue of the *Comparative State Politics Newsletter*.

My discussion of Ken Kramer's early life and career is drawn largely from a profile in the *Denver Post*, "Ken Kramer's Political Style: Sharp, Steely," by Mark Obmascik, published January 26, 1986. A useful article on the constraints against gubernatorial power in Colorado is "Lawmakers' Control of State Budget Limits Influence of Colorado Governor," by Fred Brown, in the *Denver Post* of

February 29, 1989. I wish to thank the library staff and the state capitol reporters of the *Post* for allowing me access to their files.

NATIONAL POLITICS
(CHAPTERS 11–14)

My primary source of information on congressional elections in the 1970s and 1980s is my own experience covering these events for *Congressional Quarterly* and the *Washington Star.* Most of the politicians I write about in Chapter 11 are people whose careers and campaigns I watched unfold. More detail about them is available in the biennial editions of *Politics in America, Congressional Quarterly*'s reference work about members of Congress, which I edited from 1982 to 1988. The most recent volume is the 1990 edition, edited by Phil Duncan and published by CQ Press.

I am far from the first writer to insist on the importance of candidate quality and ambition in determining congressional elections. En route to my current views on the subject, I have learned from the following books: *Unsafe at Any Margin,* by Thomas E. Mann (Washington, D.C.: American Enterprise Institute, 1978); *Strategy and Choice in Congressional Elections,* by Gary C. Jacobson and Samuel Kernell (New Haven: Yale University Press, 2nd ed., 1983); *The Politics of Congressional Elections,* by Gary C. Jacobson (Boston: Little, Brown, 1983); and *Political Ambition: Who Decides to Run for Congress,* by Linda L. Fowler and Robert D. McClure (New Haven: Yale University Press, 1989). I agree with most of the arguments in these books, although none go as far as I do in singling out candidates as the answer to most of the important congressional election questions.

On the subject of Republican prospects for becoming the nation's majority party, Kevin Phillips is perhaps the most prolific and certainly the most provocative writer of the past two decades. The single most important work on this subject is still his 1969 book, *The Emerging Republican Majority* (New Rochelle, N.Y.: Arlington House). It has proven astonishingly accurate in its predictions about presidential politics, even though its failure to anticipate the congressional future led him to modify his views in two later books, *Media-*

cracy (New York: Doubleday, 1975) and *Post-Conservative America* (New York: Random House, 1982). Two later books placing the puzzle of realignment in historical context are *Dynamics of the Party System: Alignment and Realignment of Political Parties in the United States,* by James L. Sundquist (Washington, D.C.: Brookings Institution, 1973), and *Transformations of the American Party System,* by Everett Carl Ladd and Charles D. Hadley (New York: W. W. Norton, 2nd ed., 1978).

There is an enormous amount of literature, both scholarly and journalistic, that is relevant to my chapter on the institutional life of Congress. The best I can do is point to a few books and articles that have proven important to me.

The most vivid picture (and most commonly accepted view) of Congress a generation ago is in two books by William S. White: *Citadel: The Story of the U.S. Senate* (New York: Harper & Brothers, 1956) and *Home Place* (Boston: Houghton Mifflin, 1965). The quotation in Chapter 12 on the Senate and "the integrity of its oneness" is from *Citadel.* Two other excellent books are *A Senate Journal, 1943–45,* by Allen Drury (New York: Da Capo Press, 1972), and *The U.S. Senate,* by George Reedy (New York: Crown Publishers, 1986).

The most familiar scholarly work on the Senate of this period is *U.S. Senators and Their World,* by Donald Matthews (Chapel Hill: University of North Carolina Press, 1960). The crucial early accounts of how this congressional system began to unravel are by Nelson W. Polsby. Particularly important are his article "The Institutionalization of the U.S. House of Representatives" in the March 1968 issue of the *American Political Science Review,* and the chapter on the Senate in his *Congress and the Presidency* (New York: Prentice-Hall, 4th ed., 1986).

Several books offer a convincing portrait of what congressional life has become over the past twenty years. Richard F. Fenno was ahead of everyone in explaining the influence of home-district political situations in shaping congressional careers; I am particularly glad to have read his book *Home Style: House Members in Their Districts* (Boston: Little, Brown, 1978). Other excellent books on the Congress of the 1970s are *The Senate Nobody Knows,* by Bernard Asbell (New York: Doubleday, 1978), and *The New American Politician: Ambition, Entrepreneurship and the Changing Face of Political Life,* by

Burdett Loomis (New York: Basic Books, 1988).

Morris P. Fiorina and David Mayhew have influenced the entire debate on modern congressional life by arguing that members of Congress arrange the legislative institution mainly to suit electoral needs. This argument is developed in Mayhew's *Congress: The Electoral Connection* (New Haven: Yale University Press, 1974) and Fiorina's *Congress: Keystone of the Washington Establishment* (New Haven: Yale University Press, 1977). These ideas have generated volumes of criticism; in general, though, I think they are right, and I have made considerable use of them.

There are two political biographies of Tip O'Neill and one enormously detailed book on the speakership of Jim Wright. One of the O'Neill books is his autobiography, *Man of the House: The Life and Political Memoirs of Speaker Tip O'Neill,* written with William Novak (New York: Random House, 1987). A more dispassionate and useful account of O'Neill's early career is *Tip: A Biography of Thomas P. O'Neill, Jr.,* by Shirley Elder and Paul Clancy (New York: Macmillan, 1980). Wright's story is told in *The Ambition and the Power: The Fall of Jim Wright,* by John Barry (New York: Viking Penguin, 1989).

A useful book dealing with the public policy failures of Congress in the 1980s is *Can Government Govern?* edited by John E. Chubb and Paul E. Peterson (Washington, D.C.: Brookings Institution, 1989). A good book on the most conspicuous legislative success of the decade, the Tax Reform Act of 1986, is *Showdown at Gucci Gulch,* by Alan Murray and Jeffrey H. Birnbaum (New York: Random House, 1987).

So much has been written on the presidential nominating process that singling out a few books seems arbitrary and presumptuous. My inclination is to spare the reader any further list making. I would merely suggest that, however trite it might seem to say so, Theodore H. White's *The Making of the President 1960* (New York: Atheneum, 1961) remains the best source I know of on the process as it used to be. I think *Consequences of Party Reform,* by Nelson W. Polsby (New York: Oxford University Press, 1983), is the single most useful book on what has happened to the system.

My discussion of Dwight D. Eisenhower and Robert A. Taft as presidential candidates draws upon *Mr. Republican,* by James T. Patterson (Boston: Houghton Mifflin, 1972); *The Eisenhowers,* by

Steve Neal (Lawrence: University of Kansas Press, 1978); and *Eisenhower: Captive Hero,* by Marquis Childs (New York: Harcourt, Brace, 1957).

Most of the ideas in this book took shape for me during my years as political editor of *Congressional Quarterly,* years in which I was privileged to be part of a small community of reporters at the back of the room who saw American politics as endlessly fascinating and saw their work as a way to educate one another. It is important to me to thank them by name: Rhodes Cook, Phil Duncan, Rob Gurwitt, Tom Watson, Peter Bragdon, and Bob Benenson. Warden Moxley was part of that group for a while, and my mentor and teacher for a decade before that. I miss him.

The book itself was conceived and in part written during a year's leave of absence in 1987 and 1988 as a visiting scholar in the political science department at the University of California, Berkeley. That year was made possible by Andrew Barnes, chairman of the Times Publishing Company of St. Petersburg, Florida, and chairman of *Congressional Quarterly.* Without his generosity, the book could not have been written.

Nelson Polsby invited me to Berkeley and was my host, adviser, and neighbor during ten months there. It is hard to imagine anyone performing better in any of those capacities. Ray Wolfinger and Austin Ranney also helped me negotiate the complexities of the Berkeley environment, as well as offering ideas and insights that, through no intention of theirs, found their way into the pages of this book.

I returned to Washington in 1988 and joined the ongoing experiment that is *Governing* magazine. There I was reunited with Peter Harkness and Elder Witt, my colleagues and friends of nearly twenty years at *Congressional Quarterly;* reintroduced to Eileen Shanahan, my old friend from the *Washington Star;* and privileged to meet and work for John Martin. All four of these people have been enormously supportive of this project and tolerant of the editorial digressions into which it sometimes led me. When I told Peter I wanted to write a chapter about Utica or about the Alabama legislature and asked if we could make a place for it in the magazine, he always said yes. If he hadn't, I'm not sure there would be a book now.

I was incredibly lucky when it came to editors. Steve Wasserman believed in this project and stuck with it through a tortuous round of corporate twists and turns that might have done it in. Paul Golob gave me the editorial advice I needed to stay afloat and read the manuscript with a patience and thoughtfulness for which I will always be grateful. I don't know how many old-fashioned editors are left in the publishing business; I know there is one.

My final gratitude is to Suzanne, Lizzie, and Jennie. I am deeply indebted to them for being themselves.

Index

Watergate, 116
Colorado politics and, 192, 203
congressional candidates and, 209,
212–15, 217, 238
fundamentalist Christians and, 97
presidential politics and, 35–36, 263
Sioux Falls mayoral campaigns and,
66–67, 72
Waxman, Henry, 28
Weber, Vin, 226
Weicker, Lowell P., Jr., 163
Weir, Steven, 46, 52, 60, 63, 68, 143,
214, 269
background of, 49
Campbell compared with, 62
governing skills of, 55–56
professionalism of, 48–50
on utility users' tax, 55
welfare programs:
in Concord, 275
Congress on, 249–50
West, Rebecca, 85–87
Wham, Dorothy, 197–98, 205
Wheeldon, Fay, 70–71
White, Jack, 82
White, William S., 233, 235, 286
Who Governs? (Dahl), 30, 278
Wickensimer, Paul, political
commitment of, 100–101
Williams, Pat, 241
Willkie, Wendell, 261
Wilson, Woodrow, 262
Winegarden, Vern, 74–75
Wingler, Harold, 74–75, 79
Wisconsin, University of, at
Milwaukee, 127, 136
Wisconsin Association of
Manufacturers, 133
Wisconsin Historical Society, 128
Wisconsin legislature, 125–42, 152,
164, 214, 251, 255

campaigning for, 126–31, 133–34,
139–40
consumer and environmental
programs enacted by, 275
Democrats in, 126–29, 131–42,
273
generational differences in, 140–41
as haven for liberal experiment, 136
on homosexuality, 131, 136
PACs and, 139–40
political caucus support staff in,
137–39
political leaders in, 282
reform legislation and, 134–36
Witte, Dave, 71, 74
WMUU (World's Most Unusual
University), 101
women:
in Alabama politics, 173
in Colorado politics, 7, 191,
196–202, 204–7
in Concord politics, 43, 53–54,
57
in Sioux Falls politics, 78–79, 81–83
Wisconsin legislature on, 136, 141
Woods, John, 185
Workman, Bill, fundamentalist
Christians cultivated by, 103
Works Progress Administration
(WPA), 108
W. R. Grace, 93
Wright, Jim, 242, 287
fall of, 240–41, 250
Wright, Ruth, 204
Wyden, Ron, 242
Wyoming legislature, 13

Yale University, 17, 30, 153, 259
York, Harry, 58
Young Americans for Freedom, 196
Young Democrats, 49, 173

About the Author

Alan Ehrenhalt is executive editor of *Governing* magazine in Washington, D.C. Born in Chicago in 1947, he received his bachelor's degree from Brandeis University and a master's degree from the Columbia University School of Journalism. He has been a reporter for the Associated Press, *Congressional Quarterly,* and the *Washington Star,* and for twelve years was political editor of *Congressional Quarterly.* In 1983 his biweekly column, "Congress and the Country," earned him the Everett McKinley Dirksen Award for distinguished reporting of Congress. He has been a Nieman Fellow at Harvard and a visiting scholar at the University of California, Berkeley. Ehrenhalt was the creator and editor of the reference book *Politics in America* and served as a consultant to ABC News for four congressional elections. He lives in Arlington, Virginia, with his wife and two daughters.